Welfare Economics

A LIBERAL RESTATEMENT

York Studies in Economics
GENERAL EDITORS: Professors Alan T. Peacock and Jack Wiseman

ECONOMIC POLICIES AND SOCIAL GOALS
edited by A. J. Culyer

Welfare Economics

A LIBERAL RESTATEMENT

Charles K. Rowley
UNIVERSITY OF NEWCASTLE-UPON-TYNE

Alan T. Peacock
UNIVERSITY OF YORK

A Halsted Press Book

JOHN WILEY & SONS · New York

First published in 1975 by Martin Robertson & Co. Ltd.
17 Quick Street, London N1 8HL

Published in the U.S.A. in 1975 by
Halsted Press, a Division of John Wiley
& Sons Inc., New York

Library of Congress Cataloguing in Publication Data

Rowley, Charles Kershaw.
    Welfare Economics.

    "A Halsted Press book."
    Bibliography: p.
    1. Welfare economics.   I. Peacock, Alan T.,
1922—   joint author.   II. Title.
HB99.3.R68 1975   330.15'5   75-22430
ISBN 0-470-74362-X

Printed in Great Britain at The Pitman Press, Bath

Contents

Preface

Although this book was started while both authors were at the University of York, England, and was all but completed while one author was on leave at Virginia Polytechnic Institute, USA — institutions both of which are widely viewed as bastions of economic liberalism — it would be incorrect to categorise it as a product of its environment. For there is a sense in which the scholarship of both schools for the most part is at odds with the thrust of the book, adhering to Paretian rather than to liberalist ideals and in closer conformity with the present orthodoxy. We are of course heavily indebted to both institutions as also to the University of Newcastle-upon-Tyne for the atmosphere of free and vigorous discussion which they offer and for their toleration of all ideas reasonably and rationally presented.

Our interest in the subject matter of this book was sparked off by a seminar given by Alan Peacock at the University of York in 1971, which was followed by lengthy discussions on the coercive implications of Paretian welfare economics. The outcome was two articles on liberalist welfare economics published in *The Journal of Political Economy* and in *The Journal of Public Economics* in June 1972, and a joint commitment to develop our ideas further in book form. Some preliminary drafts of chapters were written during 1973, but our decision to expand the application of our ideas, followed by the unexpected secondment of Alan Peacock to the post of Chief Economic Adviser, Department of Trade and Industry, in October 1973, pointed towards a long delay in completion through his exclusion from further writing during his period of office. The dilemma was resolved by Charles Rowley's willingness to expand the work along the agreed lines, but this left him with the major share of the burden of preparing extra chapters and drafting the final text. In the event, we are glad to say that the book is still a joint product in the sense that we have both contributed to its entire development and that we both endorse without reservation the analysis and conclusions as outlined. If nothing else, this book establishes one limited but widely denied possibility theorem — it is possible for at least two liberals to agree both on matters of philosophy and on its economic implications.

Various parts of the book have been pilot-tested at a wide range of staff economic seminars in the United Kingdom, the United States and Switzerland. A draft of chapter 4 was presented at the University of Glasgow, a draft of chapter 5 at a meeting of the SSRC Industrial Economics Study Group at the University of Newcastle-upon-Tyne, drafts of chapter 7 at the Universities of Liverpool, Newcastle-upon-Tyne and Stirling (UK) and at Virginia Polytechnic Institute, UCLA and the Universities of Kentucky and Virginia (USA) and at a meeting of the Public Choice Society in Basle (Switzerland). A draft of chapter 8 was also presented at Virginia Polytechnic Institute. We are very grateful to our academic colleagues in these institutions for their interest and encouragement and for the many fruitful and penetrating comments which have improved the quality of our book.

We acknowledge a great debt in our exposition of liberal political and economic philosophy to John Stuart Mill and to his modern interpreters, such as F. A. Hayek, Isaiah Berlin and Fritz Machlup. It would be presumptuous for us to claim more than to have restated in contemporary economic form the principle tenets of liberalism as developed and refined by these authorities. We must also thank those arch-Paretians James M. Buchanan and Gordon Tullock, who have looked kindly upon our attempt to breach their citadel and who, during Charles Rowley's stay at Blacksburg, offered help, comment and criticism far beyond the call of duty. Among the many others who have contributed to this book we would mention Peter Bernholz, William Breit, Antony Culyer, Harold Demsetz, Jack Hirshleifer, Edgar Olsen, Roger Sherman, Hirofumi Shibata, Steven Sugar, Nicolas Tideman and George Yarrow. With such a distinguished list of commentators, we are not entirely sure that we should accept full responsibility for remaining errors. But as good liberals, valuing individual responsibility in decision-making, we shall do so.

As always, we are grateful to the several secretaries who have typed away so cheerfully and so efficiently on various drafts of the book and especially to Christine Garner of the University of Newcastle-upon-Tyne, who has worked so conscientiously and so accurately in the preparation of the final draft. Most important of all, we would like to thank our wives, Margaret Peacock and Marjorie Rowley, always the most forthright of our critics, who have kept an especially vigilant eye on the contents of this book and who have requested for the household the freedoms that we urge for the economy. During the writing of this book they have both suffered, willingly and without coercion, the privations that authorship brings to family life. We hope that they find the product worthy of their sacrifices.

C.K.R. and A.T.P.

This book is dedicated to our intellectual forbears in the classical tradition of political economy whose writings provide an essential basis for liberalist welfare economics as we here develop it.

Introduction

Following forty years of unprecedented critical inquiry, both at the theoretical and at the empirical levels, economics is currently in a state of flux, with controversies raging in almost all its branches, and with the monism of the neoclassical message effectively replaced by a pluralism of competing viewpoints. Given the complexity and instability of the structures with which it deals, and the inadequacy of information required for the rigorous testing of hypotheses, this pluralism is to be applauded as a healthy indication of a vigorous and open profession still at the genesis of its potential. There is, however, a single important exception to this encouraging story, namely welfare economics, the subject matter of this text. The dominating effect of the substantial input of resources into welfare economics throughout the Western world, during the renaissance period of economic science, has been that of tightening the grip exercised by Paretian dogma over members of our profession until we are now faced with a dangerous hegemony in the economic theory of public policy. It is to the destruction of this supremacy and to the effective restatement of a viable (and in our view a superior) liberal alternative that this text is dedicated. It is perhaps worth emphasising that our attack is directed essentially not at the Paretian position itself, but at its unquestioned domination of the welfare economics battlefield.

In pursuit of this objective, we charge those who deal in Paretian welfare economics with being implicated, in greater or lesser degree, knowingly or in ignorance, in a professional misdemeanour which forms the basis for the established dictatorship. In its most serious form, the misdemeanour amounts to a policy of presenting a value-based dogma as value-free, immutable and incontestable[1,5] in the hope that those who endorse its internal logic will not inquire too closely as to its fundamental assumptions — this the oldest technique of the religious fanatic. Less seriously, but more commonly, the Paretian principles are endorsed and defended as a set of 'ethically neutral propositions, tolerant of all ethical systems'[3] and the product of 'consensus among reasonable men',[2] phrases that are designed to capture the favour of the unwary scholar, but which, in our view, are misleading within the welfare economics context. For, as we shall demonstrate, consensus does not connote neutrality in welfare economics matters and it is an illusion to infer that Paretian welfare judgements lead to non-authoritarian solutions in matters of economic policy simply because they are derived from individual preferences. Nor should it be inferred, as too often is the case, that those who deviate from consensus economics on matters of this kind necessarily are to be classified either as intellectual fools or as authoritarian knaves — indeed, we shall urge just such a deviation in the later sections of this text.

Furthermore, we shall challenge the tendency, apparent within certain sections of the Paretian orthodoxy, to distinguish in public policy discussion between economic objectives on the one hand and political and social objectives on the other; for in our view this is a false dichotomy. In so far as individuals in society have any objectives — be they social, political or economic — that are achievable via economic adjustments, then economists are best equipped to analyse the institutional implications, albeit within a suitably formulated welfare economics framework. As such, this is no criticism of Paretian welfare economics, which is fully capable of such treatments, but rather of the obsessive narrowness of its applications at the hands of certain of its practitioners.

It is not our intention to join forces with the small band of economists who have mounted a critical attack on Paretian welfare economics without presenting a constructive alternative. Indeed, we have scant respect for such negative contributions. Rather, have we welcomed this opportunity to demonstrate how an alternative political philosophy which we both embrace is translatable into an economic policy analysis radically different from that of Paretian welfare economics. In so doing, it has proved essential to distinguish in the sharpest possible way between the value assumptions of Pareto and those of liberalism, not least because of the widespread belief within the economics profession that the two approaches are identical.[4] Even Amartya Sen,[6] who himself has concluded that 'in a very basic sense liberal values conflict with the Pareto principle' (cf. chapter 5), in our view remains confused as to the true nature of liberalism, which is not concerned, as he would have it, with the primacy of individual preferences, but rather with the maintenance and extension of individual freedoms, defined as the absence of coercion of certain individuals by others. In our view, certainly, the differences between Paretian and the liberal approaches are too great for a synthesis or a reconciliation to be possible. But the incompatibility between the two philosophies is more profound than the mere existence of interdependences between individual preference functions upon which the Sen paradox is completely reliant.

The first three chapters of this book are devoted to a detailed, if critical, account of the present state of Paretian welfare economics, noting the remarkable survivorship-capacity of this hardy dogma, while underlining its essential weaknesses and limitations. It is not our wish to debunk an approach to issues of economic policy which has many attractive features which amply justify it a continuing place in the welfare economics hierarchy. Rather are we concerned to clarify the precise value judgements on which it rests and the rather special assumptions on which it is applicable so that those who select to make use of it do so in full knowledge of what is implied.

Chapter 4 presents a philosophical challenge to the Paretian hegemony arising from the New Left — not a philosophy with which we are able to associate ourselves, disagreeing as we do with respect to its value assumptions, its inner logic and its factual interpretations. Yet, we must confess a reluctant sympathy with those, like ourselves, who do not feel it necessary to swallow the Paretian value judgements in order to preserve their intellectual integrity; and, like Keynes, we maintain a sneaking — some might say a quixotic — regard for the 'dissenting underworld' while rejecting as utopian and irresponsible the main thrust of its policy implications.

The remaining chapters expound liberal philosophy and develop its implications for the analysis of economic policy, with a detailed application to a selective set of important topics. It will soon be clear to the reader that what he is being offered is classical political economy with modern trappings, adjusted to take account of the institutional constraints of the modern advanced economies. But we offer more than this. Economics is no longer written today primarily for an intelligent public of professional people, businessmen and politicians as was the case for example with Adam Smith's *Wealth of Nations* and even with Marshall's *Principles*. As we write on this occasion to persuade our fellow economists, we must demonstrate that Paretian welfare economics can be attacked successfully on its own ground, using the standard weapons of modern economic analysis. For in no other way can we penetrate the citadel and assault the inner temples of a dogma that has protected itself with the moat of mathematics and the portcullis of set-theoretic logic.

REFERENCES

1. Bohm, P. *Social Efficiency: A Concise Introduction to Welfare Economics* London, Macmillan (1973)
2. Buchanan, J. M. 'Positive Economics, Welfare Economics and Political Economy' *Journal of Law and Economics* (October 1959)

3. Culyer, A. J. *The Economics of Social Policy* London, Martin Robertson (1973)
4. Dobb, M. *Welfare Economics and the Economics of Socialism* Cambridge, Cambridge UP (1969)
5. Harberger, A. C. 'Three Basic Postulates for Applied Welfare Economics: An Essay' *Journal of Economic Literature* (September 1971)
6. Sen, A. 'The Impossibility of a Paretian Liberal' *Journal of Political Economy* (January/February 1970)

PART I

Paretian Welfare Economics

1. The Optimality Conditions

The Paretian value judgement is only a value judgement. It may well be rejected by some. But before it is rejected by economists, either explicitly or by implication, it must be remembered that virtually the entire edifice of economic theory as we know it today is built on Paretian premises. If those premises are rejected, that theory becomes irrelevant to the world in which we live. [D. M. Winch *Analytical Welfare Economics* Penguin Modern Economics (1971) pp. 199–200]

The Paretian approach[i]* is now so widely and so automatically employed in the economic theory of public policy, and is so pre-eminent in the literature of welfare economics, that there is a growing tendency to ignore the important value premises that underpin it (the acceptance of which is essential for its validity) and to claim for it a value-free place in economic doctrine to which certainly it is not entitled.[ii] Since we intend in this book to challenge the desirability of the hold exercised by Paretian welfare economics over the economics profession and to press for consideration the liberal alternative,[iii] it is essential to outline the precise value premises on which Paretian welfare economics rest and to evaluate in detail the technical assumptions and the necessary conditions for the attainment of a Paretian welfare optimum. If the Paretian approach is to be reduced to its proper status as one of many alternative value bases for public analysis, its limitations and weaknesses must be systematically exposed.

I THE VALUE ASSUMPTIONS

Paretian welfare economics rests on the assumed value judgement that, if a particular change in the economy leaves at least one individual better off, and no individual worse off, social welfare may

*Lower case roman numerals refer to notes, which appear at the end of each chapter; arabic numerals refer to references and source notes, which follow the notes at the end of each chapter.

be said to have increased. In this sense, an individualistic approach to social welfare is defined, with concern extending to all individuals in society, and with an explicit rejection of any 'organic' concept of 'the State'. It is important to define carefully the content of its initial value judgement:

(i) The concern is to be with the welfare of all members of society. This implies an ordinal social welfare function of the form:

$$W = W(U^1, U^2, \ldots U^s) \tag{1.1}$$

where W represents social welfare and U^1, $U^2 \ldots U^s$ represents the level of welfare (or utility) of each of the s individuals who, collectively, comprise the society under consideration. Commodities are relevant to social welfare only in so far as they influence the welfare of individual members of society.

(ii) An individual is to be considered the best judge of his own welfare (which is viewed entirely subjectively). No individual may impose his/her own preferences upon any other individual, no matter how well founded those preferences may appear in terms of prevailing ethical standards. Albeit uneasily, minors and lunatics are sometimes excluded from the scope of this important value judgement,[iv] but there are no other exceptions. It is this proposition that leads many economists (erroneously) to believe that Paretian welfare economics is synonymous with liberalism. It should be emphasised that this value assumption is not implicit in its predecessor (i) above. For it is quite possible to evaluate social welfare by reference to individual welfare without in any way assuming that the individual should be the judge of his/her own welfare. Indeed, the debate on paternalism and on so-called 'merit wants'[v] centres attention precisely on the dichotomy between assumptions (i) and (ii) of the Paretian welfare model.

Value assumption (ii) (restricted for the moment to cases where there are no interdependences between the welfare functions of separate individuals) implies the following ordinal utility function for each of s individuals:

$$U^g = U^g(X_i^g, v_j^g) \qquad (g = 1, 2, \ldots, s) \tag{1.2}$$

where X_i^g is the ith commodity consumed by the gth individual and where v_j^g is the jth productive service of the gth individual in the society under consideration. The X_is are presumed to exert a positive influence and the v_js a negative influence upon social welfare.

(iii) If any change in the allocation of resources increases the welfare of at least one individual without reducing the welfare of any other individual, then this change is treated as improving social welfare. This value assumption, which denies the possibility of making interpersonal welfare comparisons, is frequently referred to as *the* Paretian value judgement, so profound is its impact upon Paretian welfare economics. It implies that W is a monotonically increasing function of any U, i.e.

$$\frac{\partial w}{\partial U^g} > 0. \qquad (1.3)$$

It is this assumption, sometimes referred to erroneously as the unanimity assumption,[vi] which forms the basis for the Paretian ranking, and so important is it that a formal treatment is essential at this stage.[12]

Let the symbol R be read as 'is at least as preferred as, in the Pareto sense' and P and I denote 'is Pareto-superior to' and 'is Pareto-indifferent to' respectively. The unanimity rule then has the following implications:

(a) Given a set of states of the economy S, where X', $X''\epsilon$S, then X'RX'' if X'RgX'' for all $g = 1, \ldots, s$. (A state X' is said to be at least as preferred as X'' in the Paretian sense if each individual in the society regards X' as at least as preferred as X''.)

(b) X'PX'' if X'RgX'' for all $g = 1, \ldots, s$ and X'P$_k X''$ for some k. (A state X' is said to be Pareto-superior to a state X'' if each individual in the society regards X' as at least as preferred as X'', and if for at least one individual X' is regarded as strictly preferred to X''.)

(c) X'IX'' if X'IgX'' for all $g = 1, \ldots, s$. (A state X' is Pareto-indifferent to a state X'' if each individual considers X' to be indifferent to X''.)

(d) A state $X^*\epsilon$S is said to be a Pareto-optimal state in S if there does not exist a state $X\epsilon$S such that XPX^*. (A state X^* is said to be Pareto-optimal if no state in S is Pareto-superior to X.)

As Quirk and Saposnik[12] have emphasised, the Paretian ranking of states must be viewed as a partial rather than as a complete ranking since every element of the set under consideration cannot be ranked in terms of the ranking principle. For example, in the Paretian ranking, if, as between two states of society, certain individuals prefer the first to the second, while others prefer the second to the first, no ranking is defined between these two states. The two states are then said to be Pareto-non-comparable. Thus, whenever a change is under consideration which improves the welfare of some at the cost of a reduction in the welfare of others, Paretian welfare economics necessarily is silent, crippled by its own value assumptions. For this reason, the Paretian approach must be viewed as conservative, offering intellectual support to those who would maintain the status quo.[vii] A single objection is sufficient to cloud the welfare issue and to render unambiguous policy judgement impossible. Unanimity for public policy recommendations of any substance is rare indeed in the real world despite the emphasis placed upon 'consensus politics'.

The Paretian value judgements, outlined above, are in no sense trivial, nor indeed are they likely to prove universally acceptable. Indeed, as we shall urge in subsequent chapters, they are incompatible in important respects with the value judgements that underpin New Left philosophy[6] and (from our viewpoint more importantly) the liberal ethic.[10,11] Yet, if these value judgements *are* denied — and we are each of us free to reject them in whole or in part if we so decide — the essential relevance of Paretian welfare economics for the public policy debate immediately is undermined. In this respect, Paretian welfare economics is far more vulnerable than most of its disciples and practitioners are willing to allow. There can be no doubt at all that recent extensions in the mathematical formalisation of Paretian welfare economics have diverted attention quite unjustifiably from the shaky foundations upon which the entire edifice has been constructed.

II   THE ORTHODOXY AND ITS HERETICS

As with any religion, Paretian welfare economics contains its own heretical fringe, with whose views we shall be concerned in subsequent chapters of this book, and with whose position we share a modicum of sympathy. In brief, the Paretian heretics take a fundamentalist view of their dogma, emphasising the consensus requirement that, unless we can all be observed to agree, then we can say nothing as welfare economists about any change of situation, and caring little about the obsession of the orthodoxy with optimisation technicalities. In essence, the heretics attempt to apply the Wicksellian unanimity rule to its logical extremities and nothing more, with the inference that moves commanding universal consent, and such moves alone, can be said unambiguously to improve social welfare. If, in consequence of such adjustments, social contracts arise which involve coercive interventions, then so be it. The heretics accept the legitimacy of constitutional orders — unanimously endorsed — which contain coercive rules. They also accept the essentially conservative nature of a dogma that enables any one individual to veto a change that otherwise would meet with universal consent. James M. Buchanan is the undisputed leader of this heretic fringe, whose approach steadily is eroding the orthodox position.

But in this chapter we devote attention to the orthodoxy alone, whose views dominate the textbook and still permeate the journal literature, and whose hegemony it is our principal intention to destroy. Let us commence, therefore, by defining Paretian welfare economics by reference to its most narrow and naive set of technical assumptions, recognising that we are outlining the polar extreme, which is no longer adhered to even by many of the orthodoxy, but which yet forms the basis for many Paretian welfare economics pronouncements in the textbook and even the journal literature.[viii]

The principal technical assumptions of naive Paretianism are then as follows:

(i) The underlying analytical structure is static, with decisions assumed to take place at a point in time and to be implemented costlessly and instantaneously. In such a timeless economy, uncertainty as to the future does not exist. Furthermore, perfect knowledge about the present is commonly assumed. The size of the working population is assumed constant, and there is no involuntary unemployment. The static assumptions conventionally adopted imply that individual utility functions do not change, and that there is no technical progress.

(ii) It is assumed, unless otherwise stated, that each individual consumes some of each of the commodities and supplies some of each of the factors in the economy.

(iii) Each individual's preference ordering over states of the economy is characterised by selfishness or, more precisely, by solipsism; i.e., his preference ranking is defined over the commodity bundles that he receives and is not influenced by the commodity bundles allocated to other individuals. On this assumption, neither malevolence nor benevolence is recognised as having any relevance for individual welfare.

(iv) Each individual's preference ranking can be represented by a continuous (twice-differentiable) utility function characterised by strong convexity. By this assumption, lexicographic orderings are excluded as are straight-line indifference curves.

(v) All production functions are continuous, twice-differentiable, and are assumed to demonstrate non-increasing returns to scale (no indivisibilities). The iso-product curves display diminishing marginal rates of substitution between any two factors. The relevant functions possess sufficient curvature to yield tangency solutions and to satisfy the stability conditions.

(vi) All commodities and all factors of production are assumed to be perfectly divisible.

(vii) It is assumed that individuals seek to maximise their individual utilities, that producers seek to maximise their profits, and that all parties rationally pursue their respective objectives.

III   THE NECESSARY CONDITIONS FOR PARETO OPTIMALITY

Texts on welfare economics abound with comprehensive analyses of the necessary conditions for Pareto optimality.[5,9,12,14] There is no point, therefore, in treating this important topic at length. It is important however, for our purposes, to distinguish sharply between efficiency in exchange and efficiency in production[ix] and to outline the relationship between each of these 'lower-level' optima and the concept of a top-level optimum which is normally implicit in discussions of Pareto optimality.

Efficiency in exchange is concerned with the ability of individual consumers to direct the pattern of resource allocation from any given initial distribution of income. The relevant questions are how much of each commodity should be produced and how these commodities should be allocated among the various consumers. The Paretian approach provides a technical response to these questions in the form of certain necessary marginal conditions, the satisfaction of which ensures efficiency in exchange, always provided that the technical assumptions hold.

The first condition, which ensures efficiency in the distribution of commodities between consumers, is the requirement that the marginal rates of substitution between any pair of consumer goods must be the same for all individuals who consume both goods. If this condition does not hold, one or more consumer(s) could benefit from further exchange without any consequential damage to other consumers. This condition is usefully illustrated, in the two-person, two-good case, by reference to the Edgeworth box diagram, as in figure 1.1.

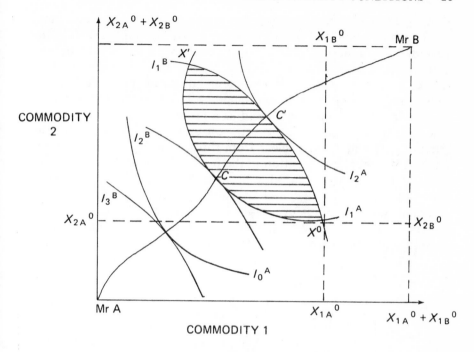

Figure 1.1

In figure 1.1 Mr A enters the market with X_{1A}^0 units of commodity 1 and X_{2A}^0 units of commodity 2; Mr B enters with X_{1B}^0 units of commodity 1 and X_{2B}^0 units of commodity 2. The joint holdings point is the point X^0, through which point are drawn indifference curves for Mr A and Mr B, labelled I_1^A and I_1^B respectively. The shaded area represents the set of reallocations of commodities 1 and 2 that are Pareto-superior to the point X^0. The point X' is Pareto-indifferent to the point X^0. The points C and C', defined by the points of tangency between indifference curves of Mr A and Mr B, and implying equality of the separate marginal rates of substitution, are optimal positions in the Paretian sense. The set of all such optimal positions is the extension of the locus CC' from Mr A's origin to Mr B's origin and is designated 'the contract curve'. Only for points on the contract curve is the necessary condition for efficiency in the distribution of commodities between consumers satisfied.

The second condition, which ensures that the quantity of each commodity produced conforms with consumer preferences, is the requirement that the marginal rate of transformation in production must equal the marginal rate of substitution in consumption for every pair of commodities and for every individual who consumes both such commodities. If this condition does not hold, a shift in the pattern of commodity production is possible which would benefit certain consumers without injuring others. This condition is illustrated, for the one-consumer, two-commodity case, in figure 1.2. TT' represents the way in which commodity 1 can be transformed into commodity 2 and may be viewed as a production possibility curve. The indifference map of the sole consumer is represented by the curves I_0, I_1 and I_2. It is clear from this figure that if production is allowed to rest at any position in the production possibility set other than X^* (the point of tangency between TT' and I_1), the welfare of the consumer could be raised by shifting to X^*. At this point, the marginal rate of transformation in production is equal to the marginal rate of substitution in consumption, and the second necessary condition for Pareto optimality thereby is satisfied.

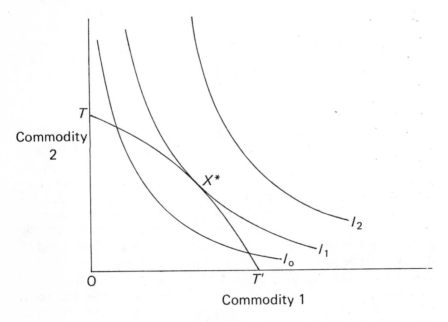

Figure 1.2

Note that we did not define the curve TT' in figure 1.2 as the outer-bound production possibility curve of the economy under consideration. For we cannot locate such a curve without reference to the third marginal condition necessary for efficiency in production. Efficiency in production is concerned with the ability of producers to provide the required range of commodities in the most efficient manner possible. The necessary condition, which ensures optimal conditions of factor substitution, is the requirement that the marginal rate of technical substitution between any pair of factor inputs must be the same for all producers who use both factor inputs. If this condition does not hold, a reallocation of factor inputs is possible which would result in a greater aggregate output without any corresponding reduction in the output of any single commodity. This condition is illustrated, for the two-commodity, two-factor input case, in figure 1.3.

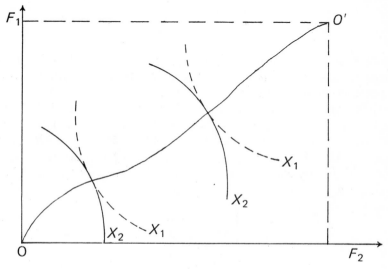

Figure 1.3

Figure 1.3 represents a box diagram with width equal to the amount of factor input 2 (F_2) and with height equal to the amount of factor input 1 (F_1). The iso-product curves for the commodity X_1 are plotted with O as the origin, and those for commodity X_2 are plotted with O' as the origin. At each point of tangency between the iso-product curves of X_1 and X_2 the marginal rates of substitution between F_1 and F_2 are equal. Each such point is a production optimum. The locus of these points is the production contract curve, from which the 'outer-bound' production possibility curve is derived.

A 'top-level' optimum is established by achieving simultaneously the necessary conditions for efficiency in exchange and efficiency in production. It requires that the rate of substitution (common to all individuals) should be equated with the rate of transformation for all pairs of goods in the economy. Once a top-level optimum is achieved, it is not possible to define a higher level of social welfare, by reference to Paretian criteria, given the initial distribution of property rights.

Following Mishan,[8] it is possible to demonstrate formally that the necessary conditions for a top-level optimum, as defined above, can be derived from the allocative rule. Let us express the equality of the value of the marginal product in all lines of output as:

$$P_x \frac{\partial x}{\partial A} = P_y \frac{\partial y}{\partial A} = \qquad (1.4)$$

$$P_x \frac{\partial x}{\partial B} = P_y \frac{\partial y}{\partial B} = \qquad (1.5)$$

where x and y are products, A and B are factor inputs, P_x, P_y are prices of the products x and y, $\partial x/\partial A$ is the marginal physical product of factor A in the production of x, etc.

Then: (1) Exchange efficiency follows from there being but a single set of product prices facing each individual; (2) productive efficiency follows from dividing (1.4) by (1.5) to give $\partial B/\partial A$ in x equal to $\partial B/\partial A$ in y; (3) top-level optimality follows if we divide (1.4) through by P_y and $\partial x/\partial A$, and (1.5) through by P_x and $\partial x/\partial B$ to obtain:

$$\frac{P_x}{P_y} = \left[\frac{\dfrac{\partial y}{\partial B}}{\dfrac{\partial x}{\partial A}} = \frac{\dfrac{\partial y}{\partial B}}{\dfrac{\partial x}{\partial B}} \right] = \dots = \frac{\partial y}{\partial x} \qquad (1.6)$$

P_x/P_y faces each individual, so that, to each, the rate of substitution is $\partial y/\partial x$, and this is equal to the rate of transformation $\partial y/\partial x$ between the products, using any of the factors at the margin. This demonstrates why perfect competition satisfies the necessary conditions for a top-level Pareto optimum.

Satisfaction of the conditions necessary for efficiency in exchange and in production provide a top-level Pareto optimum; but this in no sense implies that such a solution is the best attainable, even if the Paretian value judgements are accepted. For there is an infinite number of Paretian optima, each associated with a specific distribution of property rights and each located on the utility possibility frontier of the economy in question. Given the Paretian restriction on interpersonal utility comparisons, it is not possible either to compare alternative efficiency points or indeed to assume that any efficient point necessarily is better than inefficient points associated with different distributions of property rights.[x] If an 'optimum-optimorum' is to be located, a specific social welfare function must be employed which ranks alternative property right distributions. For those Paretians who cling fast to the individualistic approach that forms the cornerstone of the Paretian system, the notion of a social welfare function[xi] poses a number of important problems (cf. chapter 3). Nevertheless, it is widely used within the Paretian orthodoxy.

IV   ALTERNATIVE MECHANISMS FOR ACHIEVING A PARETIAN OPTIMUM

Although there is a range of alternative mechanisms for achieving a Paretian optimum, by far the most widely discussed in the welfare economics literature is the mechanism of universal perfect competition.[xii] For, on certain restrictive assumptions — notably the coincidence of private and social valuation — it can be demonstrated that perfect competition in all goods markets and in all factor markets is a sufficient condition for top-level Pareto optimality.[12]

In perfectly competitive markets, equilibrium prices (and therefore price ratios) are uniform for all consumers. Thus, the marginal rate of substitution for a utility-maximising consumer is equated with a price ratio which is identical for all consumers, thereby satisfying the first condition for efficiency in exchange. The marginal rate of transformation between any two goods will also be equated with the prevailing price ratio between them, since otherwise total revenue could be increased with no change in cost, by producing more of one and less of the other. Since all producers are governed, in equilibrium, by the same price ratios, a common marginal rate of transformation exists throughout such an economy for each pair of goods, and this rate of transformation is equated with the rate of substitution in consumption. Thus, the second condition for efficiency in exchange is satisfied. Similarly, each firm must equate the marginal rate of technical substitution between any pair of factor inputs with the price ratio that prevails between them, if profits are to be maximised, while each household must equate the marginal rate of substitution between each pair of factors to the price ratio that prevails between them if utility is to be maximised. Thus, the third condition necessary for efficiency in production is also satisfied.

In the past, there has been a regrettable tendency among welfare economists to depict perfect competition as the socially desirable market form by reference to Paretian criteria. There are two important reasons why this temptation must be denied. First, although perfect competition is indeed a sufficient condition for top-level Pareto optimality (on the restrictive assumptions usually employed), it is quite definitely not a necessary condition. A situation in which prices are equated with marginal cost in all markets — which fundamentally is the requirement for a top-level optimum — could equally be achieved by perfectly discriminating monopoly or by an appropriate set of instructions in a controlled (socialistic) economy. There is no obvious *a priori* reason for preferring the perfectly competitive mechanism to these alternative mechanisms for achieving Pareto optimality.

Secondly, it is self-evident that the assumptions upon which perfect competition rests not only *do not* but indeed *can not* exist within the modern complex industrial economy. Perfect knowledge does not and can not exist even concerning the present, to say nothing about the future. Firms and factors are not and can not realistically be made to be price-takers in all markets. Products and factors are not and cannot realistically be made to be homogeneous even within closely drawn classifications. Scale economies do not always peter out at output rates that are insignificant from the total market standpoint. Entry into all markets is not and cannot reasonably be rendered free. Indeed, the costs of adjustment in general are far more substantial than perfect competition theory conventionally suggests. In such circumstances, those who advocate perfect competition as a solution to the economic problem demonstrate only their ignorance of real-world conditions. At most, perfect competition is relevant only as a polar model, useful in that it provides an insight into real-world divergences which pose problems (in the Paretian sense) for economies that give free rein to market forces.

The prevailing orthodoxy in Western welfare economics, which evaluates market failure and supports state intervention very much by reference to real-world divergences from perfect competition, has been subjected to increasing criticism in recent years. In particular, many 'radical' economists[6] argue, to some extent justifiably, that this initial bias in favour of markets is unwarranted and that the choice between allocative mechanisms (even accepting Paretian criteria) must be made on much more fundamental philosophic grounds (cf. chapter 4). It is certainly worth re-emphasising now that perfect competition is but one of several mechanisms for allocating resources by reference to Paretian criteria.

V   THE GENERAL THEORY OF SECOND-BEST

Prior to the formal presentation by Lipsey and Lancaster[7] in 1956 of the general theory of second-best, Paretian welfare economists had pursued, virtually without reservation, an approach of 'piecemeal' welfare economics, applying to only a small part of the economy welfare rules that would lead to a Paretian optimum if they were applied everywhere simultaneously. For example, a nationalised industry would be urged to conduct its price—output policy according to the 'Lerner—Lange' marginal rule, even though it operated in an imperfectly competitive economy, on the assumption that *any* movement towards satisfying the necessary conditions for Pareto optimality must lead to an improvement in overall efficiency. The general theory of second-best condemned 'piecemeal' policy prescriptions of this kind as being futile and inappropriate:

It is well known that the attainment of a Paretian optimum requires the simultaneous fulfillment of all the optimum conditions. The general theorem for the second best optimum states that if there is introduced into a general equilibrium system a constraint which prevents the attainment of one of the Paretian conditions, the other Paretian conditions, although still attainable, are, in general, no longer desirable. In other words, given that one of the Paretian optimum conditions cannot be fulfilled, then an optimum situation can be achieved only by departing from all the other Paretian conditions. The optimum situation finally attained may be termed a second best optimum because it is achieved subject to a constraint which, by definition, prevents the attainment of a Paretian optimum.

The theorem embodying this negative conclusion was proved by maximising a welfare function subject to the conventional constraints (the production function, etc.) plus an additional constraint in the form of an inequality of one of the conventional marginal conditions. The first-order conditions resulting from this exercise were not the conventional marginal conditions for a Paretian welfare optimum, but were relatively complex expressions. Let us illustrate by reference to a single example.[9]

We wish to maximise a utility function, for a single individual, of the form

$$U = U(x_1, \ldots, x_n) \tag{1.7}$$

subject to the transformation function

$$t(x_1, \ldots, x_n) = 0 \tag{1.8}$$

where x stands both for goods (1 to s) and for factors of production $(s + 1 - n)$. The necessary conditions for a maximum are

$$\frac{\partial U/\partial x_i}{\partial U/\partial x_n} = \frac{\partial t/\partial x_i}{\partial t/\partial x_n} \quad (i = 1, \ldots, n) \tag{1.9}$$

Suppose, however, that a technical constraint prevents the fulfilment of one of these necessary conditions, viz.:

$$\frac{\partial U/\partial x_1}{\partial U/\partial x_n} = K \frac{\partial t/\partial x_1}{\partial t/\partial x_n} \text{ where } K \neq 1. \tag{1.10}$$

The utility function must now be maximised subject to two constraints and the conditions necessary for a second-best maximum are:

$$\frac{\partial U}{\partial x_i} - \lambda \frac{\partial t}{\partial x_i} - \Pi \frac{\left(\dfrac{\partial U}{\partial x_n} \cdot \dfrac{\partial^2 U}{\partial x_1 \partial x_i}\right) - \left(\dfrac{\partial U}{\partial x_1} \cdot \dfrac{\partial^2 U}{\partial x_n \partial x_i}\right)}{\left(\dfrac{\partial U}{\partial x_n}\right)^2}$$

$$- K \frac{\left(\dfrac{\partial t}{\partial x_n} \cdot \dfrac{\partial^2 t}{\partial x_1 \partial x_i}\right) - \left(\dfrac{\partial t}{\partial x_1} \cdot \dfrac{\partial^2 t}{\partial x_n \partial x_i}\right)}{\left(\dfrac{\partial t}{\partial x_n}\right)^2} = 0. \tag{1.11}$$

These conditions will differ from the earlier conditions unless the coefficient of π is zero. Detailed knowledge would be required as to the nature of the particular goods and factors involved in order to determine whether or not π is likely to be zero.

The general theorem of the second-best states that, if one of the Paretian optimum conditions cannot be fulfilled, a second-best optimum situation is achieved only by departing from all other optimum conditions. In general, nothing can be said about the direction or the magnitude of the secondary departures from optimum conditions made necessary by the original non-fulfilment of one condition. In particular, it is not true that a situation in which all departures from the optimum conditions are of the same direction and magnitude is necessarily superior to one in which the deviations vary in direction and magnitude. Indeed, in the more complex cases involving third-order derivatives (to establish that the second differential of the expression is negative), it will not be possible, for the most part, even to determine whether or not a second-best solution exists, since the relevant functions are rarely specified in sufficient detail for such an exercise. (But see chapter 3 for an optimistic Paretian view of this problem.)

Although the theorem of the second-best rapidly entered into the main body of Paretian welfare economics, and although its disturbing implications were widely recognised at the theoretical level, the theorem has exercised in practice only a limited influence upon applied welfare economics and upon the economic theory of public policy. This lack of impact is certainly not due to any lack of applicability of the theorem to real-world situations. For economists are only too well aware that they are examining economic systems that are riddled with institutional and policy constraints. For example, the virtual absence of perfect competition, referred to earlier in this chapter, almost certainly implies a failure to satisfy the marginal conditions for a top-level optimum in any private market transaction. In such circumstances, it would appear that the general applicability of Paretian welfare economics is drastically curtailed. How is it that the orthodox Paretian dogma has so successfully survived this onslaught?

Two avenues of escape have been utilised. The first, less tortuous and more popular, is that of paying lip service to the second-best theorem while proceeding (more or less brazenly, according to sensitivity) to an analysis based upon the 'piecemeal' principle. D. M. Winch[14] (more honestly than many[xiii]) has advocated openly that this approach should be widely adopted: 'The rules of first-best optimality, coupled with the caveat of second-best, do, however, constitute part of the fund of guidelines from which good, if not perfect, policy might be formulated.'

The second avenue of escape is that of restricting the generality of the second-best theorem via further analysis. The intellectual springboard for this exercise in rehabilitating 'piecemeal' analysis is the 1965 paper by Davis and Whinston,[4] which has not received perhaps the attention that it deserves. Davis and Whinston centred attention upon situations in which at least one actor within a system has an unadjustable preference ordering, a criterion function or a technology which deviates from that required for the attainment of Pareto optimality. Granted the behaviour of this deviant, they examined the behavioural rules for the other actors which would compensate best for the deviant's behaviour. They concluded that, whenever there was deviant behaviour in which only prices and the variables under the deviant's control entered into his decision rule, the market would take that behaviour into account, since the price mechanism takes into account inter-connectedness caused by scarcity. In such circumstances, piecemeal policy was all that was required. But wherever interdependence caused non-price variables not directly under the actor's control to be in his behavioural rule, the policy-maker must consider the entire system in order to avoid undesirable consequences.

In Davis and Whinston terms, therefore, the relevance of second-best considerations becomes an empirical issue concerning the degree of interdependence between utility functions and production functions within an economic system. Some ground for comfort undeniably is provided to those addicted to Paretian dogma. But, in view of recent extensions of Paretian economics into the field of utility interdependences, such comfort as there is must be somewhat chilled.

VI   CONCLUSIONS

Orthodox Paretian welfare economics has had a good run. It is still very much on the advance, and indeed it still threatens to establish a complete stranglehold over the economics profession. As we shall demonstrate in subsequent chapters, Paretian welfare economics has been extended with ingenuity to encompass such problems as interdependent preferences and income redistribution, previously regarded as outside its province.[xiv] Indeed, recent Paretian advances into the analysis of optimal rates of love and hate, crime prevention and revolution extend well beyond the limits of what is conventionally regarded as economic territory. Has it over-reached itself?

There are two answers to this question. In one sense, any analysis based upon a process of logical deduction from a set of clearly formulated premises is to be encouraged in a field (social science) that has suffered in the past an excess of hunch and intuition. On this basis, our answer to the question posed must be in the negative. In another, and perhaps more profound sense, however, the answer must be a resounding positive. For the practitioners of the Paretian dogma are now so confident in their approach, so enraptured by the formal elegance and mathematical rigour of their exercises and so contemptuous of their less highly formalised and less elegant competitors that they incline increasingly to the passing off of their normative policy judgements as positive contributions. The policy-makers are expected, by those who perpetrate this misdemeanour, to regard the mechanics of the welfare exercise with the awe accorded by the early Church of Rome to the contents of a Papal Bull, though, perhaps thankfully, in practice they are justifiably suspicious of economic analysis that appears to offer clear-cut solutions to complex politico-economic problems.

The message of this chapter is that the orthodox Paretians do their profession a disservice by their excessive claims in the field of policy formation, that there are other approaches and that there are better value judgements. Their attempt to develop a welfare economics consensus and to stamp out those who do not accept its teachings as undemocratic or illiberal not only is fundamentally misguided but indeed paves the way to intellectual serfdom.

NOTES

i This approach is based upon the writings of Vilfredo Pareto, whose *Manual of Political Economy* (1897, translated in 1971) provides the framework for Paretian welfare economics.

ii Perhaps the most consistent advocate in this respect is J. M. Buchanan.[2] Viz.: 'This Pareto rule is itself an ethical proposition, a value statement, but it is one which requires a minimum of premises and one which should command wide assent.'

iii Following the approach adopted in our recent joint publications, viz. Peacock and Rowley.[10,11]

iv Buchanan[2] has urged that 'unreasonable' members of a community might be excluded for purposes of Paretian welfare analysis. But who is to decide the criteria for 'unreasonableness'?

v We examine merit wants more closely in chapter 3.

vi Strictly, it is a Nem. Con. Rule.

vii Perhaps this is why so many apparent conservatives ascribe to Paretian welfare economics. For example, we have urged elsewhere that this is the case with 'Virginian-blend' Liberals of the Buchanan, Tullock, Hochman and Rodgers school.[10]

viii We shall review the implications of relaxing certain of these assumptions in chapter 3

ix It is our view that the detailed consideration of exchange efficiency has resulted until recently in a comparative neglect of production efficiency. Leibenstein's seminal work on 'X-Efficiency' has done much to redress this imbalance.

x Viz. Boulding[1] (p. 31): 'Thus instead of a relatively simple problem of climbing the preference mountain along the opportunity fence until we reach the highest point – which is the essential principle of maximising behaviour and of welfare economics – we find ourselves climbing a quaking jelly of a mountain that dips and sags as we walk across it, along a nightmarish fence which shifts and wavers as we walk beside it. It is little wonder that mankind has generally retreated from the quagmire of rationality to the solid highroads of taboo and principle, even though they may not go where we want them to.'

xi We discuss the social welfare function approach in some detail in chapter 3.

xii Indeed, Henderson and Quandt,[5] for example, discuss the 'efficiency' of perfect competition before introducing the Paretian model (pp. 202—8).

xiii Including (alas!) Rowley:[13] 'Despite this important caveat, policy discussion in this book ignores the problems presented by second best theory and proceeds as if the marginal conditions were already satisfied in non-steel sectors of the economy.'

xiv For a typical illustration of Paretian empire-building see Culyer:[3] 'The Paretian approach is essentially tolerant of all ethical systems and it is this generality that makes it attractive in social science which, like all science, seeks generality rather than specificity. It is also suited to the normative analysis of social policy in democratic and democratic socialist societies.'

REFERENCES

1. Boulding, K. 'Welfare Economics' in B. F. Haley (ed.) *A Survey of Contemporary Economics* Homewood, Ill., Irwin (1952) chapter I

2. Buchanan, J. M. 'Positive Economics, Welfare Economics, and Political Economy' *Journal of Law and Economics* (October 1959)

3. Culyer, A. J. *The Economics of Social Policy* London, Martin Robertson (1973)

4. Davis, O. E. and Whinston, A. 'Welfare Economics and the Theory of Second Best' *Review of Economic Studies* (1965)

5. Henderson, J. M. and Quandt, R. E. *Microeconomic Theory* New York, McGraw-Hill (1958) chapter 7

6. Lindbeck, A. *The Political Economy of the New Left* New York, Harper and Row (1971)

7. Lipsey, R. G. and Lancaster, K. 'The General Theory of Second-Best' *Review of Economic Studies* (1956)

8. Mishan, E. 'A Survey of Welfare Economics 1939—59' *The Economic Journal* (1960)

9. Nath, S. K. *A Reappraisal of Welfare Economics* London, Routledge and Kegan Paul (1969)

10. Peacock, A. T. and Rowley, C. K. 'Pareto Optimality and the Political Economy of Liberalism' *Journal of Political Economy* (May/June 1972)

11. Peacock, A. T. and Rowley, C. K. 'Welfare Economics and the Public Regulation of Natural Monopoly' *Journal of Public Economics* (August 1972)

12. Quirk, J. and Saposnik, R. *Introduction to General Equilibrium Theory and Welfare Economics* New York, McGraw-Hill (1968)

13. Rowley, C. K. *Steel and Public Policy* London, McGraw-Hill (1971)

14. Winch, D. M. *Analytical Welfare Economics* Harmondsworth, Penguin (1971)

2. Market Failure

> Given a social welfare function, and given the absence of all technological and taste externalities, and given universal constant returns to scale, there would be needed only one type of public policy — redistributive transfers. [P. A. Samuelson 'Aspects of Public Expenditure Theories' *Review of Economics and Statistics* (November 1958) p. 333]

Adam Smith, writing in 1776, felt able to conclude that each individual, pursuing his own self-interest, was led as if by an invisible hand to activities that promoted the general welfare of all. Such expansiveness is denied to the present-day welfare economist who is circumscribed by adherence to the Paretian dogma. At most, he can argue that, on certain restrictive assumptions, perfect competition satisfies the necessary conditions for a top-level Paretian optimum, though whether or not that optimum is socially desirable there is no means of deciding. Since perfect competition not only does not but indeed cannot exist as a universal phenomenon in the modern advanced economy, the policy relevance of the Paretian approach, save under conditions of socialism, cannot be considered extensive. It should be remembered that any divergence of price from marginal cost (as occurs even in the large-group monopolistic competition case) debars the attainment of a Paretian optimum.

Too often, this point is ignored by Paretian welfare economists who proceed from the rigorous formal analysis of the Paretian model to casual if not careless policy discussion in which the word 'perfect' is dropped (by accident or by design) and competition, of whatever kind, is treated (incorrectly) as a sufficient welfare-maximising mechanism. It is an interesting reflection on the dominance of theoretical rigour over practical relevance in modern economics that the 'Arrow Impossibility Theorem'[1] (elegantly formulated though of dubious practical importance) has received so much attention while the 'practical impossibility of perfect competition' hypothesis (so central to conventional Paretian analysis) has received so little. There are no Nobel Prizes for those who claim that the Paretian approach cannot be implemented in practical terms.

In any event, even the universal presence of perfect competition does not in itself ensure the attainment of a Paretian optimum. For such an outcome is contingent upon the assumption that there are no external effects in consumption and production, i.e. that the utility level of a consumer does not depend upon the consumption levels of others and that the total cost of a firm does not depend upon the output levels of other firms. Where these assumptions do not hold, even universal perfect competition unaided may be incapable of providing a Paretian optimum.[i]

Although there is a tendency in the welfare economics literature to analyse separately the problems posed by the presence of joint products, externalities, indivisibilities and public goods, these phenomena are related by the common feature that, somewhere, one or other of the marginal rates (of substitution or of transformation) is meaningless, with varying implications for efficiency in exchange and/or in production. For illustrative purposes, in this chapter we centre attention on the problems posed by public goods and by externalities.[ii]

In analysing market failure from this viewpoint, it is helpful to distinguish between three kinds of goods. The first is the case of the private good, the consumption of which by one individual automatically deprives others of its use. Private goods $(X_1, \ldots, X_n)$ can be parcelled out among different individuals $(1, 2, \ldots, i, \ldots, s)$ according to the relations

$$X_j = \sum_{i=1}^{s} X_j^i.$$

Such goods are characterised by an opportunity cost in any individual's consumption as well as an opportunity cost in production. With an appropriate resource-allocating mechanism (viz. perfect competition), market forces can provide a Paretian optimum. The second is the case of public goods $(X_{n+1}, \ldots, X_{n+m})$ that are enjoyed by all in common, in the sense that each individual's consumption of such a good leads to no subtraction from any other individual's consumption, so that $X_{n+j} = X_{n+j}^i$ simultaneously for each ith individual and for each public good. Thus, although there is an opportunity cost in production, zero opportunity cost attaches to its consumption from the individual's viewpoint and in this respect public goods are a special case of joint production. The third is the case of mixed goods which possess both private and public characteristics. It is with this category of good that the conventional externality literature is centrally concerned. Public goods and mixed goods present problems in attaining a Paretian optimum which perfect competition alone cannot resolve and in this sense they constitute a Paretian problem in market failure. In this chapter, we shall review the Paretian positions concerning these categories of market failure, from the viewpoint of the established orthodoxy.

I   PUBLIC GOODS

By reference to Samuelson's criterion,[17],[18],[19] the pure public good is located at one extreme of the commodity spectrum which distinguishes between commodities by reference to their degree of non-rivalryness in consumption. As such, there are few if any practical examples of the pure public good polar case. Nevertheless, let us retain the Samuelson tradition (the high-priest of Paretian orthodoxy) in reviewing the market failure implications of the public good category by reference to the extreme case.

Assume that each individual in society has a consistent set of ordinal preferences concerning the consumption of all goods, private and public:

$$U^i = U^i(X_1{}^i, \ldots, X_{n+m}^i). \tag{2.1}$$

Assume suitably convex and smooth production possibility schedules for all outputs, private and public:

$$F(X_1, \ldots, X_{n+m}) = 0 \tag{2.2}$$

with $\partial F/\partial X_j > 0$ and $(\partial F/\partial X_j)/(\partial F/\partial X_n)$ determinate and subject to generalised diminishing returns.

The necessary conditions for Pareto optimality in such circumstances are defined mathematically as follows:

(i) $$\frac{\partial U^i}{\partial X_j{}^i} \bigg/ \frac{\partial U^i}{\partial X_r{}^i} = \frac{\partial F}{\partial X_j} \bigg/ \frac{\partial F}{\partial F_r} \quad (i = 1,2, \ldots, s; r, j = 1, \ldots, n) \tag{2.3}$$

(ii) $$\sum_{i=1}^{s} \frac{\partial U^i}{\partial X_{n+j}^i} \bigg/ \frac{\partial U^i}{\partial X_r{}^i} = \frac{\partial F}{\partial X_{n+j}} \bigg/ \frac{\partial F}{\partial X_r} \quad (j = 1, \ldots, m, \ r = 1 \ldots, n)$$
$$\tag{2.4}$$

Equation (2.3) is the standard condition for a Paretian optimum in the case of private goods (characterised by a non-zero opportunity cost in individual consumption). In such cases, a decentralised, perfectly competitive solution technically can satisfy the necessary conditions for Pareto optimality, with goods produced at minimum cost and sold at marginal cost and with all factors receiving the value of their marginal product. In pure theory terms, at least, therefore, the issue of market failure need not be confronted. Equation (2.4), by contrast, is the special condition for a Paretian optimum in the case of public goods (characterised by a zero opportunity cost in individual consumption) in which the marginal rate of transformation is equated with the aggregate marginal rate of substitution summed over all individuals. In such circumstances, a decentralised, perfectly competitive solution must fail to satisfy the necessary conditions for Pareto optimality; and, to Samuelson and the Paretian orthodoxy, at least, some form of collective choice clearly is justified.

A Paretian optimum is less 'fulsome' in the case of public than of private goods, merely by the nature of the public good itself, though this point is rarely elaborated in the Paretian literature. For, in the pure public good case, each individual consumes an identically equal amount of the good in question.[iii] Since tastes will differ, so will the marginal evaluations of that good, in terms of a private good *numeraire* at the point of equilibrium in the public good provision. In such circumstances, efficiency in the allocation of a public good between individuals cannot be pursued and, instead, attention is centred on the lower-level objective of the optimal provision of the good in question. This implication is demonstrated in figure 2.1. MRS^1 and MRS^2 represent the respective marginal rates of substitution of the public good X_2 in terms of the private good X_1 for two persons comprising society. ΣMRS is derived by vertically summing MRS^1 and MRS^2. MRT represents the marginal rate of transformation of X_2 into X_1. The equality at E between ΣMRS and

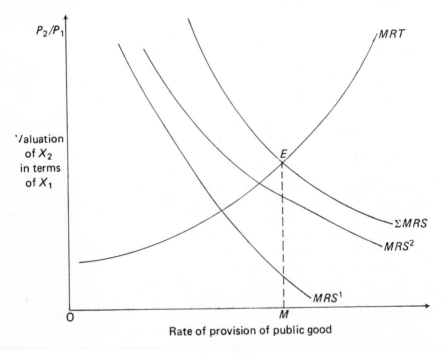

Figure 2.1

MRT determines the optimal rate of provision of the public good at $0M$ per period. At this rate, $MRS^1 \neq MRS^2$ and the necessary condition for efficiency in exchange is violated.

The optimality condition depicted in equation (2.4) and in figure 2.1 theoretically could be satisfied by an 'omniscient calculating machine' if fed the details of all relevant utility and production functions. Thus Samuelson:[18]

The failure of market catallactics in no way denies the following truth: given sufficient knowledge the optimal decisions can always be found by scanning over all the attainable states of the world and selecting the one which according to the postulated ethical welfare function is best. The solution 'exists'; the problem is how to 'find' it. [p. 389]

Unfortunately, the 'omniscient calculating machine' does not exist in the real world — though certain of the Paretian orthodoxy write as though it does — and, as we have noted, the market analogue of such a machine — perfect competition — does not work in the public good situation. How then, in practice, do the Paretians resolve their policy dilemma? Certainly, the incentives exist for individuals to act collectively in the provision of public goods at rates defined by equation (2.4); how best they might do so is still a matter of controversy.

A plethora of simple trading models in recent years has demonstrated that Pareto optimal outcomes are feasible in public good situations as a consequence of private bargains, but only where highly restrictive assumptions are deemed to hold. If the number of individuals concerned is small, and yet if each individual behaves *vis-à-vis* other individuals as though the numbers were large, ordinary exchange may generate outcomes of an optimal nature. In itself, this is no mean achievement. For, in the conventional bargaining model, involving only private goods, individuals need agree only on the terms of exchange between those goods, while reserving the right to consume varying amounts of each. In the public good case, in contrast, they must agree on the quantity of the good to be commonly consumed and also on the division between them of its cost (measured in terms of a private good *numeraire*).[iv]

In practice, however, the public good problem, for the most part, is a large-numbers problem, to which the simple trading models do not apply. It is true that, if full participation could be ensured, the large-numbers solution is more determinate than the small, with strategic bargaining impossible and with the solution at a unique point on the contract locus. But this is precisely where the problem lies, since full participation in a public good's bargain is not easily achieved when large numbers are involved, even if ordinary bargaining costs are ignored, on account of the 'free-rider' problem. The pressure for each individual to reveal his preferences is progressively lowered as the numbers rise, if the exclusion principle cannot or will not be invoked. For each individual can seize an advantage by remaining aloof from the bargaining process in the expectation that he will gain common access to the public good provisions without contributing to the costs.^{v} Thus, although everyone may wish to have the public good provided in accordance with equation (2.4), it is predictable, in the large-numbers case, that rates of provision arising in the bargaining solution will be sub-optimal, to the detriment of all concerned.

The orthodox Paretian response to the public good problem is that of recommending state intervention often in the form of public provision, at zero prices, financed by lump-sum taxes and, upon occasion, via fiscal instruments or mandatory legislation. In a fundamental sense, therefore, the public good problem is viewed by orthodox Paretians as a rationale of government. Thus Samuelson:[19]

Indeed, I am rash enough to think that in almost every one of the legitimate functions of government that critics put forward there is to be found a blending of the extreme antipodal models (public and private goods). One might even venture the tentative suspicion that any function of government not possessing any trace of the defined public good ... ought to be carefully scrutinised to see whether it is truly a legitimate function of government. [p. 356]

In this view, the individuals concerned are assumed to submit to the judgement of an 'ethical observer' or 'impartial referee', embodied as the State and charged with the responsibility of applying the Paretian rules in pursuit of a welfare maximum, and of correcting for any 'adverse' income redistribution implicit in its interventions by reference to some God-given social welfare function. For many of the orthodoxy, this 'nirvana' view of government is embraced unquestioningly in a touching, if dangerously unrealistic, obeisance to paternal authority.[2] But even the more perceptive Paretians accept the myth in their eagerness to spell out the policy implications. Thus Winch:[24]

Whether such a function represents the will of God, Superman or a dictator, the formal analytics of maximising it are straightforward once it is known, for the process is simply that of maximising the objective of the single source, whatever it may be.

There is always a danger that those who play games with such analytical devices will formulate their policy pronouncements as though the underlying assumptions in practice hold, i.e. that

'Superman' exists. This is the charge that we now level against the Paretian orthodoxy concerning public good analysis. The Paretian debate on public goods centres almost exclusively upon the issue of what precisely constitutes a public good. It is taken for granted that collective intervention must follow once public good characteristics are discovered — and this without reference to the nature of the collectivity in which important economic powers so freely are to be vested.

One does not have to probe far into political philosophy to raise serious doubts about the validity of this approach. Indeed, one has only to turn to Thomas Hobbes to read of 'that great *Leviathan* or rather, to speak more reverently, of that mortal god' to whom citizens surrender all power as the only means of resolving conflicts among themselves, to learn of the ineptitude of the orthodox Paretian viewpoint. Thus Hobbes:

. . . for all men are by nature provided of notable multiplying glasses, that is their passions and their self-love, through which every little payment appeareth a great grievance; but are destitute of those prospective glasses, namely moral and civil science, to see afar off the miseries that hang over them, and cannot without such payments be avoided.

It is not surprising, therefore, that the more perceptive of the Paretian camp, the heretics, have denied Hobbes's 'mortal god' and have sought out alternative approaches to the public good problem, in the spirit of John Locke rather than of Thomas Hobbes, relying upon consensus as a basis for public policy pronouncements. To this approach and its limitations, we defer discussion until chapter 6, in which we outline also the liberal alternatives for the public good dilemma.

II   EXTERNALITIES

Externalities arise whenever economic activity on the part of one individual (in consumption or in production) generates an effect (beneficial or detrimental) on some other individual who is not party to the activity. Beneficial externalities usually are referred to as external economies; detrimental externalities as external diseconomies. Where such externalities are Pareto-relevant, and where private solutions are not possible, the orthodoxy for the most part advocate some form of fiscal intervention, though there is controversy concerning the balance of fiscal instruments required Let us illustrate the essential Paretian position by reference to this controversy which raises a fundamental issue, namely, whether the existence of a desire for trade between two parties involved in a single externality relationship can always be viewed as proof that the existing solution is not one of Pareto-optimality. Buchanan and Stubblebine, in an authoritative contribution,[10,11] have urged that this indeed is so. Shibata[21,22] has recently challenged their position in a determined bid to resuscitate the old Pigovian orthodoxy.

Buchanan and Stubblebine consider two individuals, A and B, whose utility functions are given respectively as:

$$U^A = U^A(X_1, X_2 \ldots, X_m, Y_1) \qquad (2.5)$$

and

$$U^B = U^B(Y_1, Y_2 \ldots, Y_m) \qquad (2.6)$$

while B confronts the production function given as

$$f^B = f^B(Y_1, Y_2 \ldots, Y_m) \qquad (2.7)$$

where X_is and Y_is are called activities.

When B carries out the activity Y_1, he maximises his own utility when the following holds:

$$\frac{\partial U^B Y_1}{\partial U^B Y_j} = \frac{\partial f^B Y_1}{\partial f^B Y_j} \text{ where } Y_1 = \bar{Y}_1. \qquad (2.8)$$

Buchanan and Stubblebine define a Pareto-relevant marginal externality to exist when:

$$(-)\frac{\partial U^A Y_1}{\partial U^A X_j} > \left(\frac{\partial U^B Y_1}{\partial U^B Y_j} - \frac{\partial f^B Y_1}{\partial f^B Y_j}\right), Y_1 = \bar{Y}_1 \qquad (2.9)$$

assuming

$$\frac{\partial U^A Y_1}{\partial U^A X_j} < 0.$$

Buchanan and Stubblebine define Pareto equilibrium (with zero opportunities for further trade) as

$$(-)\frac{\partial U^A Y_1}{\partial U^A X_j} = \frac{\partial U^B Y_1}{\partial U^B Y_j} - \frac{\partial f^B Y_1}{\partial f^B Y_j}. \qquad (2.10)$$

They introduce an ideal Pigovian tax, levied on B as he performs activity Y_1, at a marginal rate equal to the negative marginal evaluation of the activity to A. B's new private equilibrium is given as

$$\frac{\partial U^B Y_1}{\partial U^B Y_j} = \frac{\partial f^B Y_1}{\partial f^B Y_j} - \frac{\partial U^A Y_1}{\partial U^A X_j} \text{ where } Y_1 = \bar{\bar{Y}}_1. \qquad (2.11)$$

At the activity rate $\bar{\bar{Y}}_1$ Buchanan and Stubblebine accede that there is no divergence between marginal private cost and marginal social cost in the usual sense. But they deny that the position is either one of Pareto optimality or one of Pareto equilibrium, since at $Y_1 = \bar{\bar{Y}}$ the necessary condition for Pareto-relevance defined in equation (2.9) is now modified to read:

$$(-)\frac{\partial U^A Y_1}{\partial U^A X_j} > \left(\frac{\partial U^B Y_1}{\partial U^B Y_j} - \frac{\partial f^B Y_1}{\partial f^B Y_j} + \frac{\partial U^A Y_1}{\partial U^A X_j}\right), Y_1 = \bar{\bar{Y}} \quad (2.12)$$

Since the bracketed terms must sum to zero for B to be in private equilibrium, so long as the left-hand term in the inequality is non-zero, a Pareto-relevant marginal externality remains, despite the application of the Pigovian tax. A full Pareto equilibrium will be reached only when (2.12) is satisfied as an equality:

$$(-)\frac{\partial U^A Y_1}{\partial U^A X_j} = \left(\frac{\partial U^B Y_1}{\partial U^B Y_j} - \frac{\partial f^B Y_1}{\partial f^B Y_j} + \frac{\partial U^A Y_1}{\partial U^A X_j}\right) Y_1 = \bar{\bar{\bar{Y}}}_1 \quad (2.13)$$

The essence of the Buchanan—Stubblebine approach is recognition that every externality relationship is necessarily reciprocal and that equilibrium is attainable only if both decision-makers have the same marginal rate of substitution between the activity in question and a *numeraire* commodity. If the behaviour of B is modified by the imposition of a marginal tax, then so must the behaviour of A, or B be further modified, e.g. by a marginal subsidy, if potential gains from trade are to be eliminated and a true Pareto equilibrium achieved. The Pigovian tax solution — by ignoring the change in property rights implicit in the tax imposition — falsely seeks out a solution that is no longer optimal in the post-tax situation.

The Buchanan—Stubblebine point is usefully summarised in figure 2.2. *BC* is the 'marginal net benefit to the producer' curve for an activity that gives rise to external diseconomies. *OA* is the 'marginal damages to the consumers' curve. Let us assume that property rights lie with the producer and that bargaining is ruled out on grounds of cost. Private equilibrium would then be at *C* despite the welfare gains reflected in the triangle *ADC*, which are available by shifting to *E*, which represents a Pareto optimum, The Pigovian tax solution would

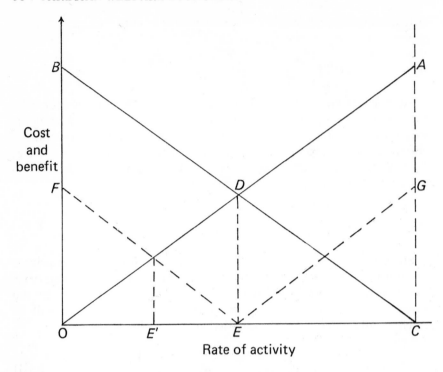

Figure 2.2

operate effectively by shifting *BC* downwards to *FE*, thereby rendering *E* a position of private equilibrium. According to Buchanan and Stubblebine, however, the tax imposition changes the institutional framework so as to render *E* irrelevant from the policy viewpoint. *E'* is the new Pareto optimum, in the post-tax situation and this will not be achieved via the tax imposition. To ensure that *E* is attained following fiscal intervention as a true Pareto optimum, Buchanan and Stubblebine require simultaneously a marginal subsidy to the consumers designed to lower the marginal damages curve to *EG*, in which case there are no potential gains from trade at the position of private equilibrium.

Shibata's criticism of the Buchanan—Stubblebine contribution denies that the imposition of a Pigovian tax changes the necessary conditions for Pareto-optimality, emphasising that the mere imposition of the tax *per se* does not alter any of the technical production possibilities, while the newly imposed tax wedge implies that B's private marginal cost in the production of Y_1 is no longer the same as the marginal cost confronted by the economy. Thus, the Buchanan—Stubblebine proof, it is urged, is based upon an inadequate recognition of the necessary conditions for Pareto-optimality. In particular, Shibata questions their failure to discuss the destination of the tax proceeds, which in his view is crucially important in the Pigovian solution. In the two-person case, Shibata infers that B should be compensated following the tax imposition by a lump-sum subsidy in order that the Paretian value judgement should not be violated, in which case his private equilibrium will occur where:

$$(-) \frac{\partial U^B Y_1}{\partial U^B Y_j} = (-) \frac{\partial f^B Y_1}{\partial f^B Y_j} + \frac{\partial U^A Y_1}{\partial U^A X_j} \qquad (2.13A)$$

which satisfies the necessary condition for Pareto-optimality specified by Buchanan and Stubblebine in equation (2.13).

Crucial to the Shibata formulation in the two-person case is the notion that B is aware both of the source of his lump-sum subsidy and of its one-to-one correspondence with his tax outgoings. For, in such circumstances, B will recognise that the value of damage imposed by each unit of Y_1, for which he is chargeable, is precisely offset by the value of the returned subsidy — in effect, the lump-sum subsidy is viewed by B as a *marginal subsidy*. Since the marginal subsidy is central also to the Buchanan—Stubblebine formulation, there is no real conflict, in such circumstances, between them and Shibata. Shibata can retain his Pigovian mantle only because the lump-sum subsidy becomes *de facto* marginal in the perception of the recipient. More generally, in a real-world situation in which compensation typically is not paid, or, when paid, is not associated directly with the externality intervention by those concerned, the Shibata criticism does not hold and the Buchanan—Stubblebine position must be accepted.

In one sense, the debate is one of semantics concerning the nature of a lump-sum subsidy. More fundamentally, however, the debate typifies the gap between the Paretian orthodoxy (Shibata) and the heretics (Buchanan and Stubblebine),[vi] even when treating conventional issues, with the former emphasising the technical requirements and the latter seeking out potential gains from trade in pursuit of the Paretian nirvana.[6,7,9,10,11]

III   PUBLIC CHOICE AND THE ARROW DILEMMA

Even under the assumptions most favourable to decentralisation of decision-making, the Paretian orthodoxy concede the irreducible need for public choice on distribution grounds. Furthermore, since the most favourable assumptions are rarely, if ever, found in the modern advanced economies, there are many other situations in which some form of public choice finds Paretian advocacy. The question thus arises as to precisely what form public choice should take in a society governed by the Paretian dogma, and in particular what relationship should be established between individual preferences and collective decisions. It is to this question that we now address ourselves.

In the context of public choice,[1,15,16,17,21] each individual may be assumed to have a preference ordering over all possible states, expressing not only his desire for his own consumption, but also his social attitudes and his judgements on matters concerning public choice. Given the breakdown of decentralised decision-making, what is required is a group decision rule (or constitution) which associates to each possible set of individual preference orderings a public choice rule. A public choice rule, in turn, is a rule for selecting a publicly preferred action out of any set of alternatives that may be feasible. Serious problems are encountered, however, in the process of deciding just what conditions are to be imposed upon the constitution as an instrument of public choice. For, where choices must be made among more than two alternatives, Kenneth Arrow[1,4] has proved that no constitution — other than one based upon the Wicksellian unanimity principle — can satisfy simultaneously a set of apparently reasonable and widely accepted conditions.

If the preference orderings of all individuals were always identical for all states, the Arrow dilemma would not arise, since a constitution based upon the unanimity principle would be operational — veritably a Paretian paradise! Idyllic though such a constitution might be, however, the Paretian principle is too weak to be applied generally in the real-world situation, where conflict between individual preference orderings is common and where consensus requirements would lead to ultraconservatism in the public choice situation. In such circumstances, even the most orthodox of Paretians concede the case for less-than-unanimity constitutions,[vii] though they seem not to recognise the enormity of this concession to public choice realities (cf. chapter 6). In any event, attempts to restrict the constitution along less-than-unanimity lines encounter serious logical criticisms, in the guise of the Arrow Possibility Theorem, to which we now must address ourselves.

There are five conditions which Arrow requires a constitution (or group decision rule) to fulfil:[1,16,17,21]

Condition 1 (the condition of collective rationality). This condition ensures that, for any given set of individual preferences, the group decision rule defined by them should satisfy the technical conditions of an ordering, namely that all possible alternative social states should be capable of being ranked and that the social choice from any particular set of alternatives should be the most preferred alternative, according to the ordering, in the available set. Given any three social states, the social ranking R must provide a complete, transitive and reflexive ranking of the states for any set of well-behaved individual preference rankings over the states.

Condition 2 (the Pareto principle). This condition ensures that the group decision rule will never yield an outcome if there is another feasible alternative that everyone prefers according to his preference ordering. If the individual orderings remain exactly the same except that one state rises in some person's orderings, then that state will not fall *vis-à-vis* any alternative state in the social preference pattern in the new situation. Formally, let $R_1, \ldots, R_m$ be the rankings of individuals $1, \ldots, m$ over two states of the economy Z' and Z''. Let $R_1', \ldots, R_m'$ be some other set of rankings over Z' and Z'' such that Z' is ranked higher for some individuals and no lower for any individual as compared with the previous rankings. Then, if under the rankings R_j, $Z'PZ''$, it must follow that $Z'PZ''$, where the social ranking R' is associated with the individual rankings R_j'.

Condition 3 (independence of irrelevant alternatives). This ensures that the social choice made from any set of alternatives will depend only on the orderings of individuals among alternatives in that set. Formally, let $R_1, \ldots, R_m$ and $R_1', \ldots, R_m'$ be two sets of rankings by individuals $1, \ldots, m$ over any set of states of the economy, and let Z^* and $Z^{*'}$ be the socially most preferred states, respectively, corresponding to individual rankings R_j and R_j'. Assume that for any two states Z', Z'' in the set, $Z'R_jZ''$ if and only if $Z'R_jZ'$ for every $j = 1, \ldots, m$. Then $Z^* = Z^{*'}$.

Condition 4 (the non-imposition condition). The social ranking is not to be imposed independently of the preferences of the members of a society. Such an imposition would occur if, for some pair of distinct social states, Z' and Z'', the social ranking is $Z'PZ''$ for every set of individual rankings $R_1, \ldots, R_m$ over the states Z' and Z''. Conditions 2 and 4 are referred to jointly by Arrow as a 'citizens' sovereignty condition'.

Condition 5 (the non-dictatorship condition). The social ranking R is not to be dictatorial. This ensures that the group decision rule will not be such that there is an individual whose preferences automatically become those of society regardless of anyone else's preferences. Formally, a social ranking R is said to be dictatorial if there exists an individual K such that for all states Z' and Z'', $Z'P_K Z''$ implies $Z'PZ''$, for any rankings $R_1, \ldots, R_m$ of all individuals other than individual K.

Arrow's General Possibility Theorem tells us that no constitution R (other than that of unanimity) exists that satisfies simultaneously conditions 1 to 5 where the collective choice set contains at least three distinct elements. It follows, as a perfectly general result, that if such a constitution satisfies all but one of the Arrow conditions then it must violate the remaining condition. The significance of this result for the various kinds of less-than-unanimity constitutions will depend on: (a) how persuasive the conditions themselves are supposed to be; (b) how great a value is placed upon internal consistency; and (c) how frequently in practice the problem of internal inconsistency might be expected to arise. Inevitably, there are differences of opinion on these matters.

It is widely acknowledged that certain of Arrow's conditions are more plausible than others as a basis for a constitution designed to reflect individual preferences in public choice. Conditions 4 and 5 in this respect clearly are crucial and we shall say no more about them. Condition 2 is unexceptional to those who endorse the Paretian value judgements and deny the relevance of preference intensities in public choice. For this reason it has provoked relatively little criticism, given the Paretian hegemony. However, if preference intensities *are* deemed relevant, it is possible that one state might move up in the orderings of some individuals, with individual orderings otherwise unchanged, and yet that some change in preference intensities might occur, rendering that state less preferable to certain alternatives even though it was preferred in the original situation. Since we are not constrained by the Paretian value judgements, we feel entirely free to criticise condition 2 as unrealistic of the real-world situation, and to recognise the public choice implications of changes in preference intensities. Thus also Pattanaik:[15]

So far as Condition 2 is concerned, its acceptability depends, to a large extent, on whether we consider preference intensities to be relevant or not. The individual orderings remaining the same otherwise, x might have moved up in the preference orderings of some individuals. But preference intensities of other individuals, as between x and y, might have undergone a change. If we think that preference intensities are relevant in social choice, then we may not require the group decision Rule to declare x to be necessarily better than y in the changed situation, even though it declared x to be socially better than y before the change. [p. 44]

Condition 3 has provoked widespread criticism both within and without the Paretian camp, and indeed Arrow himself only somewhat hesitantly endorses it in his latest discussion of the public choice dilemma.[4] Suppose that a society has to make a choice among some alternatives, and does so. Subsequently, a new alternative is introduced purely as a logical possibility. Condition 3, in ruling out any possibility that this new event might disturb the ordering of the original alternatives, essentially also denies preference intensities any role in the group decision rule. To many, even within the Paretian camp, who shrink from challenging condition 2, the restrictive nature of condition 3 is unacceptable. For, as Quirk and Saposnik put it,[16] 'one need not accept wholesale the interpersonal comparability of utility to argue that preference rankings alone are inadequate to reflect the tastes of consumers as they are to be incorporated into a social welfare function'. For those concerned to rescue public choice from apparent destruction, preference intensities offer a tempting — if for Paretians an especially treacherous — salvation. Thus Winch[24]

That the political problem of social choice should be insoluble without some means whereby individuals can indicate strength of preference should come as no surprise to economists, for no system of resource allocation, through the market or otherwise, could function efficiently without such a mechanism. [p. 181]

Condition 1 also has been the subject of considerable criticism in the course of the Arrow debate, but only with respect to certain of its requirements. Reflexivity of R does not impose any serious restriction; it is a trivial matter to say that a state socially is at least as good as itself! To require that public choice should be connected is only to require that society should be able to choose between any two alternative states or to express indifference between them, i.e. to rule out non-comparabilities. Only occasional doubts are raised as to the plausibility of this requirement. Transitivity, however, is quite another matter. It is argued, essentially, that transitivity of social preferences, unlike transitivity of individual preferences, cannot be justified as a value in itself — for behaviour that denotes lunacy in the individual does not do so at the public choice level. At best, therefore, transitivity in public choice can be justified by reference only to its consequences. The danger, in relaxing the transitivity requirement, is that public choice may run around in circles, with evidently high costs in social instability. But, for many economists, the harm attributable to intransitivity in the group decision rule is negligible.

For example, Bergson[5] has emphasised the safeguards of ever-changing circumstances which strictly limit the circularity of public choice, while Graaf[14] actually claims intransitivity as a virtue under democratic conditions since there is protection for minorities in the intransitivity of majority-based decisions. By contrast, and with much justification, Pattanaik[15] points out that the protection of minority interests can hardly be squared with the dictates of majority decision-making — an issue that we pursue in detail in chapter 5. With equal justification, Pattanaik is sceptical of the Bergson apologia, which relies on fortuitous shifts in circumstances as an outlet from the consequences of intransitivity. On the other hand, Pattanaik does allow that intransitivity may be avoided if policy decisions are made on the bases of pairwise comparisons, with defeated policies ruled out for further consideration — albeit at the cost that the final outcome *may* depend on the nature of the sequence itself.

Let us now relate the Arrow dilemma to the most commonly encountered group decision rule in so-called democratic societies, namely that of majority voting. The majority decision (MD) rule has a number of desirable properties. It satisfies not only Arrow's conditions of the Pareto principle, irrelevant alternatives, non-imposition and non-dictatorship, but also such desirable conditions as decisiveness, neutrality, positive responsiveness and anonymity. However, inevitably, given the Arrow theorem, the MD rule has a restricted domain as a group decision rule — it violates Arrow's condition of collective rationality. For, as Condorcet noted as early as 1785, the MD rule may not lead to an ordering, as a consequence of instransitivity. Consider the following example, due to Arrow.[4] There are three alternatives x, y, and z, among which a choice is to be made. One-third of the voters have the ranking x,y,z; one-third, the ranking y,z,x; and one-third, the ranking z,x,y. Then a majority of the voters prefer x to y, a majority prefer y to z, and a majority prefer z to x. There is no way of removing this impediment in the MD rule without violating other of the Arrow conditions.

For example, the constitution might provide vote-trading (log-rolling)[12,13] facilities to allow individual voters to reflect differing preference intensities in the public choice process. If the market in vote-trading were perfect, the public choice outcomes with log-rolling can be shown to be Pareto-superior to those where it is not — though even here intransitivity may persist. But in any event, log-rolling infringes conditions 2 and 3 of the Arrow theorem by introducing preference intensity implications into the group decision rule. Similar problems arise if resort is made to pressure and propaganda in public choice as a counter-intransitivity device.

Attempts have been made, within the Paretian camp, to establish that the Arrow theorem is insubstantial in the real-world situation. Most notably, Tullock[23] has argued that, once a plausible type of interdependence is assumed between the preference functions of choosing individuals,[viii] the intransitivity problem disappears in the large-numbers situation. In essence, the Tullock theorem does not establish full transitivity in public choice. It asserts the existence of a preferred point in any *convex* set, thereby ruling out of consideration all cases of increasing return — which arguably comprise a substantial portion of public choices. Arrow[3] interprets convexity of majority preference sets to imply a similarity of attitudes and points out that, with respect to the income distribution issue — where majority preference sets are not convex — intransitivity is certainly present in majority decision-making. This is not to deny Tullock the point that in practice intransitivity may prove a rare occurrence in societies that use the MD rule — and certainly the evidence does not contradict his hypothesis — but the logical criticism remains as a source of nagging doubt for those who wish to employ the MD rule as a basis for public choices required as a consequence of Paretian-based market failure.

In our view, the Arrow dilemma is trivial by comparison with the predictable consequences of majority-vote decision rules as employed, not in the direct democracies of the Arrow ivory tower, but in the real-world systems of representative government. To these problems, let us now briefly address ourselves.

IV AN ECONOMIC THEORY OF DEMOCRACY

Until recently, the economic theory of public choice offered virtually no insight into the working of the political process but sheltered instead behind the postulate that government was the impartial and omniscient servant of the public good. The discussion generated by Arrow did not improve matters in that it centred attention upon a theoretically sterile and practically useless subject. It is small surprise that such approaches contributed to a growing public scepticism as to the relevance of economic theory for the public policy debate. This scepticism has been checked of late by the more realistic and arguably more useful analyses of the public choice mechanism developed initially by Downs[13] for two-party, majority-vote systems of representative government.

Downs grounded his model upon the conventional self-interest axiom of economic theory, with politicians pursuing a vote-maximising objective function and with political parties adopting vote-maximising electoral platforms. By the application of Hotelling's theory of spatial competition, Downs demonstrated that the elected government must adopt a vote-maximising policy programme if it is not to surrender control over the governing apparatus to its political rival. The election process itself, therefore, is viewed as a political market in which votes are exchanged for policies.

In situations in which voter preferences on any issue of collective choice are clearly registered, are known to be firmly held and are arranged in a single-peaked (unimodal) distribution, the Downs model predicts that both political parties will be pressed into adopting policies favoured by the median preference voters and that the government will enact such a policy programme. Only rarely, in such circumstances, would future-orientated parties sacrifice present for future votes in the expectation that voter tastes would shift within a relevant political time period. But in the main, the policy preferences of voter minorities are not expected to exert much influence on the pattern of collective choice.

In many situations, of course, voter preferences are not clearly registered and/or are suspected to be only loosely adhered to. The Downs model then predicts that the policy utterances of both parties will be ambiguous and that the policy actions of the government will be inconsistent — evidenced either by incompatible pieces of legislation or by legislation that is not supported by the necessary finance. For to formulate clear-cut policies would be to run the risk of major net vote losses, should voter preferences shift or be misinterpreted.

In contrast to Arrow-type discussions, the Downs approach is easily adjusted to take account of imperfect knowledge in the political process and of the transaction costs of communicating information on voter preferences to the politicians. Pressure group activities are seen as the most likely response mechanisms to the imperfect knowledge situation, with the prediction that public policy is likely to be 'disproportionately' influenced by producer groups (widely defined) to the detriment generally of consumers. For the interests of producer groups in any single issue of public policy inevitably are more specific than those of consumers, with the inference that the producer pressure group activities will be the more rewarding for any given outlay. This may well prove to be a major 'imperfection' in the majority-vote systems of public choice.

Although a great deal of work remains to be done on the Downs model, by way both of tightening the model's specifications and of evaluating its predictions by reference to the evidence of public choices, the essence of the Downs approach rings true (at least to us). For it allows a key role to the (not-so-silent) voting majority in policy formation; it emphasises the reflective rather than the leadership characteristics of the political parties; it takes account of log-rolling activities and of pressure group lobbying. These are all features of the real-world scene that are suppressed in conventional Paretian welfare analysis. It is not surprising, therefore, that the more perceptive Paretians have shown disquiet at the lack of relevance of 'nirvana' policy prescription in the face of market failure, and that they have parted company on this issue with the strict Paretian orthodoxy (cf. chapters 6—8).

NOTES

i Strictly, for market failure to occur in such circumstances the externalities must be Pareto-relevant (cf. section II of this chapter).

ii Problems arising as a consequence of indivisibility are analysed in chapter 8.

iii In less extreme cases, this implication often requires modification. See Buchanan.[8]

iv These models provide an optimal solution in the rate of provision of the public good, provided that the division of its cost between the bargainers is negotiable. This is the so-called Lindahl solution.

v Viz. Buchanan,[8] p. 87: 'While he may recognise that similar independent behaviour on the part of everyone produces undesirable results, it is not to his own interest to enter voluntarily into an agreement since, for him, optimal results can be attained by allowing others to supply the public good to the maximum extent while he enjoys a "free-ride"; that is, secures the benefits without contributing towards the costs. Even if an individual should enter into such a cost-sharing agreement, he will have a strong incentive to break his own contract, to chisel on the agreed terms.'

vi At least this is the Buchanan—Stubblebine perception. Viz. p. 203—4:[11] 'Shibata, and others, have failed to recognise that the position or positions of Pareto-optimality in any system depend not only on the technological production and preference relationships, but also on the structure of rules, or institutions, within which individuals are forced to behave.' In point of fact, it is our view, for reasons outlined, that Shibata and Buchanan and Stubblebine are much closer than they would believe on the tax-subsidy issue.

vii Indeed, they make the concession more readily than do the public choice heretics who are more alert to the consequences of such a concession for the implementation of Paretian principles (Buchanan[9]).

viii Viz. Arrow,[3] pp. 107—8: '[Tullock] assumes (a) that the number of voters is large, so large that we may consider them to constitute a continuum, (b) that the indifference curves of each individual in the space of social issues are circles concentric, about a global optimum (as seen by the individual), and (c) the global optima of the different voters are uniformly distributed over the issue space, taken to be a rectangle. From (b) an individual will prefer point A to point B if and only if his global optimum is closer to A than to B. If we draw the perpendicular of the line joining the two points and thus divide the rectangle into two regions, then those individuals whose global optima are in the region containing A are precisely those who prefer A to B. In view of (c), then a majority prefer A to B if the area of the region containing A exceeds that of the region containing B. It is then easy to infer that A is preferred to B if and only if it is closer to the center of the rectangle. Since the relation "closer to the center" is certainly transitive, it follows that majority decision yields a true ordering under these circumstances.'

REFERENCES

1. Arrow, K. J. *Social Choice and Individual Values* New York, John Wiley (1951).
2. Arrow, K. J. 'Economic Welfare and the Allocation of Resources for Invention' in R. R. Nelson (ed.) *The Rate and Direction of Inventive Activity* Princeton, Princeton UP (1962) pp. 609–28.
3. Arrow, K. J. 'Tullock and an Existence Theorem' *Public Choice* (Spring 1969).
4. Arrow, K. J. 'General Economic Equilibrium: Purpose, Analytic Techniques, Collective Choice' *American Economic Review* (June 1974)
5. Bergson, A. 'On the Concept of Social Welfare' *Quarterly Journal of Economics* (May 1954)
6. Buchanan, J. M. 'Positive Economics, Welfare Economics, and Political Economy' *Journal of Law and Economics* (October 1959)
7. Buchanan, J. M. 'Politics, Policy and Pigovian Margins' *Economica* (February 1962)
8. Buchanan, J. M. *The Demand and Supply of Public Goods* Chicago, Rand McNally (1968)
9. Buchanan, J. M. *The Limits of Liberty: Between Anarchy and Leviathan* Chicago, University of Chicago Press (forthcoming)
10. Buchanan, J. M. and Stubblebine, W. C. 'Externality' *Economica* (November 1962)
11. Buchanan, J. M. and Stubblebine, W. C. 'Pareto-Optimality and Gains-from-Trade: A Comment' *Economica* (May 1972)
12. Buchanan, J. M. and Tullock, G. 'The Calculus of Consent' Ann Arbor, University of Michigan Press (1965)
13. Downs, A. 'An Economic Theory of Democracy' New York, Harper & Row (1957)

14. Graaf, J. de V. 'On Making a Recommendation in a Democracy' *Economic Journal* (June 1962)
15. Pattanaik, P. K. *Voting and Collective Choice* Chicago, University of Chicago Press (1971)
16. Quirk, J. and Saposnik, R. *Introduction to General Equilibrium Theory and Welfare Economics* New York, McGraw-Hill (1968)
17. Samuelson, P. A. 'The Pure Theory of Public Expenditure' *The Review of Economics and Statistics* (November 1954)
18. Samuelson, P. A. 'Diagrammatic Exposition of a Theory of Public Expenditure' *The Review of Economics and Statistics* (November 1955)
19. Samuelson, P. A. 'Aspects of Public Expenditure Theories' *Review of Economics and Statistics* (November 1958)
20. Sen, A. *'Collective Choice and Social Welfare'* Edinburgh, Halden-Day and Oliver and Boyd (1971)
21. Shibata, H. 'Pareto-Optimality, Trade and the Pigovian Tax' *Economica* (May 1972)
22. Shibata, H. 'Pareto-Optimality and Gains-from-Trade: A Further Elucidation' *Economica* (February 1974)
23. Tullock, G. *Towards a Mathematics of Politics* Ann Arbor, University of Michigan Press (1967)
24. Winch, D. M. *'Analytical Welfare Economics'* Harmondsworth Penguin (1971)

3. Empire-Building

And so, having made my plea, let me salute the profession with what might well have been the title of this paper, with what is certainly the key that points to the solution of most problems in applied welfare economics, with what surely should be the motto of any society that we applied welfare economists might form, and what probably, if only we could learn to pronounce it, should be our password:

$$\int_{z=0}^{z^*} \sum_i D_i(z) \frac{\partial X_i}{\partial Z} \, dz.$$

[A. C. Harberger 'Three Basic Postulates for Applied Welfare Economics: An Interpretative Essay' *Journal of Economic Literature* (September 1971) p. 796]

For many people at the present time, the central issue in the economic debate concerns not efficiency in production and exchange (indeed, the word 'efficiency' itself is a bourgeois anathema to the disciples of the New Left), but rather the existence of inequality in income and wealth and the corresponding 'need' for social justice. The economic solution is sought out on this basis not, for the most part, in terms of consensus politics and the mutual benefits of trade, but in the politics of conflict and in the economics of revolution.[18] On these matters, as we have emphasised, the *conventional* Paretian dogma has nothing to say, emasculated as it is by its own self-denying ordinance.

For a dogma with the evident survival capacity of the Paretian, however, one might predict that attempts would be made by the more perceptive members of the priesthood to encompass the challenge to its relevance and thereby to extend the scope of its empire. Indeed, such attempts have been forthcoming, albeit in our view with very limited success. It is to such attempts at empire-building by Paretian welfare economics that we must now turn.

I   THE COMPENSATION PRINCIPLE

The making of interpersonal utility comparisons as a means of evaluating the welfare implications of resource shifts is denied by the third value assumption of the Paretian dogma. Thus, if there is a change in resource allocation which increases the welfare of certain individuals at the cost of decreasing the welfare of others, the Paretian dogma offers no guidance to those who would evaluate that change. In a world of ongoing major resource shifts, where some individuals inevitably must suffer if others are to gain, this denial is severely restrictive; and, indeed, if policy were to be conducted entirely upon Paretian lines, conservatism must surely prevail. Since not all Paretians are conservative, and of those who are many do not relish revolution, an avenue of escape acceptable to the dogma clearly was required. The compensation principle seemed to promise just such a Paretian outlet.[12]

The notion underlying the compensation principle is that, if a resource shift would result in some individuals being better off and others being worse off, and the gainers could compensate the losers while themselves remaining better off, then the resource shift is Pareto-preferred. This notion is widely known as the Kaldor—Hicks criterion,[13] since it was formulated by these economists during the late 1930s in response to a damning attack on the Paretian approach (and indeed on welfare economics in general) by Lionel Robbins. The debate generated by this notion — which continues at the present time — is one of the most extensive and perhaps fundamental controversies ever to break out within the Paretian dogma.

The Kaldor—Hicks version of the compensation principle took the following form. Assume two alternative situations, Q_1 and Q_2. If, in situation Q_2, real income (welfare) is such that those who would gain in the switch from Q_1 to Q_2 could compensate those who would lose without thereby returning to their Q_1 level of real income (welfare), then Q_2 is adjudged socially preferable to Q_1 *even if no compensation is paid*. This notion is depicted diagrammatically in figure 3.1 by reference to Scitovsky community indifference curves.[i] A two-good, two-individual situation is depicted. Q_1 is the initial bundle of the two goods (X and Y) which are divided between the two individuals (A and B) as at point C' on the contract curve OQ_1. The situation reflects exchange efficiency in the Paretian sense. I_1 represents the community indifference curve relevant to the division at C'. Q_2 is the alternative bundle of the two goods which are divided between the two individuals as at point C'' on the contract curve OQ_2. I_2 represents the community indifference curve relevant to the division at C''. If I_1 and I_2 were directly comparable, a move from the one to the other would satisfy the Paretian criteria. In figure 3.1, however, they are non-comparable, since they intersect; the strict Paretian criteria are not satisfied, in that a move from Q_1 to Q_2 benefits A to the detriment of B.

In such circumstances, Kaldor—Hicks would ask whether it is yet

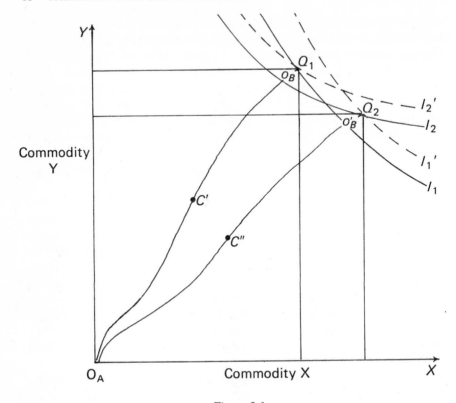

Figure 3.1

possible, by a lump-sum redistribution of Q_2, to render individual B no worse off than was his case at Q_1 while still leaving individual A better off. To test for this, we construct through Q_2 a community indifference curve I_1' that is comparable with I_1. Since I_1' lies above I_1 it is apparent that there is some division of the Q_2 bundle (that from which I_1' has been generated) that would satisfy the Kaldor–Hicks criterion. If such were the case, and if compensation were actually to be paid, there would be a welfare improvement even by reference to the strict Paretian criteria. The Kaldor–Hicks criterion of potential compensation of course might well fail to satisfy these criteria.

In any event, the Kaldor–Hicks criterion suffers from a serious weakness, namely that a move from Q_1 to Q_2 which satisfies the potential compensation test may provide a situation in which a return move to Q_1 then also satisfies that test. Such is the case indeed in figure 3.1, where it is possible to construct the community indifference curve I_2' through Q_1 comparable with and above I_2.

This apparent paradox, first noted by Scitovsky, is the consequence of a particular change in the common marginal rate of substitution between the two goods, X and Y, induced by their (hypothetical) redistribution between the two individuals, A and B. As Mishan has noted,[12,13] this interrelationship between relative valuation and distribution is a major source of paradox in the welfare economics field.

In an attempt to resolve the paradox, Scitovsky proposed a stricter test, known as the Scitovsky double-criterion, whereby the Kaldor—Hicks criterion is applied first to assess the move from the initial to the alternative position and (if successful) secondly to assess the return move to the initial position. Only if the first test is successful and the second test *unsuccessful* is the move to be considered a welfare improvement by reference to the Scitovsky criterion. It is perhaps worth noting that a social ranking based on this criterion is not necessarily transitive.

Despite the evident expediency of the hypothetical compensation approach, a number of the Paretian priesthood remained concerned at the possible distributional implications of such a method of circumventing the Paretian strait-jacket. To set their minds at rest, Little proposed a more comprehensive criterion which embodied distributional objectives. To assess whether a movement from an initial to an alternative situation constituted a welfare improvement, Little requested that three questions should be answered in the positive, namely: (i) is the Kaldor—Hicks criterion satisfied? (ii) is the Scitovsky criterion satisfied? and (iii) has the alternative a better distribution than the initial situation? As is so often the case, the posing of the additional question satisfied the misgivings of the disciples while the evident impossibility of answering the question from within the faith conveniently was forgotten. On such bases are dogma protected and indeed extended in the face of successful criticism. To judge from the extensive application of the compensation criteria in contemporary cost—benefit analysis, the Paretians owe a considerable debt to Kaldor—Hicks, to Scitovsky and to Little.

Such rankings of alternative situations by reference to potential Paretian comparability based upon hypothetical compensation criteria surely must raise suspicion in all but the most naive, complacent and/or committed of Paretian intellects. For the approach is shot through with problems both of a theoretical and a practical nature, and, indeed, where it is applicable it is not required. If transfers of income were costless, and if the process of identifying other collections of goods on the same community indifference curve also was costless, there would be no need to invoke the hypothetical compensation criterion, since direct comparisons could be made and the appropriate Paretian adjustments could be implemented. In the absence of such conditions, hypothetical compensation becomes a treacherous instrument, not least because of the problem of ensuring that those affected by the adjustment correctly reveal their preferences. For, if it is known that compensation actually will not be paid, there is no incentive whatsoever for either party to the conflict correctly to reveal his preferences, as might arguably occur in small group-bargaining situations over real compensation. Rational protagonists in bartering over *hypothetical* compensation would contend that the compensation they would pay or must receive approached in each case the limit of infinity. Paretians who rely upon an omniscient arbiter to resolve this conflict fall foul of the nirvana fallacy.

It is now clear, despite the despairing attempts by Paretians to resolve the paradox, that contradictable alternatives cannot be ranked by reference to allocative criteria, but only by reference to distributional considerations. Moreover, following a detailed reappraisal of the compensation test approach, Mishan[13] recently has further restricted the scope of the compensation test by demonstrating that even the apparently 'non-contradictable' case, in which one collection manifestly has more of every good than the alternative collection, may turn out, on further investigation, to present essentially the same sort of contradiction. These cases, also, could be ranked only by reference to distributional criteria. Thus Mishan:[13]

In the light of the above analysis, a conclusion that criteria based on potential Pareto comparability should be used with greater circumspection is hardly necessary. The transparently 'contradictable' case, which is resolved in this paper, has always been a source of dissatisfaction. What is more disconcerting is the disclosure that the apparently 'non-contradictable' case — in which one collection has manifestly more of every good than the alternative collection — may turn out, on further investigation in goods space, to produce essentially the same sort of contradiction. Such cases are then resolved only by reducing them to a distributional ranking of the collections in question. [p. 765]

This conclusion has serious implications for the policy relevance of Paretian welfare economics. For, as Mishan[13] has emphasised, 'The set of alternative states likely to occur in the real world for which in fact "everyone" in the one state will be better off than he is in an alternative or existing state cannot be very large.' If, in all cases of conflict, actual compensation is deemed impracticable and hypothetical compensation ineffective, the Paretians are forced to rest their judgement upon distributional criteria. Yet by their own ordinance, the Paretians are not allowed a distributional judgement.

In such circumstances, the Paretians can say nothing whatsoever about the welfare implications of the vast majority of important policy alternatives. It is fortunate indeed, therefore, that as yet, at least, we are not all committed to the Paretian dogma.

It is not unfair to claim that hypothetical compensation was developed by Paretian economists, who resented their (voluntary) imprisonment in the Paretian strait-jacket, in a bold attempt to hoodwink the policy-makers into believing that the Paretian criteria were more powerful than in fact was the case. Once this hoax is exposed, the Paretian voice on matters of policy prescriptions becomes muted indeed and those who continue to practice within the strict Paretian framework are seen to be emasculated by their own ideology. Such however is the instinct of preservation of Paretian practitioners that even the most critical and independent of their fellowship draw back from the full implications of their analysis. Thus Mishan:[13]

Yet the belief that our attachment to potential Pareto criteria springs chiefly from mundane professional considerations is going to be difficult to swallow. There is always hope that a little more thought may enable us to discover some redeeming features of such criteria. In that hope, I forbear from proposing that we abandon them. [p. 766]

The fact that so outspoken a critic of conventional economic thinking felt it necessary to stay his pen and to obfuscate his final paragraph is perhaps the best possible testament to the grip exercised by Paretian dogma over the economics profession.

II   INTERDEPENDENCES BETWEEN UTILITY FUNCTIONS

Until recently, Paretian welfare economics was grounded unambiguously upon a self-centred (or strictly a solipsist) concept of human nature, characterised by strict independence of individual preference functions. Neither malevolence nor benevolence was recognised as having relevance for behaviour in the private or in the public market place. An assumption less descriptive of the human condition is difficult to imagine; for our lives clearly are dominated by interdependences between individual utility functions. To quote Boulding:[2]

Selfishness, or indifference to the welfare of others, is a knife edge between benevolence on the one side and malevolence on the other. It is something that is very rare. We may feel indifferent towards those whom we do not know, with whom we have no relationships of any kind, but towards those with whom we have relationships, even the frigid relationship of exchange, we are apt to be either benevolent or malevolent. We either rejoice when they rejoice, or we rejoice when they mourn.

Paretian economists over the past decade have come slowly to recognise the restrictive nature of the solipsist assumption and have reacted characteristically in an empire-building fashion. Benevolence and malevolence, love and hate now feature widely in welfare analyses, both at the theoretical and at the applied level. Orthodox Paretians have seized upon this avenue of escape from the distribution problem. The manner in which they have done so indicates the fundamental resilience and yet the bounded and essentially conservative nature of their dogma.

In essence, the approach adopted is that of generating Pareto-preferred income redistribution by assuming the existence of interdependence between individual utility functions. A typical example is that by H. M. Hochman and J. R. Rodgers,[10] who analysed Pareto-optimal income redistribution between Mutt (the rich member of a two-person economy) and Jeff (his poorer counterpart) where their respective utility functions took the form:

$$U_M{}^o = f_M(Y_M{}^o, Y_J{}^o) \tag{3.1}$$

and

$$U_J{}^o = f_J(Y_M{}^o, Y_J{}^o) \tag{3.2}$$

where $U_M{}^o$ and $Y_M{}^o$ were the initial values of Mutt's utility index and income respectively prior to any redistribution and where $U_J{}^o$ and $Y_J{}^o$ were the corresponding values for Jeff.

Given specific restrictions on the nature of the utility functions — namely that $\partial U_M/\partial Y_M$, $\partial U_J/\partial Y_J > 0$ and that $\partial U_J/\partial Y_M \leqslant 0$ at $Y_M{}^o$ (or if $\partial U_J/\partial Y_M > 0$ then $\partial U_J/\partial Y_J > \partial U_J/\partial Y_M$) — it follows that all transfers are entirely a matter of Mutt's volition, and that the process of determining a Pareto-optimal redistributive transfer can concentrate on Mutt's preferences alone. Since transfers large enough to reverse the initial distributional ordering are not allowed, it follows in the two-person case that the transfer cannot be greater than

$$\frac{(Y_M{}^o - Y_J{}^o)}{2}.$$

The degree of income redistribution which is Pareto-optimal in the context of the Hochman—Rodgers model is a function of the initial distribution of real income and of Mutt's marginal rate of substitution between the utility derived from income retention and that derived from income redistribution. It is important to note therefore that this redistribution is secondary in nature and is dependent on the initial distribution of income which is exogenous to the Hochman—Rodgers model.[14] Indeed, the Hochman—Rodgers model precludes all discussion of primary redistribution.[ii] For primary income redistribution is a function of society's view of equity, which, in the case of conflict, must be resolved by the political process or, in extreme cases, by revolution.

Given the two-person economy postulated in their model, Hochman and Rodgers present no convincing case why Pareto-optimal redistribution should not take place through private charity. Thus, their justification of a system of state intervention through fiscal instruments is less than convincing. Once the model is extended to an N-person economy,[7] in which each rich person cares about his own welfare and the welfare of the poor, however, the process of optimal redistribution via private charity is obstructed by the free-rider problem.

In a society of N persons, of which $k < N$ are poor, suppose that the government were to raise £1 each from the rich (that is, £$N - k$) to be distributed equally among the poor. The utility gain of R_i would be

$$\left[\frac{N}{k} - 1\right] \sum_{j=1}^{k} \frac{\partial UR_i}{\partial Y_j} \tag{3.3}$$

while his utility loss is $\partial UR_i / \partial YR_i$ so that the net gain from the tax and redistribution is

$$\left[\frac{N}{k} - 1\right] \sum_{j=1}^{k} \frac{\partial UR_i}{\partial Y_j} - \frac{\partial UR_i}{\partial YR_i}. \tag{3.4}$$

If, instead, R_i had given through charity and the £1 had been distributed in the same way, the gain would have been

$$\frac{1}{k} \sum_{j=1}^{k} \frac{\partial UR_i}{\partial Y_j} - \frac{\partial UR_i}{\partial YR_i} \tag{3.5}$$

which is clearly smaller as long as $N > (k + 1)$, that is, as long as there is more than one rich person. The reason for the possibility of gains through collective action is clear, namely the free-rider argument, which renders the level of voluntary transfers suboptimal. In such circumstances, a large government poverty programme may be Pareto-optimal even though private charity programmes for the poor do not receive any contributions. Indeed, it has been suggested that taxes will be the more preferred to charity as a means of Pareto-preferred income redistribution, the greater the gap between N and k (i.e., the greater the proportion of rich to total population). In practice, however, the process of public choice itself is susceptible to distortion in the face of the free-rider problem. Certainly, there is little reason to suppose that a two-party majority voting system will provide a Pareto-optimal redistribution of income via collective choice. Indeed, if utility functions do take the form suggested by Hochman and Rodgers, the evidence of actual redistribution in the UK and the USA almost certainly indicates a welfare distortion. For, as Tullock[18] has noted (pp. 247–57), the vast majority of income transfers take place between the middle-income groups:

What we actually observe in democracy is that majority voting does not redistribute much money to the poor and does redistribute a great deal of money to people who are by no means poor. This last activity . . . is almost a total social waste. [p. 253]

The Hochman–Rodgers model effectively precludes all discussion of secondary redistribution in kind and centres attention exclusively upon the case for cash transfers. In certain circumstances, however, the nature of utility interdependence may suggest, by reference to Paretian criteria, that redistribution should be effected by transfers of specific commodity bundles. Specifically, such a situation would arise when interest in the consumption of other persons derives from externalities accruing from the consumption of a particular commodity, with utility functions taking the form:

$$U^A = U^A(X_1^A, X_2^A, \ldots, X_n^A, X_1^B) \tag{3.6}$$

and

$$U^B = U^B(X_1^B, X_2^B, \ldots, X_n^B) \tag{3.7}$$

where X_1 is the commodity whose consumption by B provides external benefits to A.

More specifically, by way of example, Lindsay[11] has recently argued, with particular reference to medicare consumption, that a more equal consumption is desired among individuals demonstrating the same 'medical need'. This suggests a utility function of the form:

$$U^J = U^J(X_1^J, X_2^J, \ldots, X_n^J, ei) \tag{3.8}$$

where

$$ei = - \sum_{i=1}^{s} (\bar{X}_1 - X_1{}^i). \qquad (3.9)$$

In such circumstances, Lindsay justified the public provision of medicare as a redistributive mechanism, by reference to the costs both of administering a suitable subsidy/rationing programme and of identifying individuals suffering from clinically identical medical conditions. Lindsay urged that a single-course medicare programme such as the British National Health Service might be adopted as the most efficient instrument (in second-best terms) for optimising medicare provisions given the equality of consumption constraint. Not all Paretians would follow Lindsay in this policy interpretation.[iii] Nevertheless, some mechanism for redistribution in kind (private or public) is required where Pareto-relevant marginal externalities exist in the form outlined by Lindsay.

So far, discussion of Pareto-preferred income redistributions has centred attention upon cases where the rich are concerned about the income levels of the poor. Buchanan and Tullock[7] have demonstrated, however (pp. 192—8), that provision for income redistribution may be made for more self-centred reasons. Suppose that the marginal utility of income declines for each individual in society and that each individual recognises this phenomenon. Further suppose that each individual anticipates that his income will fluctuate over time, but unpredictably, thereby rendering an insurance solution inappropriate. In such circumstances the individual may favour a collective redistribution of income to an extent indicated by his utility function even though the risk of income falls remains essentially uninsurable. In practice, however, as Buchanan and Tullock recognise, collective decisions are based upon voting procedures which do not necessarily supply Pareto-optimal solutions. Individuals who are sufficiently sophisticated economically to assess the insurance principle are unlikely to misconceive the true nature of the political process in so far as it might impinge upon their own welfare. Only in terms of some social contract thesis, therefore, is it possible to interpret actual redistributions effected by government as reflecting a Pareto-preferred shift as explained by the interdependent utilities or the insurance principle. For those who find the social contract approach unappealing, some alternative approach is required. For many neo-Paretians, the Bergson social welfare function approach serves.

III   BERGSON SOCIAL WELFARE FUNCTIONS

It is important to distinguish at the outset between the group decision rule of Arrow and the social welfare function of Bergson,[1] not least because both concepts commonly are referred to as social welfare functions while possessing quite different characteristics. The Bergson social welfare function is a real value function, the arguments of which consist of magnitudes representing different aspects of a social state, the values of which indicate the social welfare indices corresponding to different social states. It may be written as:

$$W = W(U_1, U_2, \ldots, U_n) \qquad (3.10)$$

where U_i is the level of the utility index of the ith individual. In this sense, a Bergson social welfare function is an ordinal index of society's welfare and is a function of the utility levels of all individuals. It is not unique, and its form depends upon the value judgements of those who deem it desirable since it expresses their views as to the effect upon society of the utility level of the ith individual.

In contrast, the Arrow group decision rule is more general in scope in that it specifies the method of deriving the social ordering implied by a Bergson social welfare function. For, in many instances, it may prove impossible to decide upon an acceptable form for the social welfare function by consensus, in which case a group decision rule (dictatorial or otherwise) is clearly required. The Arrow group decision rule fulfils this important requirement and is a necessary though not a sufficient condition for the existence of a Bergson social welfare function. Henceforth, in this chapter, all references are to social welfare functions of the Bergson type.

It may well be imagined with what relief the social welfare function approach was seized upon by neo-Paretians who were anxious to have their say on matters of public policy while recognising the futility of the hypothetical compensation test. For the indeterminacy that arises in Paretian analysis whenever income is redistributed can be removed by introducing a social welfare function in which society's preferences among alternative utility distributions are explicitly specified. With the distribution problem thereby solved, the conventional Paretian criteria may be applied to secure a welfare optimum.

In truth, of course, the social welfare function approach is anathema to strict Paretians,[3,4] in that it incorporates judgements that are not derived from individual preferences.[iv] Certainly, it is far from clear why one should be concerned with following the dictates of individual preferences in allocation when the fundamental issue of distribution is to be decided by the whim of a philosopher—king or of some eccentric economist. Moreover, in the absence of very considerable public finance ingenuity, it is by no means obvious that the incomes thrown up in the allocative solution can be made compatible with the distributive dictates of the social welfare judgement without some damage to allocative efficiency[v] unless the social welfare judgement is neutral with respect to distribution. The fact that the most commonly utilised social welfare function *is* neutral with respect to distribution perhaps is explained by this potential problem.

Neo-Paretians, nevertheless, show themselves increasingly willing to utilise the social welfare function approach as a means of circumventing the distribution obstacle without necessarily endorsing its full implications. Let those who create policy decide for themselves whether they endorse the value judgements of the social welfare function. If not, they may reject the policy implications, however logically these may be derived. Where the value judgements are accepted and the logic of the analysis is impeccable, however, the policy prescriptions should be implemented. The final section of this chapter is devoted to an extreme example of just such an approach to resolving the income distribution dilemma.

Many Paretian economists are strongly attracted, in principle at least, by egalitarian principles, and not a few have sought hard for a method of reflecting this principle in their policy pronouncements without consequently having to discard the Paretian approach for the evaluation of economic efficiency. The assumption of universally diminishing marginal utility — which served their predecessors well in this respect — is no longer helpful given their unwillingness to make interpersonal utility comparisons. Instead, the conventional Paretian now seeks refuge in a suitable social welfare function. For the simple-minded (and overtly honest) economist, the problem immediately is resolved by writing income equality as an independent variable in the social welfare function. For the more sophisticated economist, it is deemed superior to specify an innocuous-looking social welfare function whence income equality magically is derived as an implication — the rabbit out of the hat! Since there is a growing tendency among economists to blind the unwary by science on these matters we shall illustrate the dodge by reference to a contribution by Amartya Sen.[17]

Sen was concerned to rescue Lerner's 1944 'equality of distribution' theorem from its reliance on utilitarian assumptions and to provide a more general foundation. To do so, he made four assumptions:

Assumption 1 (total income fixity). There is a fixed income $y*$ to be divided among n individuals, i.e. $y_1 + \ldots + y_n = y*$.

Assumption 2 (concavity of the group welfare function). Social welfare W, a symmetric and increasing function of individual welfare levels $W(U_1 \ldots, U_n)$ is concave.

Assumption 3 (concavity of the individual welfare functions). There are n individual welfare functions $U^1(y) \ldots, U^n(y)$, and each of them is concave.

Assumption 4 (equi-probability). If p_i^j is the probability that person i has the welfare function U^j then for all j, $p_i^j = p_h^j$ for individuals i,h.

Sen proceeded on this basis to prove theorem 1 — that the mathematical expectation of social welfare is maximised by an equal division of income. Assumption 4 of course is his sleight of hand. Given the symmetry of W, a group welfare function can be defined $W = F(y^1, \ldots, y^n)$ in which y^i is the income going to the person with the jth welfare function U^j. For any income distribution $(y_1, \ldots, y_n)$, any reordering of it $(y^1, \ldots, y^n)$ essentially reflects a particular assignment of individual welfare functions to the persons in the group. For any distribution vector y, there are $n!$ such reorderings $\tilde{y}(k)$, $k = 1 \ldots, n!$, and corresponding to each k, there is a specific value of social welfare given by $F[\tilde{y}(k)]$. Since assumption 4 implies that each of the possibilities are exactly equally likely, the mathematical expectation E of social welfare is given by:

$$E(y) = \frac{1}{n!} \sum_{k=1}^{n!} F[\tilde{y}(k)] . \tag{3.11}$$

If x is an equal-distribution vector, i.e., $x_1 = \ldots \ldots = x_n$, then clearly

$$E(x) = F(x). \tag{3.12}$$

By assumption 1 it is obvious that:

$$x = \frac{1}{n!} \sum_{k=1}^{n!} \tilde{y}(k). \tag{3.13}$$

By assumptions 2 and 3, $F(.)$ is a concave function, and therefore from equations (3.11), (3.12) and (3.13) it must be the case that:

$$E(y) \leqslant E(x). \tag{3.14}$$

Since (3.14) holds for all y, evidently theorem 1 must be true, Q.E.D.

IV THE HARBERGER FINAL SOLUTION

In September 1971, with a *bravura* that is encountered rarely even within the Paretian camp, Arnold Harberger[9] presented an open letter to the economics profession, pleading that three basic postulates should be accepted as providing a 'conventional' framework for all applied welfare economics. The postulates were:

(a) the competitive demand price for a given unit measures the value of that unit to the demander;
(b) the competitive supply price for a given unit measures the value of the unit to the supplier;
(c) when evaluating the net benefits or costs of a given action (project, programme or policy) the costs and benefits accruing to each member of the relevant group (e.g. a nation) should normally be added without regard to the individual(s) to whom they accrue.

These postulates underlie most analyses that use the concepts of consumers' and producers' surplus as evaluated within the Paretian framework. Indeed, although Harberger refers misleadingly to consumers' surplus only throughout the remainder of his tract, it is quite clear both from the postulates themselves and from his illustration in his figure 1, that he has redefined consumers' surplus to incorporate producers' surplus also, presumably on the basis of postulate (c). In fact, Harberger's plea is for the general acceptance by economists working in the field of welfare economics of a social welfare function that maximises the sum of consumers' and producers' surplus over competitive cost and which is neutral with respect to income distribution. Viz:

$$\text{Maximise } W = TR + S - (TC - R) \qquad (3.15)$$

where W = net economic welfare, TR = total revenue, S = consumers' surplus, TC = total cost and R = inframarginal rent.

Assuming (for illustrative purposes) that all factors are available in completely elastic supply, inframarginal rents will be zero and the net welfare gain is:

$$W = TR + S - TC \qquad (3.16)$$

Now $TR + S = \int_0^Q P(\acute{Q})d\acute{Q}$ where $P(\acute{Q})$ is the demand curve. Differentiating this expression with respect to Q yields

$$(TR + S) = \int_0^Q P(\acute{Q})d\acute{Q} \qquad (3.17)$$

$$= P(Q) \qquad (3.18)$$

and

$$\frac{d}{dQ}(TC) = MC \ [\text{marginal cost}]. \qquad (3.19)$$

Thus, the necessary and sufficient conditions for a net economic welfare maximum are seen to be the familiar relations:

$$\frac{dW}{dQ} = \frac{d}{dQ}(TR + S) - \frac{d}{dQ}TC = 0 \qquad (3.20)$$

whence

$$P - MC = 0 \qquad (3.21)$$

and

$$\frac{d^2 W}{dQ^2} = \frac{dP}{dQ} - \frac{d^2}{dQ^2}, (TC) < 0. \qquad (3.22)$$

In essence, therefore, the Harberger social welfare function accepts the individualistic thrust of the first two Paretian value assumptions (as outlined in chapter 1) while rejecting the constraint upon policy discussion imposed by the third value assumption. Implicit in this approach is the view that public policy analysis should be concerned principally with issues of efficiency in resource allocation, leaving equity considerations in the hands of the fiscal authorities. Those who reject this viewpoint may well find themselves at odds with the Harberger policy blueprint, even though they adhere to the Paretian framework.

Harberger developed a measure of welfare change, consistent with the aforementioned social welfare function, which emphasised the general equilibrium nature of the surplus concept. His measure took the form:

$$\Delta W = \int_{z=0}^{z^*} \sum_i Di(z) \frac{\partial Xi}{\partial z} dz \qquad (3.23)$$

where Di represents the excess of marginal social benefit over marginal social cost per unit of activity i, Xi represents the number of units of activity i, and z is the policy variable, the effects of a change in which we are concerned to evaluate.

To illustrate how distortions elsewhere in the system might be incorporated into his measure, Harberger discussed the implications of a tax imposition which would drive a wedge between demand price and supply price. In the absence of any other distortions, a tax placed on a single good j would be reflected in terms of (3.23) as follows:

$$\Delta W = \int_{T_j=0}^{T_j^*} T_j \frac{\partial Xi}{\partial T_j} dT_j \qquad (3.24)$$

which is equal to the familiar Marshallian triangle. However, if taxes · on other goods already exist when T_j is imposed, the effects of its imposition are given by:

$$\Delta W = \int_{T_j=0}^{T_j^*} T_j \frac{\partial Xi}{\partial T_j} dT_j + \int_{T_j=0}^{T_j^*} \sum_{i \neq j} Ti \frac{\partial Xi}{\partial T_j} dT_j \qquad (3.25)$$

This is equal to the Marshallian triangle plus, with constant Tis, the expression $\Sigma_{i \neq j} Ti \Delta Xi$, where ΔXi measures the change in the equilibrium quantity of Xi occasioned by the imposition of T_j^*. Any of the terms in this expression can be either positive or negative depending on the nature of the distortion. Optimistically, Harberger suggests that the task of locating the general equilibrium solution in practice is 'entirely manageable'!

Harberger's plea is for the 'conventionalisation' of all applied welfare economics on the basis of his social welfare function.[vi] He rests his case for such a proposal on the alleged simplicity, robustness and long tradition of his three basic postulates. His paper was published, so far without comment or criticism, in one of the world's most respected and widely read professional journals of economics. Yet at no point does Harberger outline (let alone attempt to justify) the value basis of his proposal, if indeed he even recognises that value judgements are involved. Is this to be the final consequence of the formalisation of welfare economics? Are we all about to rush blindly, lemming-like, into murky Paretian waters? It is the principal purpose of this book to ask economists to pause before the plunge, to reconsider their value premises, and ask of themselves whether or not they truly are Paretian or neo-Paretian dogmatists.

NOTES

i Most welfare economics textbooks show how these curves are derived. See, e.g. Mishan[12] for a detailed discussion.

ii For this reason, the treatment of income redistribution via utility interdependences essentially is a conservative approach. It is much utilised by 'Virginian-blend' economists (e.g. Hochman and Rodgers,[10] Buchanan[5] and Tullock[18].

iii Lindsay[11] himself was not entirely convinced. Viz.: 'Such an examination might reveal factors not considered here which act to thwart the egalitarian aims of the Health Service. For example, to a certain extent medical care is clearly rationed among individuals on the basis of the doctor's evaluations of the relative "medical needs" of competing patients' (p. 362). For a realistic assessment of the economics of medicare provision by the state in two-party majority-vote systems, see J. M. Buchanan.[6]

iv See especially J. M. Buchanan.[5] 'In my view, a consistent methodological position does not allow the introduction of non-individualistic norms in *either* allocation *or* distribution. It will be objected that my approach amounts to an "opting out" of the discussion of many interesting and highly important issues of applied economic policy. So it does, but I can see no personal excuse for joining other economists in an attempt to hoodwink the public into thinking that we make more sense out of these issues than analysis allows.'

v Even lump-sum taxes may have allocative effects once the profit-maximisation assumption is abandoned.

vi We can recall nothing similar in the form of this 'open sesame' economics since *Heinrich v. Thünen* invented his famous formula for the natural wage — $w = \sqrt{ap}$ — with which he was so impressed that he had it engraved on his own tombstone!

REFERENCES

1. Bergson, A. 'A Reformulation of Certain Aspects of Welfare Economics' *Quarterly Journal of Economics* (February 1938)
2. Boulding, K. 'Economics as a Moral Science' *American Economic Review* (March 1969) pp. 1–12
3. Buchanan, J. M. 'Positive Economics, Welfare Economics, and Political Economy' *Journal of Law and Economics* 2 (October 1959) pp. 124–38
4. Buchanan, J. M. 'Politics, Policy and Pigovian Margins' *Economica* (February 1962)
5. Buchanan, J. M. 'What Kind of Redistribution Do We Want?' *Economica* (May 1968) pp. 185–90
6. Buchanan, J. M. *The Inconsistencies of the National Health Service* (Occasional Paper No. 7) London, Institute of Economic Affairs (1965)

7. Buchanan, J. M. and Tullock, G. *The Calculus of Consent* Ann Arbor, University of Michigan Press (1965)
8. Goldfarb, R. S. 'Pareto Optimal Redistribution: Comment' *American Economic Review* (December 1970) pp. 994—6
9. Harberger, A. C. 'Three Basic Postulates for Applied Welfare Economics: An Interpretative Essay' *Journal of Economic Literature* (September 1971) pp. 785—97
10. Hochman, H. M. and Rodgers, J. R. 'Pareto Optimal Redistribution' *American Economic Review* (September 1964) pp. 652—7
11. Lindsay, C. M. 'Medical Care and the Economics of Sharing' *Economica* (November 1969) pp. 351—62
12. Mishan, E. 'A Survey of Welfare Economics 1939—59' *Economic Journal* (1960)
13. Mishan, E. 'Welfare Criteria: Resolution of a Paradox' *Economic Journal* (September 1973)
14. Musgrave, R. A. 'Pareto Optimal Redistribution: Comment' *American Economic Review* (December 1970) pp. 991—3
15. Peacock, A. T. and Rowley, C. K. 'Pareto Optimality and the Political Economy of Liberalism' *Journal of Political Economy* (May/June 1972) pp. 476—90
16. Quirk, J. and Saposnik, R. *Introduction to General Equilibrium Theory and Welfare Economics* New York, McGraw-Hill (1968)
17. Sen, A. *On Economic Inequality* London, Oxford University Press (1973)
18. Tullock, G. *Private Wants, Public Means* Scranton, Pa., Basic Books (1970)

PART II

The Philosophical Challenge

4. The New Left

In any given situation the resources and the choice of alternatives which lie before the individual are restricted and in a capitalist society most notably restricted by the class to which the individual belongs. In this given situation in which the individual finds himself there may be one path consistent with his best advantage, which it will profit him to take; but that path is determined for him by external circumstances and is not the path he would have trodden had his situation been different. [Maurice Dobb 'The Trend of Modern Economics' in *Political Economy and Capitalism* (1960 reprint)]

I INTRODUCTION

The criticisms we have made so far are designed to expose the 'limitations of Paretianism', though our ultimate aim is to expose the confusion in the minds of those who equate Paretian welfare economics with liberalism, and to offer as precise guidance as we can on the reasons why liberalism is an alternative to and is not co-terminous with a Paretian approach. This requires us to move at some stage from a critique to a positive statement of the liberal point of view, but before we do so we must pay attention to the views of those who have anticipated us in at least the destructive part of our task and particularly those heirs of the dissenting 'underworld', as Keynes called it, commonly termed 'The New Left'.

There are some initial difficulties facing even the more sympathetic critics of the New Left in providing a distillation of their views. Firstly, in the house of the 'mortal God' of materialistic thinking characterising the New Left, there are many mansions. At one wing of the edifice, there are traditional Marxian apologists, some of whom have tried to beat the capitalist apologists of high-flown economic theory at their own game by developing highly sophisticated models of capitalist development.[3] At the other, there are those who, following the tradition of Veblen, have eschewed the use, and explicitly denied the relevance, of mathematical techniques in exposing the 'fallacies' of establishment economics. While a taxonomy of leftist economics would be a fascinating study, it is more germane to our task to identify those elements in its thinking that deny the applicability of Paretian welfare economics to the problems of policy, and this means that we largely confine ourselves to the younger members of American economics faculties, many of whom have undergone the rigours of US graduate economics training but who have found themselves — or so they believe — ill-equipped to solve the problems of society bequeathed to them.

Secondly, their refuge in the Marxian heritage, and possibly the need for product differentiation, has led them to bring their economic thoughts into line with modern sociological jargon. Economists of a less adventurous spirit cannot claim that they have the right to develop a jargon of their own, while others must not; but whereas the development of a jargon is usually defended on the grounds that there is need for precision, it is not certain that New Leftists who have broken with traditional economics are searching for or even desire precision in their reasoning. The most charitable interpretation one can offer for their approach is that, the more one takes account of the complexities of society, and particularly the interaction between social and economic phenomenon, the more difficult it is to express oneself clearly and precisely — though Adam Smith managed somehow.

Thirdly, also in line with Marxian tradition, the style of the New Left is polemical. To make it possible for philosophy to change the world, as Marx wished, it is necessary to employ the language of the warrior kings of the Old Testament and their colourful prophets. While this suggests a lack of confidence in the prediction of the inevitable downfall of capitalism, this style of writing has an intuitive appeal which is denied more rigorous methods of exposition. However, as our purpose is less to refute such views and more to show how they lead to the rejection of Paretian welfare economics, we have no need to indulge in stylistic emulation. But there are difficulties left in weeding out the invective from the analysis.[i]

It is fortunate for us that the work of collating the views of the New Left on traditional economics has already been undertaken by Assar Lindbeck,[5] though the attitude of the New Left on welfare economics is implicit only in his monograph.[ii] Almost simultaneously, one of the New Left School, Herbert Gintis, published a skilful attack on welfare economics,[2] which deals more specifically with the matters of concern to us. This has helped us greatly with the problem of identification and classification of New Left views.

II   THE NEW LEFT AND THE PARETIAN VALUE ASSUMPTIONS

To the New Left it appears to be essential not even to begin to define welfare in terms of some existing state of the economy and with reference to the existing preference systems of individuals, but to define it in terms of an ultimate goal which has yet to be realised. Until then, members of society, save for the 'exploiters', live in a state of abject misery. The ultimate goal is 'freedom', which is a state in which there are not hierarchical relations between individuals and all social and economic activities are carried out by co-operation, which requires individuals to fuse their individual interests for the good of the whole.

Apart from the clear indication that, in a very general sense, the concern is with the welfare of all and not with an élite few, there is very little resemblance between a Paretian value system and that of the New Left. Firstly, the notion of 'freedom', which is synonymous with 'happiness', involves something more than the sum of the 'happiness', whatever that may mean, experienced by each individual. As Marcuse,[6] one of the main prophets, has said, 'Happiness is an objective condition which demands more than subjective feelings', and he adds:

... its validity depends on the real solidarity of the species 'man', which a society divided into antagonistic classes and nations cannot achieve. As long as this is the history of mankind, the 'state of nature', no matter how refined, prevails: a civilised *bellum omnium contra omnes*, in which the happiness of the ones must coexist with the sufferings of others. The First International was the last attempt to realize the solidarity of the species by grounding it in that social class in which the subjective and objective interest, the particular and universal, coincided .... Then the Spanish civil war aroused this solidarity, which is the driving power of liberation, in the unforgettable, hopeless fight of a tiny minority against the combined forces of fascist and liberal capitalism. [p. 14]

— a fine example of the elliptical and polemical style of New Left writing!

Secondly, it follows that welfare is not defined in terms of marginal changes comparing one state with another, with preference systems of individuals given. It is a goal to be worked for, which involves the total transformation of society. It may be noted — parenthetically — that, unlike orthodox Marxian thinking, it has become quite respectable to indulge in utopian speculation. In a striking passage, Marcuse[6] justifies this deviation from orthodox Marxism:

Utopian possibilities are inherent in the technical and technological forces of advanced capitalism and socialism: the rational utilisation of these forces on a global scale would terminate poverty and scarcity within a very foreseeable future. But we know now that neither their rational use nor — and this is decisive — their collective control by the 'immediate producers' (the workers) would by itself eliminate domination and exploitation: a bureaucratic welfare state would still be a state of repression which would continue even into the 'second phase of socialism' which each is to receive 'according to his Needs'. [p. 4]

This passage illustrates an important difference between collectivists and the New Left.

Thirdly, what we have labelled *the* Paretian value judgement, which denies the possibility of interpersonal comparisons of utility and defines an improvement as one where the welfare increases when at least one individual is better off and no one is worse off as a result of some change in the economy (cf. chapter 1, p. 9), has clearly no place within this value scheme. The New Left would go further and claim that it rests on an untenable assumption, namely that, in the course of moving to a preferred position, there is nothing inherent in the movement itself that alters the preference structure. While this is a specific technical criticism by the New Left[2] of the realism of the Paretian analysis, it also points forward towards a fundamental proposition in the New Left's view of the operation of capitalism which explains its antipathy towards the market system.

III   THE NEW LEFT CRITIQUE OF THE TECHNICAL ASSUMPTIONS

Much is made in New Left literature of the simplistic view of individual decision-making postulated in Paretian welfare economics and, indeed, in market economics generally. The idea of individuals with given preference structures independent of one another acquiring goods or providing factor services within a regime of scarce resources and thereby maximising utility denies the existence of any interaction between the process of consumption and production and the alteration in the preference structure itself, and entirely ignores constraints on behaviour, other than scarcity, that limit the capacity of the individual to maximise. The first strand of this criticism requires members of the New Left to bow in the direction of Marx and the second in the direction of Veblen.

To justify the first strand of the argument, appeal is made to 'common experiences'. Take an individual who at a given level of consumption expresses the wish and is offered the opportunity of substituting silk shirts for cheaper cotton shirts. According to *the* Paretian welfare judgement, the individual will be better off. But, it is argued by Gintis:[2]

Has his/her welfare increased? Perhaps not. For the very process of consuming the new bundle changes the individual's preferences. In particular, if he/she becomes accustomed to silk shirts, he/she may be no better off after the change than before. If the reader doubts this, he/she should ask if this individual, upon being returned to his original commodity bundle, regains his/her *original* level of welfare. [p. 585]

(The passage also reveals the author's concern for the sensibilities of the Women's Liberation Movement both in the specification of gender and dress!) Similarly, Paretian economics would suggest that a favourable shift in the production frontier caused by improved technology could produce a welfare improvement (with or without compensation arrangements); but a new technology alters the pattern of work activities and thereby alters both individuals' capacities and their preferences.

The second strand puts great stress on the 'role behaviour' of the individual. This is an enormous subject, but only the essential elements need be extracted from the relevant sociological literature in order to explain its relevance to welfare economics. Veblen[12] is the outstanding exponent of the view that individual utility depends on the opinion of others and how the individual adapts his behaviour according to the social norms prevalent in the society of his time. Therefore, as later sociologists have maintained, the ability of the individual to maximise utility will depend on the extent to which he is content with the norms and the role that is assigned to him in the social structure, and his capacity (such as his physical and educational development) to perform it. It follows that, to the New Left, the Paretian technical assumptions ignore significant character-istics of individual behaviour and important influences on it. Individuals are not solipsists bound up in themselves and oblivious of the opinion of others — their preference systems are interdependent but in a different way from that postulated by those who have explored the characteristics of Paretian optimal income redistribu-tion (see chapter 3). Secondly, their utility is not only a function exclusively of market relationships but also of their social and political relationships with others.

This difference of view about the factors governing individual utility has lead the New Left to pay particular attention to the constraints that social organisation places on the individual's capacity to improve his welfare, and particularly his 'work situation'. We shall examine the relevance of this point to the criticism made by the New Left of the institutional underpinnings of Paretian welfare economics in the next section of this chapter, but a brief general example illustrates the point. Where production is motivated by profit, entrepreneurs maximise the difference between sales and costs. In competitive conditions, this requires cost minimization with a concomitant hierarchical control of work activities characterised by rigid monitoring of the work force. Thus important individual qualities of the worker which determine his capacity for enjoyment, such as aesthetic taste and personal affection, are incapable of being developed within this work situation. This is the basis of the famous Marxian concept of 'alienation'[7] about which more anon.

IV   THE ACHIEVEMENT OF AN OPTIMUM

To the New Left, the Paretian institutional requirement of perfect competition within a system of private enterprise is neither possible nor desirable.

There is no need to explain in detail the familiar reasoning which leads New Leftists to receive with acclamation the conversion of Galbraith and many others to a thesis of industrial change which is so closely associated with the Marxian theory of economic development. In our criticism of the Paretian specifications for an optimal market system, we place the main emphasis on the innate impossibility of the perfect competition model associated with the unrealism of assuming perfect knowledge, no barriers to entry and product homogeneity. The New Left position emphasises rather the process by which small-scale capitalism through technological change and associated improvements in economies of scale must inevitably increase the size of operation of profit-taking enterprises with a consequential increase in the degree of market imperfection. But the element of unrealism in Paretian welfare economics extends far beyond the inherent divergences that must exist between perfect competition and actual market forms and into the realm of political action. The policy prescriptions of Paretian welfare economics in respect of market failure, such as the use of taxes and subsidies to bring marginal social costs in line with marginal social benefits, rests on the assumption that such fiscal measures will command popular support or at least will be enforceable. Such a view, to the New Left, ignores the fact that concentration of economic power brings a concentration of political power in the hands of relatively few industrialists. The activities of government will reflect this power, not necessarily solely in opposing expansion of government activity that promotes competition or attempts to correct the distribution of income between capital and labour, but also in support of expansion of government activity, such as defence and tied foreign aid, that may stabilise and improve the turnover of large corporations. Therefore, to the New Left, the concept of an independent government operating corrective mechanisms rather along the lines of control engineering is wholly false. The correct analogy is with a cybernetic system in which there is a close interaction between the economic and social structure of society and its pattern of political decision-making.[2]

But whether or not the market economy is characterised by competition or monopoly or can be made competitive does not decide the issue for the New Left. So long as profit-taking is a major element in the objective function of firms, then the system is condemned simply because it is based on organised markets. The market is an immoral system, for it presupposes that men are to be motivated solely by a desire for pecuniary gain and that, to obtain success, the activities of producers must be designed to mesmerise and by so doing to corrupt the consumer. Thus not only are preference systems of individuals changed by consumption itself, which offers a technical objection to the Paretian approach, but the preference systems are distorted to fit bourgeois norms which emphasise materialistic emulation. In the words of the famous Appeal by the students of the Sorbonne during the 1968 'French Revolution', '. . . we are privileged in not yet being fully integrated into this infernal cycle of consumption'. Further, for the reasons already given, the individual's capacity to improve his/her welfare is severely constrained by his/her work situation because of the hierarchical control of industry which market capitalism demands. To make the point in another way, equation (1.2) was written as:

$$U^g = U^g(X_i^g, v_j^g) \qquad (g = 1, 2, \ldots, s).$$

The first partials of the Xs are usually regarded as positive, whereas those of the vs are negative, i.e. the amounts of work done can be treated as negative goods. Not only does Paretian welfare economics tend to concentrate much more attention on the basket of commodities in explaining the virtues of consumer sovereignty and efficient allocation of resources, but the pain—cost element subsumed under the variation in the values of the vs is grossly neglected.

The intense barrage of criticism by the New Left of market capitalism and, on occasion, of centralised collectivism is in strong contrast to the lack of clear delineation of an economic organisation which best fits their idea of an optimum. New Leftists share with traditional Marxists the view that human motivation is a function of economic organisation and therefore that the destruction of capitalism, which exalts greed and reduces the bulk of the population to zombies in the face of materialist incentives, will by itself result in a transformation in human personality. The ideals engendered by the common cause of revolution will themselves create the identity of interests and selflessness which will make it possible for individuals to live in harmony with one another, once the market system is overthrown.[iii]

The economic system that will replace market capitalism is never described in detail. We only know what its characteristics will *not* be, rather than what they are likely to be. Thus money as a medium of exchange is rejected, as is any form of hierarchical organisation of production, whether or not the means of production are collectively owned. There also appears to be a strong antipathy towards urban living and culture as manifestations of the capitalist 'achievement', for urban life symbolises the intense specialisation and division of labour on which an industrialised society depends. By a process of elimination we appear to be left with a utopian vision either of a peasant-type culture where individuals are self-sufficient[iv] or of a kind of bucolic paradise where scarcities no longer exist and where, in the caustic words of a critic of previous generations of socialists, 'roast pigeons will in some way fly into the mouths of the comrades'.[10]

The inspired vision of the future has curious antecedents in the aristocratic homage paid to pastoral life in the eighteenth century and the bourgeois yearnings for a retreat to the country of the Lake Poets, or again the remote exclusive love nest of Baudelaire — 'Là, tout n'est qu'ordre et beauté/Luxe, calme et volupté'. These remain unrecognised or forgotten by New Left writers who have derived their inspiration from the writings of the young Marx of 1844 who rejected the use of the tools of economic analysis in devising solutions for the allocation of resources and even, so it seems, the acceptance of division of labour. Division of labour would no longer characterise the soulless process of physical production — only the intimate act of human reproduction.

V   THE RELEVANCE OF THE NEW LEFT ATTACK

It is tempting to spend some time reviewing these arguments in detail, but this would take us far away from the main purpose of this work. This task has in any case been brilliantly performed by Assar Lindbeck.[5] Rather than reiterate the criticisms of this author and those with sympathies more in line with our own, we shall now outline the *similarities* as well as the differences in the approach used by the New Left to our own.

Firstly, we accept that any initial value judgements that are to be translated into economic policies need not be constrained by reference to some initial state of the world in which individual preference systems are fixed and immutable. While clearly we have more sympathy with the individualistic bias of Paretian economics, we do not accept that liberalism is bound by Paretian initial value judgements, its description of the real world and its policy conclusions; and, along with the New Left, we certainly reject any suggestion that the Paretian system sets a standard by which other systems are to be judged.

Secondly, it follows that we join with the New Left in condemning attempts to segregate 'economic welfare' from 'welfare' in general, a position which, incidentally, Pareto himself rejected.[11] We agree that latter-day Paretians have come to accept that individual welfare functions can embody preferences that reflect the taste for altruistic actions and even for forms of government, but, as we have already shown, the attempt to make the analysis all-embracing runs into difficulties of its own (cf. chapter 3).

Thirdly, as we explain in detail later, we share the New Left's suspicion of monolithic economic and political organisation though we are not led thereby to reject the market system.

But profound differences remain. The first is that we reject the fundamental assumption of the New Left that individuals' behaviour with respect to resource-use is conditioned exclusively by their material circumstances and more particularly by the form of economic organisation in which they work. Ours is the tradition of Hume and Smith, which maintains that human nature — 'mean sensual man' — is here to stay and that this nature will not be transformed by the demise of capitalism. The perfectibility of man which haunts the literature of utopian visionaries across the centuries is for us a chimera.

The second is that we reject the proposition that the problem of scarcity is a put-up job engineered by the capitalist system and that, therefore, the destruction of that system will remove an important source of conflict between individual members of any society.

Likewise, we must reject the proposition that, even if resources are limited, the ideal moneyless society beloved of the New Left will so alter the preference systems of individuals, in respect of both acquisition of goods and provision of factor services, that wants will be so reduced that scarcities will disappear.

With these similarities and differences firmly in view, we now investigate the liberal alternative.

NOTES

i For a revealing fusion of an anti-mathematical, jargonised and polemical approach to a critique of modern economic analysis, see the Introduction[4] written by Hunt and Schwartz.

ii For a rather different *tour d'horizon* of radical economics in the USA, see Bronfenbrenner.[1] Bronfenbrenner views radical economics as developing as a branch of welfare economics. He provides a useful bibliography.

iii For an interesting and sympathetic account of Maoist ideas on this subject, see John Gurley.[9]

iv McInnes[8] has chronicled the growing respectability among members of the New Left for utopianism. For a justification of utopianism see Paul Baran.[9]

REFERENCES

1. Bronfenbrenner, M. 'Radical Economics in America: A 1970 Survey' *Journal of Economic Literature* (September 1970) pp. 747–66
2. Gintis, Herbert 'A Radical Analysis of Welfare Economics and Individual Development' *Quarterly Journal of Economics* (November 1972)
3. Goodwin, R. 'A Growth Cycle' in C. H. Feinstein (ed.) *Socialism, Capitalism and Economic Growth* Cambridge, Cambridge UP (1967)
4. Hunt, E. K. and Schwartz, J. C. (eds) *A Critique of Economic Theory* Harmondsworth, Penguin (1972) Introduction
5. Lindbeck, A. *The Political Economy of the New Left: An Outsider's View* New York, Harper & Row (1971)
6. Marcuse, Herbert *An Essay on Liberation* Boston, Beacon Press (1969)
7. Marx, Karl *Economic and Philosophic Manuscripts of 1844* (ed. D. J. Struik) New York, International Publishers Co. (1970) pp. 107–27
8. McInnes, Neil *The Western Marxists* La Salle, Ill., Library Press (1972) chapters 6–8
9. Mermelstein, David (ed.) *Economics: Mainstream Readings and Radical Critiques* Westminster, Md, Random House (1973) articles by Sweezy, Baran and Gurley

10. von Mises, L. 'Economic Calculation in the Socialist Commonwealth' in F. A. Hayek (ed.) *Collectivist Economic Planning* East Orange, NJ, Thomas Kelly (1947)
11. Tarascio, V. 'Vilfredo Pareto and Marginalism' *History of Political Economy* (Fall 1972) pp. 406–25
12. Veblen, Thorstein *Theory of the Leisure Class* Modern Library edition (1934) chapter 2

5. Liberalism

Does this leave us with a definition of a liberal — a pure, all round liberal? Not really. Perhaps though we may say that a 'liberal is one who values liberty above all other social goals and who will never consent to the restriction of any freedom, economic, political, or intellectual except as the price to be paid for the fuller realisation of other freedoms. He must demonstrate that this price is worth paying; he must always be ready to re-examine his and other positions; and he must not place material welfare above liberty. [F. Machlup 'Liberalism and the Choice of Freedoms' printed in E. Streissler (ed.) *Roads to Freedom* London, Routledge and Kegan Paul (1969)]

Liberalism as we understand the concept is concerned essentially, though not exclusively, with the maintenance and extension of individual freedom, defined as that condition of mankind in which coercion of some individuals by others is reduced to the minimum possible degree.[11,13,14] Freedom in this sense encompasses the moral and intellectual, the political and the economic spheres and, fundamentally, is divisible, as we shall demonstrate in this chapter. To a considerable extent, the philosophical foundations of liberalism, in the sense here defined, are due to the writings of John Stuart Mill,[11] while many of the more recent applications of liberal philosophy to issues in economic policy are due to the 'Neo-Austrian' school and most notably of course to Hayek[6,7] and Machlup.[10]

In a striking passage in chapter III of *On Liberty*, which itself has the significant title 'Of Individuality, as One of the Elements of Well-Being', J. S. Mill writes:[11]

He who lets the world, or his own portion of it, choose his plan of life for him, has no need of any other faculty than the ape-like one of imitation. He who chooses to plan for himself employs all his faculties. He must use observation to see, reasoning and judgment to foresee, activity to gain materials for decision, discrimination to decide and, when he has decided, firmness and self-control to hold to his deliberate decision . . . It is possible that he might be guided on some good path, and kept out of harm's way, without any of these things. But what will be his comparative worth as a human being? It really is of importance, not only what men do, but also what manner of men they are that do it. [p. 73]

This fundamental notion that the essence of humanity lies in the capacity to choose, and not simply in the ability to reason clearly, implies that individuals must be granted the widest possible freedom of choice (and with it a corresponding responsibility) if they are to develop their capacities. Coercion of some individuals by others can only be justified as a means of resolving conflicts between the choices of individuals and even then must be minimised in the process of conflict resolution. The essence of liberalism is freedom, therefore, not as an instrument, or even as a human preference, but as an ethical value in itself. For liberals in the tradition of Mill are not convinced of the existence of objective immutable truth, but believe that a good society is one that is uncertain of its truths and dedicates itself, not to an ideal, but to an eternal search.[5] For liberals, fallibility and the right to err are viewed as necessary corollaries to the capacity for self-improvement; symmetry and finality are mistrusted as enemies of freedom, and truth is viewed as many-sided. Thus Berlin:[3]

For him [Mill] man differs from animals primarily neither as the possessor of reason, nor as an inventor of tools and methods, but as a being capable of choice, one who is most himself in choosing and not being chosen for; the rider and not the horse; the seeker of ends and not merely of means, ends that he pursues, each in his own fashion; with the corollary that the more various these fashions, the richer the lives of men become; the larger the field of interplay between individuals, the greater the opportunities of the new and the unexpected; the more numerous the possibilities for altering his own character in some fresh or unexplored direction, the more paths open before each individual, and the wider will be his freedom of action and thought. [p. 178]

In accepting Mill's philosophy of liberalism, therefore, we are concerned to assist in constructing a society which secures the maximum freedom of choice for its individual citizens (given material constraints) and which recognises individual responsibilities for such choices as are made. In our view, it is unnecessary to believe in free will in order to ascribe responsibility to individuals for their actions[3,7] — though many determinists reject the concept of individual responsibility on the ground that individual choices are merely the outcome of past events. Following Hayek,[7] we would assign responsibility to individuals, not in order to assert that they might have chosen differently, but in order to make them different, i.e. to influence the future pattern of their choices. If this view is accepted, there is no irreconcilable conflict between liberalism and determinism though we ourselves consider that in practice it is just such a belief in free will that has fostered the spirit and vitality of liberalism.[11]

Although we ourselves accept the existence of free will[i] and deny the determinist position, by no means do we believe that all mankind is automatically either able or willing to exercise free will in the absence of coercive restrictions. We acknowledge that few individuals are able to exercise their ability to choose without an intense intellectual effort — that Sartre's 'road to freedom' is by no means an easy one. We accept also that many of those, like Mill's free man, who believe themselves to be capable of exercising freedom of choice may flinch from so doing for fear of the implied responsibility — in Sartre's terminology, that they prefer the *en-soi* to the *pour-soi*. It is indeed our recognition of such obstacles to the exercise of free will, as much as anything, that confirms us in the liberalist philosophy and that leads us to part company with the Paretian dogma.

For we believe that mankind marks out its true distinction from the animal kingdom by exercising free will, by making choices and recognising the responsibility that such choices imply. We are concerned therefore to assist in the development of a society that encourages individuals to want to exercise free will, which assists them in their efforts so to do, and which confronts them with the responsibility for their decisions. In this sense, freedom is not a means to a higher political end, but itself is the highest political end attainable by mankind.[1,5]

I   LIBERALISM AND PARETO OPTIMALITY

Central to our discussion is the view that there is no essential identity between the Paretian and the liberal positions — that the two philosophies are based upon quite different value judgements — and indeed that widely divergent policy prescriptions are to be expected when Paretians and liberals engage in policy discussion. In our view, however, the incompatibility between the two philosophies commonly is confused, as a consequence of an incorrect definition of liberalism, even by those who recognise that they differ. Such, for example, is the case with the recent contribution by Amartya Sen,[15,16] which, in misrepresenting the nature of the conflict with a characteristic confusion between liberalism and individual freedom in social choice, nevertheless provides an invaluable forum within which the true conflict between Pareto and liberalism may be appreciated.

Sen proposed — and proved — that there is no social decision function that simultaneously can satisfy the following conditions (U,P, and L*):

Condition U (unrestricted domain). Every logically possible set of individual orderings is included in the domain of the collective choice rule.

Condition P (Pareto principle). If every individual prefers any alternative x to another alternative y, then society must prefer x to y.

Condition L* (minimal liberalism). There are at least two individuals such that for each of them there is at least one pair of alternatives over which he is decisive, that is a pair of x, y, such that if he prefers x (respectively y) to y (respectively x), then society should prefer x (respectively y) to y (respectively x).

Proof: Let the two individuals referred to in condition L* be 1 and 2 respectively, and the two pairs of alternatives referred to be (x,y) and (z,w) respectively. Let $x \equiv z$. Assume that person 1 prefers x to y and y to w, while person 2 prefers w to z ($\equiv$x). Let everyone in the community, including persons 1 and 2, prefer y to w. There is no inconsistency, therefore, in individual orderings. Person 1 prefers x to y and y to w, while person 2 prefers y to w and w to x. By condition U this should be in the domain of the social decision mechanism. But by Condition L*, x must be preferred to y, and w must be preferred to x ($\equiv$z), while by condition P, y must be preferred to w. Thus, there is no best element in the set ($x \equiv z,y,w,$) in terms of social preference, and every alternative is worse than some other. A choice function for the society does not therefore exist.

Next, let x,y,z, and w be all distinct. Let person 1 prefer x to y and person 2 prefer z to w. Let everyone prefer w to x and y to z. There is no contradiction for persons 1 and 2. By condition U this configuration of individual preferences must yield a social choice function. But by condition L* society should prefer x to y and z to w while by condition P society must prefer w to x and y to z. This means that there is no best alternative for this set, and a choice function does not exist for any set that includes these four alternatives. Thus, there is no social decision function satisfying conditions U,P, and L*, and the proof is complete.

The dilemma posed by Sen in this proof has been viewed widely as a disturbing one for would-be Paretian 'liberals' in societies where individuals do not necessarily respect each other's personal choices.[ii] For, in such circumstances, pairwise choices based on 'liberal' values may conflict with those based on the weakest version of the Paretian principle — in which it is not even required that if someone prefers x to y and everyone regards x to be at least as good as y, then x is socially better — which insists only that if everyone strictly prefers x to y then x must be preferred to y.

Critical reactions to Sen's theorem[2,9,12,13] have endorsed the formal validity of his argument while questioning the relevance of his assumptions — itself no easy task given the weakness of the conditions that underpin the theorem. For example, Sen does not require transitivity of social preference (required by Arrow), but merely the existence of a best alternative in each choice situation. Nor does he require the independence of irrelevant alternatives (once again imposed by Arrow), which denies recourse to preference intensities as a solution to the social choice dilemma. And still he presents an impossibility problem. The critics, for the most part, have centred attention upon two issues, namely the relevance of completeness[2] for a social decision rule and the precise nature of condition L* (of minimal liberalism). To these apparently separate but in fact interdependent issues we must now direct attention.

Suppose that condition L* does indeed capture the essence of liberalist philosophy (which it does not), from the viewpoint of *individual* decision-making. It must be noted, then, that Sen's theorem refers to the possibility not of *individual* but of *social* choice, and this is a constitutional question, which is to be resolved only after a careful evaluation of the costs and benefits under a range of different circumstances. The assumption, in condition U, of an unrestricted domain certainly is unjustified when treating constitutional rules even at the elementary level of Sen, and especially when dealing with a philosophy, condition L*, which concerns itself not only with the internal form of a social welfare function but also with just what policies a social welfare function should be called upon to decide, i.e. with the issue of the proper domain for collective choice. The Arrow-type framework is useless without completeness of the social choice rule. A complete social ordering is incompatible with condition L*. Ergo, the framework of the Sen contribution is to be rejected. Let us go yet further. Attempts such as that by Sen to reduce complex reality to mechanistic form are *doomed* from the outset if relevance has a positive value. For the notion of a lexicographic ordering of ethical values is rarely relevant in real-world circumstances where value trade-offs are so pervasive. Once the notion of trade-offs is accepted, completeness in the social decision rule is unattainable, and the debate on collective choice is rescued from Arrow-type aridity.

Worse still, Sen has grossly misinterpreted the liberalist philosophy in his condition L* as was noted by Hillinger and Lapham,[9] who unfortunately failed systematically to develop the implications of their restatement. As they view it, liberalism may be broadly defined as the desire not to coerce individuals to accept choices that they would not have made voluntarily — and on this definition they deduce that where the actions of one individual do not impinge on the welfare of others, then liberalism follows as a special case of the Paretian principle. Whenever the choices of one individual impinge on the welfare of others, they claim that there is no general presumption in favour of freedom of individual choice and that there is no clear-cut liberal solution, other than (perhaps) reliance upon the Paretian principle. Thus, they view the Paretian principle as a generalisation of liberalism and deny the possibility of conflict between the two dogmas.

Since it is our purpose in this book to establish the *separate natures* of the Paretian and the liberalist philosophies and to demonstrate the divergent consequences for the theory of public policy, it will be evident that we cannot endorse such a judgement. Suffice it to repeat that we understand liberalism to be concerned with the maintenance and extension of negative freedoms,[12,13] defined as the absence of coercion by certain individuals of others — while recognising the problem of a conflict of freedoms and the need to rank and to enforce appropriately ranked freedoms by coercive measures. Liberalism is not concerned necessarily either with the supremacy of individual preferences or with the policy of *laissez-faire*. The inadequacy of condition L* as the condition of liberalism should require no further emphasis.

Let us further clarify the divergences between the liberal and the Paretian dogmas by reference to the Paretian value assumptions outlined in chapter 1. There is no disagreement on condition (i), which determines that concern is to be with the welfare of all members of society. A dogma dedicated to the extension of negative freedom must be based upon an individualistic foundation. Condition (ii), which determines that an individual is the best judge of his own welfare, however, is endorsed only with strict reservations. For liberals do not accept Pareto-preferred moves which involve 'unnecessary' coercion, even though they are the outcome of individual's preferences.[iii] If certain individuals do not value freedom as highly as liberals would wish, there is no reason why their behaviour should be condoned by the liberal order. Condition (iii), which rules out interpersonal utility comparisons, is denied by liberalism in that the institutional adjustments required for freedom impinge significantly upon the primary structure of rights in all economies. Liberals are not prepared to sacrifice freedom to the Paretian strait-jacket. The implications of the liberal value judgement for collective choice, justice and efficiency are outlined in part III of this book. They diverge significantly from those of Pareto.

II   THE NATURE OF FREEDOM

The oldest and perhaps the most pertinent definition of freedom is simply 'independence of the arbitrary will of another'. In this sense freedom refers solely to a relation of individuals to other individuals and the only infringement on it is coercion by individuals. The wider the area of non-interference, the wider is an individual's freedom. As such, freedom is entirely a negative concept. Thus Hayek:[7]

It is often objected that our concept of liberty is merely negative. This is true in the sense that peace is also a negative concept or that security or quiet or the absence of any particular impediment or evil is negative. It is to this class of concepts that liberty belongs: it describes the absence of a particular obstacle — coercion by other men. It becomes positive only through what we make of it. It does not assure us of any particular opportunities, but leaves it to us to decide what use we shall make of the circumstances in which we find ourselves. [p. 19]

But, however highly it is valued, negative freedom cannot conceivably be unlimited, because, if it were, it would entail a state in which all individuals could boundlessly interfere with all other individuals — a situation which would culminate either in social chaos or in the domination of the weak by the strong. Inevitably, therefore, the area of men's free action must be limited by law. It is important to note however that even protective legislation of this kind is coercive, an infringement of negative freedom.

Negative freedom, as outlined above, is entirely distinct from the concept of positive freedom, which is commonly but mistakenly applied in discussions of freedom. The positive sense of the word freedom derives from the wish on the part of the individual to be his own master, to be independent of external forces of whatever kind. Although apparently closely associated with negative freedom, in fact positive freedom is its greatest enemy. Thus Berlin:[3]

The freedom which consists in being one's own master, and the freedom which consists in not being prevented from choosing as I do by other men, may, on the face of it, seem concepts at no great logical distance from each other — no more than negative and positive ways of saying much the same thing. Yet the 'positive' and 'negative' notions of freedom historically developed in divergent directions not always by logically reputable steps, until, in the end, they came into direct conflict with each other. [p. 132]

To those who profess themselves advocates of positive freedom, freedom is power, effective power to achieve specific objectives, and the demand for freedom is the demand for power to be attained and protected by legislation or by alternative coercive measures. In essence, this is the philosophy of 'bastard' liberalism as currently preached in the United States, which has developed subtly from a doctrine of freedom into a doctrine of authority and which, in other societies, has become a favoured weapon of despotism. This is not to imply that positive freedom is not demanded (and obtained) frequently for laudable social objectives such as the elimination of poverty and disease, improved standards of living and the provision of equality of opportunity, etc. Nor does it imply that those who demand effective power necessarily will fail to exercise such power in the interest, as they see it, of those from whom their authority is desired. Nevertheless, the granting of this effective power brings with it the power of coercion for some individuals to wield over others and this is the negation of freedom in the negative sense.[iv] It is unfortunate indeed that the use of such phrases as 'freedom from want' and 'freedom from disease', which imply effective power, has resulted in a misunderstanding of the important concept of freedom as serious and as deep-rooted as is the case at the present time.

III   THE PRINCIPAL CATEGORIES OF FREEDOM

The 'indivisibility of freedom' is a slogan that is frequently encountered and widely accepted. But it is incorrect. There are many freedoms, not one alone — many kinds of human activity to which the principle of non-interference may or may not be applied. Some freedoms are compatible with each other, or even complementary, but others are rivalrous. Thus Machlup:[10]

Some of these freedoms may be independent of each other, others complementary or competing in the sense that more of one may permit either more or less of another. That is to say, greater freedom in one realm of human action may make it either easier or harder to achieve freedom in another realm of action. Some freedoms support one another, others impair one another; and where there is a conflict of freedoms it is important to know it and to analyse their comparative value for the pursuit of happiness, present or future. [pp. 128–9]

Machlup's analysis of the dimensions of freedom is usefully summarised as follows.

i   Intellectual and moral freedoms

There are four principal intellectual and moral freedoms, namely: (a) freedom of conscience, (b) freedom of religion, (c) academic freedom and (d) freedom of non-conformity and eccentricity. In each case, these freedoms are negative, 'to do or not to do' as each individual might freely choose. Freedom of conscience implies that any individual may refuse to do things against his conscience even when required to do so by other individuals acting separately or as a collectivity. Examples of this freedom are: the right to conscientious objection against conscription into the armed forces, the right of refusal to assist in acts of genocide, and the right of refusal to inform upon friends and colleagues when called upon to do so. Freedom of religion implies the right of any individual to worship in any way, or not at all, as he wishes, and irrespective of the preferences of any prevailing orthodoxy. Academic freedom encompasses the rights of any individual to study, investigate and teach any subject that might interest him, irrespective of the judgement of any other individuals. Such a freedom is incompatible with the restrictive behaviour of college administrators who present a black-list of unsuitable subjects as it is of militant students who disrupt the classes of those whose viewpoints they do not accept. Freedom of non-conformity and eccentricity implies the right of any individual to be different in appearance, habits and way of life, irrespective of how abhorrent this may be to some prevailing orthodoxy. Few societies uphold this freedom. Public disapproval, social ostracism and legal punishment are commonly utilised infringements.

ii   Political freedoms

There are essentially six negative political freedoms, namely: (a) freedom of coalition, (b) freedom of assembly, (c) freedom of vote, (d) freedom of revolution, (e) freedom of expression, speech and the press, (f) freedom of privacy. Freedom of coalition implies that any individual may combine with anybody for any purpose. In practice, this freedom usually is restricted to coalitions for purposes not involving harm to others — a consequence of a conflict between freedoms. Freedom of assembly implies the right to convene or attend gatherings for discussion and deliberation of any subject. In practice, this freedom frequently is curtailed, for example in so far as assemblies for anti-race propaganda are concerned. Freedom of vote implies the right of any individual to cast his vote in free and secret balloting in periodic elections and referenda. All societies restrict this freedom to exclude minors and lunatics. Many societies further restrict the freedom to exclude aliens and illiterates. Dictatorships deprive individuals of the freedom of vote perhaps completely. Freedom of revolution implies the right to overthrow a government that denies 'essential' freedoms. In many ways, this is a strange freedom, although it was incorporated into several of the state constitutions in the United States. In so far as it implies the right of a minority to overthrow by violence a government supported by a majority, it would not in general be supportable. But specific circumstances nevertheless might seem to necessitate such a freedom where fundamental freedoms were in jeopardy, e.g. where a majority-based government pursued a policy of genocide. Freedom of expression, speech and press is self-evident as are the censorship restrictions imposed by almost all societies, though by some far more severely than by others. Freedom of privacy implies the right of any individual to live without being exposed to the view of knowledge of uninvited individuals. This freedom is invaded in many ways, even in the so-called democracies, viz. by the tapping of telephone wires, by the interception of mail, and by pressure on individuals to testify on matters that they do not wish to disclose.

iii   Economic freedoms

There are essentially seven negative economic freedoms (with some inevitable overlap between them), namely: (a) freedom of work, enterprise and trade, (b) freedom of travel and migration, (c) freedom of contract, (d) freedom of markets, (e) freedom of competition and entry, (f) freedom of choice in consumption and (g) freedom of choice in occupation. Freedom of work, enterprise and trade is self-evident. In most societies it is restricted either formally, by legislation, or informally, as a consequence of the freedoms of contract and coalition. Freedom of travel and migration implies the right of any individual to travel both domestically and abroad and to shift his place of residence again either domestically or abroad. Few if any societies allow complete freedom of travel and migration abroad. Most Western countries allow freedom of travel and migration domestically. Freedom of contract implies the right to make any kind of binding contract with anyone, except under duress or with deceit or fraud. This freedom not infrequently is in conflict with the freedoms of work, trade and enterprise and of competition and entry. Different societies impinge in differing ways and to a varying degree upon these separate freedoms in an effort to resolve the conflict. Freedom of markets implies the right of any individual to buy or sell any quantity of a commodity at any price agreeable to himself and to the other party(ies). This freedom is frequently restricted, e.g. for narcotics, alcohol, pornography and prostitution, sometimes to reflect the importance of other freedoms but frequently as a consequence of a paternalistic collectivity.

Freedom of competition and entry implies the right of any individual to enter any industry, trade or market and to compete in any way except with the use of violence, deceit or fraud. This freedom is frequently restricted by legislation and also as a consequence of the freedoms of contract and of coalition. Freedom of choice in consumption implies a right of any individual to use his buying power for any goods or services he chooses without any obstruction in the form of rationing restrictions or prohibitions. As stated, this freedom is encompassed by the freedom of markets but it may be further required that prices should reflect demand and the supply of resources required for their production as would be the case in competitive markets. In neither sense, but especially in the latter, is freedom of choice in consumption maintained in practice. Finally, freedom of choice in occupation implies a right of any individual to use his labour talents in any occupation he chooses, with wages reflecting the supply of the labour in question and the demand for the products to which it contributes as would be the case if competition prevailed both in the commodity and in the factor markets. As such, this freedom is always violated in practice — if not by legislation, then as a consequence of the freedoms of contract and coalition.

IV LIBERALISM AND THE CONFLICT OF FREEDOMS

Freedoms are in conflict and coercion is inevitable — this is the harsh reality of the human condition.[v] Liberals, therefore, cannot press for freedom without a careful definition of their preference orderings. To decide the appropriate content of coercive interventions it is necessary, therefore, to rank negative freedoms and to define their relationship with other social objectives. To this controversial task let us now address ourselves.

We attach supreme importance to the intellectual and moral freedoms outlined above and we would be prepared to defend these almost at any cost in terms of sacrificed alternatives. For, if these freedoms are not protected, and if individuals are provided with access only to a restricted range of ideas and viewpoints, the notions of political and economic freedom may be rendered meaningless, however wide they may seem to be in a superficial sense. For this reason, we would not condone restrictions on anti-liberal expositions even where potentially they might endanger a liberal order. Better to take the risk and to trust that liberalism will prevail in a society with freedom of expression than to implicate ourselves in the destruction of liberalism in a misguided attempt to protect it from criticism. As Machlup[10] has emphasised, liberalism is not a timid philosophy.

We attach also very considerable importance to certain of the political freedoms outlined above, most notable to the freedoms of expression, speech, press and assembly, which equally well might be categorised as intellectual and moral freedoms, and to the freedom of vote, which is essential if individuals are to exercise any freedom with respect to political matters. There is indeed a conflict between freedom of expression etc. and freedom of privacy, which in our view can be resolved to a considerable extent by 'separate facilities' intervention. For example, there need be no general censorship of pornography or of racialist propaganda; but those who find such expressions offensive should not have their privacy invaded either by a public display or presentation or by the invasion of their private homes. In general, liberals do not readily embrace the freedom of revolution, even in anti-liberal societies, partly because revolutions seldom extend freedoms as negatively defined and usually further restrict them, but largely because liberals place considerable faith in the intellectual and moral freedoms as a means of dissuading mankind from pursuing illiberal objectives. This does not mean that liberals upon occasion may not be sufficiently incensed as to engage in revolution, but this is a last-ditch solution. To a more limited extent, also, liberals cannot fully endorse the freedom of coalition and associations, since this may well generate discretionary power within the political and economic spheres, which significantly endangers important freedoms, of which more anon.

Inevitably, there are severe conflicts of freedoms within the economic sphere and this is where the difficulty of ranking is especially apparent. Our own view, in general terms, is that the freedoms of markets, of competition and entry and of freedom of choice, to the extent possible, in consumption and occupation are more important than are the freedoms of contract and coalition, and we are prepared to accept coercive interventions *of an appropriate nature* to ensure the dominance of the former over the latter freedoms wherever they are in conflict. Our reasoning on this is straightforward. The major threats to individual freedoms are seen to stem from concentrations of political and economic power, whether in the hands of the State, of bureaucrats, of firms or of private citizens. For the liberal is acutely aware of the potential for coercive abuses characteristic of significant discretionary power; he believes in the viewpoint that all power corrupts, and recognises the difficulty of eliminating discretionary power and its abuses once established. For this reason liberals have a preference for a system that encourages voluntary exchange through market processes, and they share a belief that some form of competitive capitalism provides the strongest safeguard for such a system. They further share a preference for some form of decentralised government rooted in the democratic tradition and an abhorrence of any philosophy of government that upholds the doctrine that the State is an organic entity, essentially independent of the individuals from which it is composed.

The fact that liberals attach importance to the extension of negative freedoms in no sense implies that they attach a zero rating to other social objectives, such as justice and material welfare. Rather it is true to say that liberals with other individuals obtain positive utility from economic advances, but that, where these are in conflict with important negative freedoms, they personally would discount the economic benefits more sharply than would non-liberals; i.e., they attach a higher value to freedom.[6] The precise nature of the trade-off will depend on many considerations, including the freedoms and social objectives that are in conflict and the stage of development of the society in question.

V   SOME LIBERAL PREDILECTIONS

In our view, the liberal approach to policy issues emphasises certain features of the economic system to a greater degree than is discernible in other treatments. Although this difference of emphasis is a matter entirely of positive interpretation, it carries with it important implications for the economic theory of public policy and is relevant to the ranking of alternative institutional solutions.

i   The importance of property rights

It is not surprising that a philosophy dedicated to the support of
freedom has paid close attention to the nature and significance of
property rights,[4a] since such rights play a central role both in the
delimitation of economic freedoms and in the resolution of conflict
between freedoms. The liberal emphasis upon a property rights
approach to the theory of production and exchange has resulted,
however, in at least three important modifications to the theoretical
framework, which impinge upon the policy debate. First, individual
decision-makers, rather than the productive organisation, assume
central importance in theories of the firm, markets and of representative government. Individuals are assumed to seek their own interests
and to maximise utility subject to the constraints of the organisational structure, arguably with non-trivial implications. Second,
account is taken of the fact that more than one pattern of property
rights can exist with varying implications for organisational
objectives, thereby directing attention to the interrelationship
between institutional arrangements and economic behaviour. Third,
the relevance of non-zero transaction costs for economic adjustment
is incorporated explicitly into public policy analysis, arguably with
significant consequences.

ii   The relevance of X-inefficiency

X-inefficiency is a phenomenon now recognised for theoretical
purposes by Paretian as well as by liberal economists, following the
seminal contribution by Harvey Leibenstein.[9a] It is noteworthy in
this section principally because of its close association with the
property rights literature and because its policy implications,
following Paretian thinking, for the most part are favourable to
liberalism. In certain respects, therefore, and quite by chance, the
recognition of X-inefficiency has drawn the Paretian approach to
market structure more closely into line with that of liberalism.

   Classical economic theory, by viewing the profit-seeking entre-
preneur as the controlling and active factor input with all other
factors passively co-operating in pursuit of his objective, had no place
for X-inefficiency. Firms were assumed automatically to combine
their factor inputs efficiently, and thereby to minimise production
costs for any selected rate of output. Once this simplistic notion of
the property rights situation is disturbed, however, X-inefficiency
possibilities emerge even within a profit-motivated organisation, save

only where survivorship is at risk.[14a] For the non-controlling factor inputs — both management and shop-floor labour — are now seen to be set on maximising their own utility functions (which are not necessarily coincidental with profit maximisation) subject to the organisational constraints established by the controlling factor. In non-survivorship conditions, the result inevitably is X-inefficiency and policing costs, both of which, on certain assumptions, may be viewed as Paretian welfare losses, with important implications for the public policy debate.

iii   The pervasion of power

Liberals have always paid close attention to the role of power in the economic system, viewing power and freedom essentially as antonyms. Only recently, however, has the power issue been recognised explicitly in conventional economic analysis and then at the instigation of J. K. Galbraith,[5a] who by no stretch of the imagination is associated with liberalism as here defined. Galbraith has strictured the profession for its failure to recognise the importance of power both in microeconomic and in macroeconomic analysis, and has urged that this omission has damaged the predictive ability of economic models and so the credibility of the professional economist. At the microeconomic level, for example, Galbraith suggests that monopoly and oligopoly, by manipulating consumers via sales promotions, engage in an over-utilisation of resources, in direct contradiction to the neoclassical predictions. At the macroeconomic level, he argues that the power of large corporations to generate inflation enables them to enter into costly wage settlements without concern for the consequences, thereby rendering conventional demand management of the economy inoperative. For Galbraith, predictably, recognition of the pervasion of power establishes a case for further direct state intervention, designed to control the corporations both in their microeconomic and in their macroeconomic activities. Predictably, also, the power of bureaucracy and its corruption are ignored in the Galbraithian model. To liberals, by contrast, the recognition of the pervasion of power does not imply blind acceptance. Nor is power especially distinguished by reference to its location. Liberals are as concerned to remove the props of power in the corporate and union spheres as they are to chain Leviathan. The policy implications of this emphasis — though in no way sympathetic to those derived by Galbraith — are nonetheless highly significant.

iv   The problem of alienation

Contrary to popular opinion, liberals[17] are equally concerned about the so-called problem of alienation as are Marxists and New Leftists, though they view it in different terms. Marx, in his philosophical and sociological critique of capitalism, centred attention upon alleged deleterious effects of the market economy upon the worker's inner life, arguing that the development of private property capitalism and the division of labour caused workers to become degraded or dehumanised, a state denoted as alienation. To Marx, alienation was a consequence of powerlessness, isolation and self-estrangement, concepts that require a brief further discussion. Powerlessness alienation is a consequence of (i) the separation from ownership of the means of production; (ii) the inability to influence general managerial policies; (iii) the lack of control over the conditions of employment; and (iv) the lack of control over the immediate work process. In full capitalism, the worker became a commodity to be hired and fired at will and coerced by the chronic excess supply of labour — the industrial reserve army. Isolation was seen by Marx as an inevitable consequence of powerlessness alienation, with alienated man becoming isolated from himself, from his fellows and from nature. Capitalists as well as workers suffer from isolation alienation — both play unreal roles in an unreal world. Self-estrangement implies that a worker becomes isolated from his inner self under capitalism, with the work process losing any semblance of individually purposeful activity, and with work becoming an external experience. Thus Marx viewed the process of capitalist accumulation as a process in which wealth had become an end in itself and in which mankind had become a commodity and thereby was alienated.

Liberals, in contrast to Marx, reject the notions of powerlessness and isolation alienation as being implicit in capitalism while acknowledging the potential problem of self-estrangement. In these respects, liberals reflect the approach of Adam Smith. Smith viewed the division of labour not as an instrument of economic bondage but as a mechanism for providing mankind with effective power in the face of a niggardly environment. The capitalist division of labour was seen by Smith as a prerequisite for cultural fulfilment which could be attained only by economic progress. To Smith, the free market economy provided a means for mutual gain — not a basis for social conflict — and division of labour was viewed as benefiting all classes. The worker in no sense was viewed as being powerless in the face of a wage-exploiting employer: rather, all productive enterprise was viewed as being subordinate to the consumer — a view that closely reflects the ideal of present-day liberalism. The very process of division of labour was seen as favouring social intercourse, thus liberating mankind from his essential isolation. This does not imply, of course, that Smith or indeed present-day liberals view work as a commodity — for clearly, it is not in that positive wage rates for the most part are necessary to call forth factor supplies. Nor was Smith (are liberals) unaware of the culturally debilitating environment of the division of labour — Smith's antidote of education was forcibly expressed in *The Wealth of Nations*. But the self-estrangement alienation of Smith is a mild version indeed of that of Marx — indeed, Smith intimates that the condition is unlikely to be recognised as a problem by workers who are happily enjoying increased opulence in the progressive division of labour. Liberals endorse this intimation at least in economies characterised by extensive negative freedoms.

In our view, the problem of alienation, in so far as it exists, is a consequence of the division of labour and not of absolute or relative deprivation, powerlessness or isolation induced by capitalism. Alienation exists because individuals do not always enjoy serving under the authority of others — an essential condition of the division of labour. Whatever the system of production — and liberals are not necessarily committed to the neoclassical paradigm — some of those who serve will suffer from self-estrangement. But this has nothing whatsoever to do with socialism or capitalism as such. To the shop-floor worker it may matter little whether he serves under the authority of Comrade Malenkov or that of Arnold Weinstock. It is less than likely that the whip in the overseer's hand will be transformed magically into an orchestral baton as a system of capitalism is subverted to one of socialism! If we have not learned this much from history we are indeed blind to its messages.

v   Nirvana economics

The most influential attack on nirvana economics is due to Harold Demsetz,[4b] who contrasts the nirvana approach with his (preferred) comparative institution approach to the economic theory of public policy. In essence, the Demsetz approach corresponds closely to that of the liberal tradition. Thus Demsetz:

In practice, those who adopt the nirvana viewpoint seek to discover discrepencies between the ideal and the real and if discrepancies are found, they deduce that the real is inefficient. Users of the comparative institution approach attempt to assess which alternative real institutional arrangement seems best able to cope with the economic problem. [p. 1]

Demsetz attacks the nirvana approach as being excessively susceptible to three logical fallacies, namely (i) the 'grass is always greener fallacy'; (ii) the 'fallacy of the free lunch'; and (iii) the 'people could be different fallacy'. The 'grass is always greener fallacy' is embedded in all attempts by Paretian welfare economists to compare a market failure situation with a solution theoretically attainable via perfect government. For, as Demsetz emphasises, 'the political or non-profit forces that are substituted for free enterprise must be analyzed and the outcome of the workings of these forces must be compared to the market solution' before an interventionist conclusion should be reached. The 'fallacy of the free lunch' occurs when Paretians derive a 'market failure' conclusion on the basis of an analysis which does not take account of relevant marketing costs, an error to which the Paretian technical assumptions render them excessively prone. The 'people could be different fallacy' occurs whenever Paretians over-ride the utility functions of the individuals concerned, for example by analysing a policy outcome on the assumption that individuals are risk-neutral when in fact they are risk-averse, and designating the outcome (incorrectly) as one of market failure.

In one sense, Demsetz's criticisms may be passed over merely as a demand for the more circumspect application of Paretian welfare economics to policy analysis. No doubt there is much need for that. In a more profound sense, however, Demsetz's strictures must be viewed as an assault on the citadel. For Demsetz is urging that the Paretian criteria just are not designed to cope with real-world problems; that once the nirvana standard is abandoned as untenable, as it must be, the Paretian ship is left drifting without a compass; that modern analysis has yet to describe efficiency in a world where indivisibilities are present and knowledge is costly to produce, and where governments are neither omniscient nor necessarily impartial. In such circumstances the concepts of perfect competition and Pareto optimality simply are unable to give much help.

VI   LIBERALISM AND COERCION

Coercion has been defined[7] as any reduction in negative freedom, such as occurs for example when the alternatives before an individual are so manipulated by other individuals as to narrow the range of effective choice. Only in the limit, where the choice set is narrowed to a single element, does this imply a complete elimination of freedom of choice. In this sense, coercion must be distinguished from power to coerce, though the two concepts of course are closely related. We have already argued that liberalism cannot imply the absence of coercion, given the conflict that exists between freedoms, and between freedoms and other social objectives. The issue thus arises as to what form coercion normally should assume. The essential answer is that, where coercion is necessary, liberals are always concerned to avoid subjecting individuals to the arbitrary will of other individuals. To the implications of this for policy we now must turn.

Central to the philosophy of liberalism is the belief that all forms of coercive intervention should conform to 'the rule of law'[10] and that this requirement should constitute a limitation on the powers of government, including the powers of the legislature. The 'rule of law' is more than 'constitutionalism'. It requires that all laws should conform to a set of principles. First, laws must always be prospective and never retrospective in their effect, since their intention is to influence current and future choices and not to punish individuals for past decisions registered in ignorance of the subsequent coercive intervention. Second, laws must be known and certain (to the maximum extent attainable) so that individuals are in a position accurately to predict the decisions of the courts. Third, laws must apply with equal force to all individuals without exception or discrimination. It is this requirement that laws apply equally to all, including those who govern, that makes it improbable that 'oppressive' laws will be adopted. It must however be recognised that 'equality before the law' is not always entirely possible since certain laws may be known to affect certain individuals to a greater extent than others. There is no general solution to this problem save a policy of vigilance to ensure that legislation does not seek out known individuals in a persistent and vindictive fashion.

Finally, once the 'rule of law' is established, liberals would urge the adoption of such constitutional safeguards as *habeas corpus* and trial by jury as additional restrictions on the exercise of arbitrary discretionary powers. It is important to recognise, however, that only when the rule of law is established — only where individual courts pass the final judgements — are these constitutional devices effective safeguards for individual freedom. Thus Hayek:[7]

To use the trappings of judicial form where the essential conditions for a judicial decision are absent, or to give judges power to decide issues which cannot be decided by the application of rules, can have no effect but to destroy the respect for them even where they deserve it. [p. 219]

VII   THE LIBERAL APPROACH TO POLICY FORMULATION

The very method of exposition of the liberal position indicates that liberalism without question is a missionary philosophy. It prescribes what it believes to be good for mankind, though under no illusion about the lack of enthusiasm which it may encounter from non-liberals. It is inevitable that in many important respects the political and social arrangements in modern societies will be incompatible with liberalism, implying that to achieve a liberal society requires a change in the existing order of individual preferences. It has been suggested that liberals, in their enthusiasm for their policy objectives, will impose their will upon society. Nothing could be further from the truth.

Liberals are good democrats, accepting as a corollary to equality before the law the requirement that all individuals (excepting minors and lunatics) should have the same share in making the law. Majority voting is a decision rule which liberals helped to establish against bitter opposition and which they still accept. This does not imply, however, that liberals are required to endorse outcomes of majority voting that result in illiberal policies. The point has been well-put by Hayek:[7]

Liberalism is a doctrine about what the law ought to be, democracy a doctrine about the manner of determining what will be the law. Liberalism regards it as desirable that only what the majority accepts should in fact be law, but it does not believe that this is therefore necessarily good law. Its aim, indeed, is to persuade the majority to observe certain principles. It accepts majority rule as a method of deciding, but not as an authority for what the decision ought to be. [p. 104]

The liberal, therefore, will abide by the decisions arrived at by majority rule, while exercising all reasonable means of persuasion available to him, short of coercion, to alter the preferences of those who would encourage illiberal policies. In this sense, liberals are not constrained by the existing order of individual preferences. Categorically, however, this does not imply that liberals are dictators. Liberals will not force individuals to be free!

NOTES

i To accept free will is not at all to deny the predictive powers of economic science, though certain scientists flinch from freedom on such grounds. Thus the notable geneticist C. H. Waddington:[7] '[Freedom] is a very troublesome concept for the scientist to discuss, partly because he is not convinced, in the last analysis, there is such a thing.' (p. 72)

ii Viz. Sen[15] (p. 157):

What is the moral? It is that in a very basic sense liberal values conflict with the Pareto principle. If someone takes the Pareto principle seriously, as economists seem to do, then he has to face problems of consistency in cherishing liberal values, even very mild ones. Or, to look at it in another way, if someone does have certain liberal values, then he may have to eschew his adherence to Pareto optimality. While the Pareto criterion has been thought to be an expression of individual liberty, it appears that in choices involving more than two alternatives, it can have consequences that are, in fact, deeply illiberal.

iii The following perceptive comment was received from Steven Morrell, a postgraduate student at Virginia Polytechnic Institute:

My fundamental value judgement is that most individuals desire to be surrounded, for the most part, by others who are alike in ideology, race, religion, physical traits, etc. The desire for homogeneity stems from a desire to be able to predict the behaviour of others in a wide range of circumstances. The informational content of individuals, as to behaviour patterns, who are similar in the aforementioned respects, is much greater relative to those who are different. Therefore, because it has been, and probably still is, less costly to prohibit diversity in views, mannerisms, etc. than to invest in information concerning the behaviour of homosexuals, lesbians, etc., we observe Barry's fact — i.e. coercers.

iv Viz. Berlin[3] (p. 166):

This [negative freedom] is almost at the opposite pole from the purposes of those who believe in liberty in the 'positive' — self directive — sense. The former want to curb authority as such. The latter want it placed in their own hands. That is a cardinal issue. These are not two different interpretations of a single concept but two profoundly divergent and irreconcilable attitudes to the ends of life. It is as well to recognise this even if in practice it is often necessary to strike a compromise between them. For each makes absolute claims. These claims cannot both be fully satisfied. But it is a profound lack of social and moral understanding not to recognise that the satisfaction that each of them seeks is an ultimate value which, both historically and morally, has an equal right to be classed among the deepest interests of mankind.

v Hayek emphasised, some twenty years ago,[6] that liberalism is not synonymous with *laissez-faire*. Viz: 'Probably nothing has done so much harm to the liberal cause as the wooden insistence of some liberals on certain rough rules of thumb, above all the principle of laisser-faire.' (p . 13)

REFERENCES

1. Acton, Lord 'The History of Freedom in Antiquity' (1862), excerpt in Alan Bullock and M. Shock (eds) The Liberal Tradition London, A. & C. Black (1956) p. 121
2. Bernholz, P. 'Is a Paretian Liberal Really Impossible?' unpublished monograph (1974)
3. Berlin, I. Four Essays on Liberty Oxford, Oxford UP (1969)
4. Culyer, A. 'Pareto, Peacock and Rowley, and Policy Towards Natural Monopoly — Comment' Journal of Public Economics (February 1973)
4a. Demsetz, H. 'The Exchange and Enforcement of Property Rights' Journal of Law and Economics (October 1964)
4b. Demsetz, H. 'Information and Efficiency: Another Viewpoint' Journal of Law and Economics (April 1969)
5. Gordon, Scott 'Frank Knight and the Tradition of Liberalism' Journal of Political Economy (May/June 1974)
5a. Galbraith, J. K. 'Power and the Useful Economist' American Economic Review (March 1973)
6. Hayek, F. A. The Road to Serfdom London, Routledge & Kegan Paul (1971)
7. Hayek, F. A. The Constitution of Liberty London, Routledge and Kegan Paul (1960)
8. Hicks, J. R. Essays in World Economics Oxford, Clarendon (1959) Introduction
9. Hillinger, C. and Lapham, V. 'The Impossibility of a Paretian Liberal: Comment by Two Who are Unreconstructed' Journal of Political Economy (November/December 1971)
9a. Leibenstein, H. 'Allocative Efficiency vs X-Efficiency' American Economic Review (June 1966)
10. Machlup, F. 'Liberalism and the Choice of Freedoms' in E. Streissler (ed.) Roads to Freedom: Essays in Honour of Friedrich von Hayek London, Routledge and Kegan Paul (1969)
11. Mill, J. S. On Liberty Oxford, Oxford UP (1912)
12. Ng, Y.-K. 'The Possibility of a Paretian Liberal: Impossibility Theorems and Cardinal Utility' Journal of Political Economy (November/December 1971)
13. Peacock, A. T. and Rowley, C. K. 'Pareto Optimality and the Political Economy of Liberalism' Journal of Political Economy (May/June 1972)
14. Peacock, A. T. and Rowley, C. K. 'Welfare Economics and the Public Regulation of Natural Monopoly — A Reply' Journal of Public Economics (February, 1973)
14a. Rowley, C. K. Antitrust and Economic Efficiency London, Macmillan (1973)
15. Sen, A. 'The Impossibility of a Paretian Liberal' Journal of Political Economy (January 1970)
16. Sen, A. 'The Impossibility of a Paretian Liberal: Reply'. Journal of Political Economy (November/December 1971)
17. West, E. G. 'The Political Economy of Alienation: Karl Marx and Adam Smith' Oxford Economic Papers (March 1969)

PART III

Liberalist Welfare Economics

6. Collective Choice

It is no less important in a democratic than in any other government, that all tendency on the part of public authorities to stretch their interference and assume a power of any sort which can easily be dispensed with, should be regarded with unremitting jealousy. Perhaps this is even more important in a democracy than in any other form of political society; because where public opinion is sovereign, an individual who is oppressed by the sovereign does not, as in most other states of things, find a rival power to which he can appeal for relief, or, at all events, for sympathy. [John Stuart Mill *Principles of Political Economy* (ed. B. Bladen and J. Robson) book V chapter xi para. 3]

The conflict between the orthodox Paretian and the liberal philosophies is nowhere more apparent than in the debate on the appropriate domain and the institutional framework of collective choice in the so-called democratic societies. To the orthodox Paretian, the presence of market failure (appropriately defined) is a necessary and sufficient condition for collective intervention, since the 'State' is viewed as an efficient, omniscient and impartial servant of the public good. Where market failure prevails, the pattern of intervention is to be decided only by reference to cost-effectiveness criteria. To the liberal, by contrast, market failure itself is an elusive concept dependent upon a *realistic* assessment of the comparative efficiencies of alternative institutional frameworks; and, even where it is located, collective choice is not an automatic consequence. For the concentration of power in collective hands is characterised in liberal utility functions by negative marginal utility, with the implication that efficiency losses due to market failure are to be traded off against the welfare losses resulting from collective choice. Moreover, since liberals are not neutral as between instruments of intervention, cost-effectiveness criteria provide only a starting point in determining the institutional framework of collective choice. This conflict between orthodox Paretians and liberals on the issue of public choice is the focal point of the present chapter.

There remains for consideration, however, the position of the Paretian heretics, who, as we explained in chapter 2, adopt a fundamentalist approach to their dogma which encompasses issues of collective choice as well as of market performance. Since, in particular respects, the Paretian heretics provide a bridge-head between the Paretian and the liberal approaches — especially with regard to the public good problem — section I of this chapter is turned over to a critical evaluation of their position. Section II, which is devoted to recent developments in the economic theory of representative government, essentially destroys the heretical position. Section III defines an alternative (and in our view a superior) liberal alternative.

I   THE PUBLIC CHOICE PARETIANS

The public choice Paretians (PCPs)[i] are concerned, in essence, to extend the Paretian unanimity principle to the process of collective choice. In this sense, they are to be associated with the 'social contract' philosophers — Locke, Rousseau, Kant and, despite their protestations,[ii] Hobbes — and they acknowledge readily their debt to Knut Wicksell whose work on the organisation of the fiscal system is an evident source of their inspiration.

In essence, PCPs are searching for a consent solution to the Hobbesian anarchistic dilemma — the war of all against all — with its corollary of a life on earth that is 'nasty, brutish and short'. But, unlike Hobbes, who found a solution based upon the notion of political obligation, PCPs ground their analysis upon the concept of the self-seeking solipsist of the Paretian paradigm, who yet sees his advantage in the general observance of conventional rules of conduct, as enshrined in a constitutional contract. Thus Buchanan and Tullock:[9]

Our basic analysis of the individual calculus that is involved in choosing among alternative organizational rules, in selecting a political constitution, has demonstrated that it will often be to the rational self-interest of the individual to select a particular rule that can be predicted to produce results on occasion that run counter to the self-interest of the individual calculated within a shorter time span. By shifting the choice backward from the stage of the specific collective decision to the stage of the constitutional decision, we have been able to incorporate the acquiescence of the individual to adverse collective action into a calculus that retains an economic dimension. . . . [p. 314]

The presence of the public good problem (or even of straightforward externalities in the absence of trade possibilities) provides a *prima facie* case for collective intervention, following Paretian criteria. Clearly, there are welfare gains available if appropriate agreement can be attained — but agreement must be universal if the Paretian principle is not to be violated. PCPs seek out a solution in which a constitutional contract, defining a collectivity and a set of decision rules, is established by universal consent. They pay particular attention to the nature and domain of the collectivity and to the likely structure of those decision rules that are to be constitutionally determined.

Fundamentally, PCPs[7,9] see the constitution as establishing on the one hand a 'protective' state — neutral as the referee or umpire in the game situation — which will carry out its 'external' function as an enforcing institution and on the other hand a 'productive' state, which will carry out its 'internal' function in facilitating the optimal provision of public goods. The interface between the protective and the productive state is seen to lie in the enforcement of internal contracts. Although unanimity is required for the constitution itself, this does not imply that the decision rules that govern collective choice should themselves satisfy the unanimity requirement. For individuals will trade off the costs of decision-making against the benefits of the veto when negotiating over the decision rule as the basis for the constitutional contract.

The problem is approached in terms of the private calculus of the individual as he confronts constitutional choices, not knowing with any certainty his own particular role in the chain of collective decisions that may be effected in the future. Such an individual can ensure his presence in the decisive group only by the voting rule of unanimity. He would surely support such a rule if the costs of decision-making were to be ignored. It is argued, however, that the anticipated costs of reaching a decision — viewed as an increasing function of the decision-rule requirement — will cause individuals to concur on group decision rules that embody a less-than-unanimity requirement. The thesis is illustrated in figure 6.1 due to Buchanan and Tullock.[9] The curve $D(n)$ represents the ith individual's view of the present value of the expected costs of reaching a decision as the number of persons whose consent is required rises from zero to N (unanimity). No decision costs are entailed by a rule of zero; whereas, at the other extreme, a rule of N entails the very high decision costs of reaching unanimous agreement. The form of $D(n)$ suggests that the cost of reaching agreement increases more than in proportion to the number of individuals required to reach agreement. The curve $E(n)$ represents the ith individual's view of the present value of external costs which he expects to be imposed on him by the operation of the various decision rules. External costs are viewed as a declining function of the size of the decision rule. In the limit,

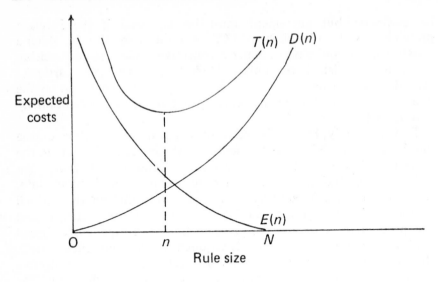

Figure 6.1

external costs are zero with the unanimity rule, since the ith individual can veto any action inimical to his interests. The vertical summation of the $D(n)$ and $E(n)$ curves gives the 'total cost of social interdependence' curve $T(n)$. The rational individual is led to seek that rule that minimises this sum, namely n in figure 6.1. Thus Buchanan and Tullock:[9]

By agreeing to more inclusive rules, he is accepting the additional burden of decision-making in exchange for additional protection against adverse decisions. In moving in the opposing direction toward a less inclusive decision-making rule, the individual is trading some of his protection against external costs for a lowered cost of decision-making. [p. 72]

Buchanan and Tullock emphasise that there is no unique outcome in this analysis. Specifically, there is no reason, *a priori*, to suppose that a simple majority will prove to be the preferred voting rule,[iii] nor that an individual will prefer the same decision rule for all issues. Moreover, the model does not deal with the question of how individual constitutional choices are combined. Buchanan and Tullock simply assume that individuals negotiate on the adoption of the constitutional rule and that the rule finally adopted must command unanimous consent. The negotiation might well be protracted save where the group held closely similar views on the cost of social interdependence. Although Buchanan and Tullock saw above-majority voting rules as the likely outcome, in practice the simple majority rule or some variant of it is most frequently adopted.[1,26]

Fundamentally, this approach to the group decision rule problem rests on a social contract theory of the State and is significantly dependent upon the society in question being composed of reasonable individuals. For otherwise, consensus as to the group decision rule is unlikely to materialise. Indeed, in the face of evident unreasonableness in real-world situations, PCPs have shown willingness to compromise. Thus Buchanan:[3,iv]

Despite our knowledge that some men are wholly unreasonable, we assume this away just as we have done in the organisation of our whole democratic decision-making processes. Insofar as 'antisocial' or unreasonable individuals are members of the group, consensus, even where genuine 'mutual gains' might be present, may be impossible. Here the absolute unanimity rule must be broken; the political economist must try, as best he can, to judge the extent of unanimity required to verify (not refute) his hypothesis. Some less definitive rule of relative unanimity must be substituted for full agreement, as Wicksell recognised and suggested. [pp. 134–5]

While recognising that the chosen group decision rule (with positive bargaining costs) is unlikely in practice to be the unanimity rule, PCPs are loath to accept the outcome of specific majority rules in the implementation of collective choice. They propose, therefore, an ingenious (if in our view an unrealistic) compromise. The Paretian welfare economist is to construct operational propositions about specific policy changes and to advance such propositions as 'presumed Pareto-optimal'. The test lies in the degree of support that the proposal obtains. If consensus in support of the change is forthcoming, the proposition is justified: otherwise, not.

PCPs recognise that any such proposition in practice will not be decided upon by a unanimity decision rule, and present two alternative solutions to the problem thereby created. The first rests upon the assumed responsibility of the welfare economist, who is urged to present propositions designed to satisfy a unanimity test, even though a majority criterion in fact exists. Thus Buchanan:[3]

In a sense, the political economist is concerned with discovering what people want. The content of his efforts may be reduced to very simple terms. This may be summed up in the familiar statement: *There exist mutual gains from trade.* His task is that of locating possible flows in the existing social structure and in presenting possible 'improvements'. His specific hypothesis is that *mutual* gains do, in fact, exist as a result of possible changes (trades). This hypothesis is tested by the behaviour of private people in response to the suggested alternatives. Since 'social' values do not exist apart from individual values in a free society, consensus or unanimity (mutuality of gain) is the only test which can insure that a change is beneficial.

Alas! The flesh is weak. PCPs have no illusion that such an approach will be maintained in practice and they explicitly accept that deviations will occur in societies that choose to conduct collective choice with 'less-than-unanimity' decision rules. Their second solution, therefore, rests heavily on the social contract notion that consensus exists concerning the nature of the group decision rule itself. In such circumstances, even though some individuals may suffer as others gain from a specific collective decision, it is argued, nevertheless, that the Paretian criteria are not transgressed, in that each individual has freely envisaged such an outcome in his choice of decision rule. Thus Buchanan and Tullock:[9]

If the constitutional decision is a rational one, the external cost imposed by 'nonoptimal' choices because of the operation of the less-than-unanimity voting rule will be more than offset by the reduction in the expected costs of the decision-making. [p. 94]

To the relevance of the PCP approach for collective choices in the real-world situation of representative government we now direct attention.

II   THE ECONOMIC THEORY OF REPRESENTATIVE GOVERNMENT

The important distinction between the direct democracies of the Arrow Possibility Theorem (implicit to some extent also in the PCP approach) and the representative governments of the real world was emphasised at the conclusion of chapter 2. It now remains to outline more fully the economic theory of representative government, following the important contributions by Downs,[13] Niskanen[17] and Breton,[2] both as a basis for criticising the PCP position and as a foundation for the liberal approach to the problem of collective choice. This section draws heavily on Breton's important model.

i   The institutional setting

In a two-party political system, the extent to which the political parties are shielded from the preferences of the voting citizens will depend upon: (i) the decision-rule(s) upon which representation is based; (ii) the length of the election period; and (iii) the degree of full-line supply.

The range of alternative decision rules is so extensive that comprehensive discussion is out of the question. Let us illustrate by reference to two practical examples, namely the British and the USA solutions. In Britain, a simple majority is required both at the constituency level, to select the representatives, and at the government level, to select the party that governs. In consequence, the preferences of only one-quarter of the electorate need be represented in the public sector in the limiting case where such voters are distributed optimally over the constituencies. Indeed, if the constituencies are uneven in size, a government concentrating upon the smaller constituencies might represent fewer than one-quarter of the electorate. In the United States, by contrast, the rules concerning the choice of the President and the governors of each state in the union require a larger proportion of the electorate — at least fifty per cent — though the congressional form of government in any event is more complex than its British parliamentary counterpart.

The length of the election period is also a highly important factor in the degree of freedom exercised by representative government; for any non-zero length must offer politicians the freedom to implement some policies at variance with the preferences of most — even of all — citizens. In the case of lengthy election periods — possibly five years in the British case — the emergence of lobbies, pressure groups etc. in part are to be viewed as a defence reaction on the part of alienated voters. In a similar manner, the fact that representative governments offer a bundle of policies to the electorate provides an opportunity for them to supply a number of policies that are at variance with citizen preferences —.once again offering a degree of freedom which is not always recognised in more traditional analyses. Indeed, one implication of federalism (and direct democracy) is to reduce the size of the policy bundle on offer and thereby to narrow the area of political discretion — as liberals have been quick to emphasise.[v]

ii   The political market place

Breton's model of representative government summarises the demand for public policies on the part of voting citizens by the equation

$$S^d = g(Q, I, Pi*) \tag{6.1}$$

where S^d is the demand for the flow of expenditure-type policies, Q is a vector of tax-prices, I is money income and $Pi*$ is a vector of political participation cost over citizens for the ith instrument. The dependence of demand upon Q and I merely incorporates conventional demand assumptions (conventionally ignored) into the analysis of political markets. But $Pi*$ requires a brief discussion.

Citizens cannot, for the most part, adjust the rate of provision of public policies to their individual preferences when differences are apparent, owing to the public/non-private goods characteristics of many of these provisions. The difference between the desired rate of provision (at existing tax prices and incomes) and that provided may be designated as the degree of coercion imposed on citizens. Those who suffer from or fear non-negligible coercion are able to improve their lot only by influencing politicians (or ultimately by fleeing the society). Thus coercion is a major source of political participation. Citizens may engage in political participation (i) via large pressure groups (though these are eroded in practice, following Olsen, by the free-rider problem); (ii) via individual and small group activities, where the free-rider problem is obviated; (iii) via social movements which may result in additional political parties; (iv) via personal adjustments (e.g. in the leisure—work relationship), which conceivably may affect the political participation of other citizens; (v) via private provisions (legal or otherwise) based on some version of the club principle; and (vi) via political mobility. The precise balance in these alternative instruments of political participation operative in a particular economy will depend upon their respective cost-effectiveness as viewed by individual citizens.[vi] In most countries we observe lobbying, pressure-groups, social movements, self-supply and political mobility. In few advanced economies is individual adjustment a significant source of participation (Britain now seems to be an important exception) and it would seem that coercion has to reach dramatic proportions before the supply of labour is affected.

From the supply viewpoint, Breton follows Downs in applying the self-interest axiom to the behaviour of political parties. He assumes that each politician who is a member of a political coalition is characterised by a utility function defined for a probability of re-election variable, and for variables such as pecuniary gain, personal power, image, idealism, etc. Viz:

$$U'p = Up(\pi, a_m), (p = 1, \ldots, P)$$
$$(m = 1, \ldots, M)$$
(6.2)

where p represents any given politician, π is the probability of re-election variable, and the a_ms are the other variables outlined above. Equation 6.2 is to be maximised subject to some level of $\pi(\pi^*)$, which is required for political survival and subject to important technical constraints (of which more anon).

Decisions in the public sector of democratic countries usually are made not by individual politicians, but rather by coalitions acting in concert. Since it is unlikely, in practice, that all members of the coalition will have identical orderings of policies, it is assumed that the coalition possesses some exchange mechanism through which policies are traded so as to reflect a group ordering, be it in the form of cabinets, committees, conventions or informal groupings. Clearly, log-rolling in all its forms is susceptible to strategic behaviour on the part of those politicians who can take advantage of institutional conditions to drive favourable bargains.

Once the coalition is formed, and its utility function negotiated, the maximisation problem must be formulated within an explicit time dimension, given the discreteness of election time. In the earlier part of the election period, parties will value policies by reference to a rate-of-time discount lower than that used by the electorate. As the re-election date approaches, however, the rate utilised by the parties will approach that of the electorate, or of such part of the electorate viewed as being politically important. The role of an effective opposition in part is to raise the memory factor of the electorate, thereby forcing the government to satisfy the preferences of the dominant section of the electorate on a more continuous basis.

The government, in maximising its utility function, faces important technical constraints. In particular, to secure re-election it must minimise the degree of 'coercion' on the decisive section of the electorate, by one or more of four basic devices. It may: (i) enact and implement discriminatory policies which favour the decisive section; (ii) discriminate similarly with regard to probability of detection and the penalty levies for those who commit legal offences; (iii) engage in implicit log-rolling combined with full-line supply so as to maintain political support; and (iv) seek to alter the preferences of citizens so that a decisive section identifies with policy provisions. The appropriate mix of such policies in any given situation will be determined by reference to cost-effectiveness criteria. The discriminatory implications of such behaviour are highly relevant for the liberal position on collective choice as we shall emphasise in a subsequent section of this chapter.

Although decisions on the supply of public policies are made by politicians, they are influenced more or less substantially by bureaucrats. Let us, following Breton,[2] assume that bureaucrats maximise a utility function defined for one variable only, namely the relative size of their bureaus, measured in terms of numbers employed. In no sense are they *directly* responsive to citizen preferences.[20] The following implications are to be derived from such an assumption. Bureaucrats typically will emphasise the benefits and under-estimate costs in cost—benefit studies, and will favour a rate of discount in estimating present values which makes large projects more profitable. They will favour complicated and labour-intensive forms of intervention to be handled administratively through their bureaus. More generally, they will favour planning and interventionist policies and decry programmes that imply some dismantling of their empires, manipulating 'information' for this purpose as it progresses through the political system — a phenomenon depicted as 'control-loss' by Gordon Tullock.

The government, aware as it is of the control-loss phenomenon, will attempt to curtail its impact firstly by the introduction of such anti-distortion devices as redundant bureaus, overlapping zones of responsibility between bureaus, the periodic flattening of the bureaucratic structure and direct citizen contacts, and secondly by bribing the bureaucrats to supply correct information. Thus, Breton argues that, on the supply side of the public sector, the dominant force in shaping the pattern of expenditure policies and tax prices is the relative power of politicians and bureaucrats.[vii] His supply equation takes the form:

$$S^g = f(Q, B) \tag{6.3}$$

where S^g denotes the quantity supplied, Q represents the vector of tax prices and B is the ratio of the power of bureaucrats to that of politicians. Q is necessary since supply decisions are determined by the coercion felt by decisive votes implicit in the relationship between S and Q.

Equilibrium in the political market place — given by the equation of supply and demand — is to be viewed differently according to the level of participation costs P^* and its impact on preference revelations. If P^* is low and the number of voters who reveal their preferences to the governing party is greater than that required by the decision rule, the government is free to select from the set of voters who reveal their preferences a decisive subset, while ignoring the rest. The subset chosen — if the politicians are more powerful than the bureaucrats — will confirm re-election. If the bureaucrats are more powerful than the politicians, however, and if the bureau-building policies do not conform with the decisive voter preferences, the government may be defeated at the polls.

If P^* is high and the number of preferences revealed falls short of the decisive limit, the government initially will not know which policy bundle to provide. All parties, in such circumstances, will engage in search procedures and will advertise so as to homogenize the preferences of the electorate. The government may also attempt to lower P^*, for example by allowing tax relief on pressure group activities, or by encouraging social movements, illegal private provisions etc. as a means of stimulating the process of preference revelations. In the limit, where the number of preferences exactly equals the decisive limit, the policy bundle will be designed to satisfy the voters in question, with the inference that those best able to participate — for whatever reason — will be disproportionately successful in influencing policy.

In any event, the issue of over- or under-provision of public goods, in the Paretian sense, cannot be generally answered by this model. Much depends on the level of political participation costs and on the relative bargaining power of politicians and bureaucrats. It is our view that Breton has captured in his model much of the essence of political markets of the kind with which we are acquainted. Let us proceed from such a basis — and not from the notion of Samuelsonian omniscience — to a review of the liberal approach to the collective choice dilemma.

III   A LIBERAL APPROACH

Liberalism, as we have defined it, is concerned essentially with the maintenance and extension of negative freedoms, defined as the absence of coercion by some individuals of others, and not with the provision of effective power as a basis for improving economic efficiency. This does not imply that liberals are indifferent to material welfare or that they insist upon a lexicographic ordering of freedoms and economic efficiency. Rather are they prepared to trade off freedoms in return for improvements in efficiency, always provided that freedoms are not substantially or irreversibly eroded in such a process. Where freedoms themselves are in conflict, liberals also will endorse coercion in so far as it is required to maintain the liberal hierarchy of freedoms and always provided that it does not violate the fundamental tenets of the rule of law. Let us now review the implications of liberal philosophy for the issue of collective choice.

i   The appropriate domain of collective choice

There is an important sense in which the concept of collective choice encompasses all aspects of state economic intervention, be it through public provision, public finance, legislation or exhortation. For, indeed, many of the implications of representative government are applicable equally to all such aspects of intervention policy. In this book, however, we make the somewhat arbitrary distinction between those areas where some form of *public provision* most commonly is encountered and accepted and those areas where it is not, treating only the former in this chapter and reserving detailed discussion of the latter for chapter 8. Inevitably, such a division implies that the present discussion is restricted, for the most part, to the problem of public and non-private goods and services.

For the more naïve Paretian, at least, the public good, character-ised by marked non-rivalness in consumption, presents an over-whelming case for public provision at zero prices financed by taxation or by an increase in the size of the national debt. Even the sophisticates,[4,5,7] who take some account of political market imperfections and of the inevitable gradations of publicness in real-world commodities, find it difficult to resist the collective choice solution. Liberals by no means are so easily persuaded of the necessity of the public good—collective choice association, though this in no sense implies a belief that government should never concern itself in economic matters. Those who castigate the classical economists as being dogmatically anti-government demonstrate only their own lack of acquaintance with the classical literature.

For liberalism cannot exist within an anarchistic vacuum, but itself is dependent upon important public provisions. Liberals have always recognised the importance of the rule of law, with its implications that property rights, once established, should be protected and enforced by central government provisions. They have widely endorsed also a further set of public provisions of commodities which, for various reasons — derived principally from extreme publicness characteristics — are especially unsuited to competitive supply. The most important such provision is that of a reliable and efficient monetary system — though many governments have proved irresponsible in this regard — but others, scarcely less important, include national defence, the maintenance of internal law and order, of prescribed standards of safety, of health and of weights and measures, and the provision of information, for example on such matters as land registration and company performance. Less un-equivocally, liberals may tolerate without undue concern the public provision of sanitary services, of road construction and maintenance, and many of the amenities provided by municipalities for the inhabitants of their cities, always provided that in these fields of endeavour the government is not issued with exclusive responsibility, but is exposed at least potentially to outside competitive substitutes.

But, in a wide range of other areas categorised by non-private good characteristics — most notably education, medicare, television, the arts, invention and innovation — liberals diverge sharply from their Paretian counterparts and turn their backs for the most part on public provision in favour of some less socialist form of intervention. They are motivated in so doing by dislike for certain of the predictions derivable from the economic theory of representative government, most especially of the coercive powers afforded by the majority-vote decision rule, lengthy periods and full-line supply, which are likely to result in discriminatory provisions to mirror the pattern of political participation and in allocative distortions arising from bureaucratic interventions. They also dislike the X-inefficiency implications of public provision, especially where commodities are marketed at zero price on a zoned basis and where private competition is banned by law, to say nothing of the implied diminution of freedoms of choice in consumption and in occupation. For reasons such as these, liberals prefer even private to public monopoly, where a competitive solution does not seem possible, though they are prepared to countenance a range of alternative instruments of intervention to tackle the public—non-private good case. To these alternatives let us now address ourselves.

ii   The alternatives to public provision

The liberal dilemma concerning public goods centres upon the problem of maintaining a tolerably efficient provision while avoiding the buildup of the power of central government and the destruction of competitive markets implicit in centralised public provision solutions. In reviewing the alternative liberal responses it is useful to remind ourselves of the three basic functions that any organisation of supply performs,[5] namely (i) determination of how much to produce — the allocative function; (ii) determination of how to cover the costs — the financing function; and (iii) determination of how to distribute the benefits — the distribution function. For, in separating out these functions, the various impacts of alternative interventions are relevantly exposed and can be compared with the collective choice solution. In the case of the polar public good, for example, collective choice implies that the allocation function is determined via the machinery of representative government, that the financing function is determined via tax—price decisions, and that the distribution function is fulfilled by the collective consumption requirement. We have already rehearsed the practical limitations of this approach.

Unregulated private provision. One solution that cannot be ruled out on *a priori* grounds by liberals is that of providing public goods through competitive markets in those areas where returns to scale do not predominate and where non-purchasers can be excluded from consumption. And it is worth emphasising that there is nothing in the public good concept itself that rules out the ability to exclude. Demsetz[11,12] has argued that such public goods may be provided *efficiently* via market processes, following Marshall's joint supply model, where exclusion is practised. Demsetz contended that the rate of production of public goods responded to demand and supply conditions in exactly the same way as jointly produced goods — that a competitive market price would direct the appropriate volume of resources into public good production — and that the only substantive problem was that of achieving an appropriate rate of consumption from existing units of the public good, given the latter's characteristic of a zero opportunity cost in consumption.

The Demsetz solution involves price discrimination — which can occur in the competitive provision of public goods since there is a zero opportunity cost to each firm in allocating any given rate of provision to additional customers — and this implies that the marginal rates of substitution of the public good for a private good *numeraire* will differ for separate individuals in the equilibrium situation. But, with public goods, equal marginal rates of substitution in the general case are inconsistent with Pareto-optimality as a direct consequence of the collective consumption characteristic.

Competition will ensure that the revenues generated via price discrimination will be just sufficient to cover costs, implying that X-inefficiency will be rooted out in a way that is unlikely in the case of public provision. Individual customers, viewing price as given in the large-numbers case, will maximise utility subject to budget constraints that contain such prices as are thrown up in their market subgroupings, with the implication that efficient price discrimination will satisfy the necessary condition for exchange efficiency. In the limiting market subgroup, where demand prices reach zero to the left of the equilibrium rate of public good provision, zero prices will prevail without posing any viability problem for the competing supplies. An omniscient and efficiency-minded government could do no better.

Of course, there are practical obstacles to the attainment of the Demsetz nirvana.[viii] Policing problems arise because customers will attempt to disguise themselves to qualify for a lower price and because those who purchase in cheaper markets will be tempted to engage in arbitrage activities. The latter problem, however, is often minimal in the public good situation since many of the commodities concerned (for example medicare and education) are services that cannot easily be arbitraged. The former problem cannot be denied, though market separation by reference to such criteria as age, sex, location and income often will prove effective. In any event, the problem of market separation in the competitive market solution is no more serious in nature than is the problem of assessing appropriate tax prices in the collective choice situation.

More serious, perhaps, is the criticism, pressed by Thompson,[24] to the effect that the Demsetz solution, by assuming that prices are equated with consumers' marginal rates of substitution (MRSs) in Pareto-optimum, essentially begs the question as to how much MRSs are in fact perceived. For this is an acknowledged weakness in all Lindahl-type solutions. If, as is likely in practice, prices are equated with MRSs for actual quantities consumed, and individuals then adjust their consumption of complementary and substitutable private goods, there is no certainty that an optimal provision of the public good will ensue in the final equilibrium. In essence, this is an information problem which may not be resolved by iteration if the rate of public good provision is locked into the system by a false set of signals. Arguably again, however, this is a problem which also menaces any collective choice solution. In terms of the Paretian criteria, there is no clear-cut *a priori* ranking of the two policy alternatives.

In the case of public goods with high exclusion costs — for example defence — competitive provision at least in its conventional form may be out of the question; for consumers who cannot be excluded from the benefits will be tempted to under-reveal their preferences, with the implication of under-provision of the good in question. Yet, even in such cases, tie-in arrangements, whereby the consumption of a second product is tied to the consumption of the public good, may go far towards resolving the market dilemma. Demsetz illustrated this point by reference to radio and television provision, assuming unrealistically[ix] that owners of receivers cannot be excluded from signal transmissions. In such circumstances, there are two private groups willing to meet the costs of broadcasting, namely advertisers who wish to transmit their messages into all homes, and the producers of radio and television receivers who have an obvious interest in an extended service. While not asserting that the tie-in solution necessarily is efficient, Demsetz yet emphasised that whether private or public production yielded the better outcome could not be determined at such a level of discourse. With this view, we have no disagreement.

In assessing the unregulated competitive market solution as an alternative to collective choice, liberals must evaluate the benefits from reduced coercion and from extensions in freedom of individual choice, and weigh such advantages against any potential efficiency losses of the conventional Paretian kind. By no means should it be supposed that collective choice will always dominate private provision, even when excludability is costly, in a comparative-institutions assessment in which liberal criteria are given full rein. Even should it do so, all is not lost for those who fear Leviathan, as we shall demonstrate in our discussion of yet further solutions.

The club principle. The economic theory of clubs[6,15,16] centres attention upon the appropriate nature of consumption ownership—membership arrangements in the hinterland between the pure private good and the pure public good of Samuelson's polar model. It is of direct relevance to those commodities involving some publicness, in which the optimal sharing group is larger than the single household but smaller than an infinitely large number of households. The central question in the theory of clubs is that of determining the membership margin for the commodity in question. The theory of clubs strictly is relevant only in cases where exclusion is feasible in economic terms.

In chapter 2, following Samuelson's contribution, private goods, defined to be wholly divisible among persons $i = 1,2, \ldots , s$, were seen to satisfy the relation

$$X_j = \sum_{i=1}^{s} X_j^i \qquad (6.4)$$

whereas public goods, defined to be wholly indivisible as among persons, were seen to satisfy the relation

$$X_{n+j} = X_{n+j}^i \qquad (6.5)$$

In intermediate situations, it becomes necessary to distinguish between 'goods available to the ownership unit of which the reference individual is a member' and 'goods finally available to the individual for consumption'. In the construction which follows (due to Buchanan),[6] the X_js are to be interpreted as 'goods available for consumption to the whole membership unit of which the reference individual is a member'. It is also necessary to incorporate into the utility function arguments that represent the size of the sharing group, since for any commodity the individual's utility in consumption depends upon the number of other persons with whom he must share its benefits. Alongside each X_j there must be placed an N_j which defines the number of persons who are to participate as 'members' in the sharing of good X_j, including the ith person whose utility function is examined. The rewritten utility function now becomes:

$$U^i = U^i[(X_1^i, N_1^i), (X_2^i, N_2^i), \ldots, (X_{n+m}^i, N_{n+m}^i)]. \quad (6.6)$$

The marginal rate of substitution in consumption between X_j and some *numeraire* commodity, Xr for the ith individual, is given by $\partial U_j^i / \partial U_r^i$ and the marginal rate of substitution 'in consumption' between the size of the sharing group and the *numeraire* is given by $\partial N_j^i / \partial U_r^i$. This latter ratio represents the rate (which may be negative) at which the individual is willing to give up the *numeraire* in exchange for additional members in the sharing group.

The cost function confronting the individual will include the same set of variables as follows:

$$F = F^i[(X_1^i, N_1^i), (X_2^i, N_2^i), \ldots, (X_{n+m}^i, N_{n+m}^i)]. \quad (6.7)$$

It is necessary to include the club-size variables, the N_js, in this cost function since the addition of members to a sharing group will normally affect the cost of the good to any single member, given the specific quantity of club facilities under consideration.

The usual marginal condition for a Pareto-optimum in respect to consumption of each good is derived from the utility and cost functions as:

$$\frac{\partial U_j^i}{\partial U_j^i} = \frac{\partial F_j^i}{\partial F_r^i}. \quad (6.8)$$

To this conventional condition must now be added:

$$\frac{\partial U_{NJ}^i}{\partial U_r^i} = \frac{\partial F_{Nj}^i}{\partial F_r^i} \quad (6.9)$$

which states that the marginal rate of substitution 'in consumption' between the size of the group sharing in the use of good X_j and the *numeraire* good Xr must be equal to the marginal rate of substitution 'in production'.

Combining equations (6.8) and (6.9), we obtain

$$\frac{\partial U_j^i}{\partial F_j^i} = \frac{\partial U_r^i}{\partial F_r^i} = \frac{\partial U_{Nj}^i}{\partial F_{Nj}^i} \tag{6.10}$$

in which circumstances the individual will have available to his membership unit an optimal quantity of X_j, measured in physical units, and also will be sharing this quantity optimally over a group of determined size.

It is now possible to classify goods by their degree of publicness, simply by directing attention to the equilibrium value for N_j in equation (6.10). Goods for which the equilibrium value of N_j is large can be classified as containing much publicness (the polar case requires that N_j should approach infinity), whereas goods with a low equilibrium value of N_j (in the limit one) can be classified as essentially private.

The club principle has been endorsed, especially by public choice Paretians, as a method of achieving Pareto-optimality in the non-private good sector without recourse to collective choice in its all-embracing sense. In practice, for a variety of reasons[x] clubs may tend to be sub-optimal in size and, indeed, in many cases the size of the collective-sharing group must be viewed as being determined exogenously. The following inequality is then apparent:

$$\frac{\partial U_j^i}{\partial F_j^i} = \frac{\partial U_r^i}{\partial F_r^i} > \frac{\partial U_{Nj}^i}{\partial F_{Nj}^i} \bigg|\, Nj = K. \tag{6.11}$$

The loss of welfare benefits (in the Paretian sense) implicit in equation (6.11) would be viewed by strict Paretians as sufficient justification for a full collective choice solution. But not so the liberal, who will wish to trade off the welfare losses against the freedom gains. In one sense, indeed, the club principle, which emphasises self-help within a voluntary group association, satisfies the basic tenets of liberal philosophy and must be viewed as an especially attractive proposition. Its widespread utilisation, especially in more affluent societies, suggests that, where economic conditions are conducive, voluntary association tends to be preferred to coercive collective association by many citizens when dealing with non-private goods. In this respect, increasing affluence may draw together the liberal and the Paretian approaches to the club principle.

It cannot be denied, however, that club solutions are inapplicable where exclusion cannot be implemented; for in such circumstances the free-rider problem will destroy it just as it will the Demsetz solution. In certain cases, however, legislation on property rights may revive the exclusion principle without major cost, and so establish a basis for market-type solutions. However debatable such solutions may appear to those imbued in the Paretian dogma — and legislation in property rights usually damages some individuals and benefits others — their attractiveness to liberals requires no further explanation. Let us briefly explore some possibilities.

Legislation on property rights. Where the structure of property rights is variable, the problem of non-excludability is seldom insuperable. For there are few commodities whose services are non-excludable solely due to physical attributes. Thus Buchanan:[6]

Consider the classic lighthouse case. Variations in property rights, broadly conceived, could prohibit boat operators without 'light licenses' from approaching the channel guarded by the light. Physical exclusion is possible, given sufficient flexibility in property law, in almost all imaginable cases, including those in which the interdependence lies in the act of consuming itself. Take the single person who gets an inoculation, providing immunization against a communicable disease. Insofar as this action exerts external benefits on his fellows, the person taking the action could be authorized to collect charges from all beneficiaries under sanction of the collectivity.

If legislation on property rights is contemplated as a solution to the free-rider problem, a first-best Pareto-optimum is an unlikely consequence. For exclusion measures inevitably result in welfare losses in the extreme cases of publicness characterised by a zero opportunity cost in consumption. Nevertheless, legislation may provide the basis for an acceptable market solution, when viewed from a comparative institutions standpoint, especially where policing and enforcement costs are low. For the very process of excluding — which forces free-riders to reveal their preferences — offers an opportunity to estimate accurately the value of diverting resources from other uses to the production of the public good. Even to Paretians, an optimal (or near-optimal) rate of provision of the public good, from the long-run viewpoint, presumably is valued more highly than the full collective consumption outcome, in the short run, which is dictated by the publicness characteristic.

It is not suggested, of course, that property rights are always adjustable — even less that they will always be adjusted — to provide optimal exclusion in the sense here outlined. In many cases the combination of policing and enforcement costs will prove too high, and the property right solution will fail at the outset. In other cases, the quirks of legal practice and the inadequacies of the existing judicial process will impede operations and provide unacceptable results.[10] Where property arrangements are adjustable, however, and where the courts are attuned to the relevant economic considerations, much can be done to reduce the burden of the free-rider problem.

The voucher principle. A wide range of voucher schemes has been debated in the economics literature,[19,21,22] mostly from the Paretian standpoint, as a means of tackling the publicness problem without resort to public provision. We shall outline a single example, due to Olsen,[19] and evaluate its implications from the liberal viewpoint. The Olsen proposal is for a voluntary voucher scheme which permits each eligible household to purchase a voucher with a specified face value for a specified cash outlay. The voucher, if purchased, must be expended upon a particular commodity (for example education) which must not be resold, with severe penalties for those who try to do so. The government will redeem these vouchers from sellers of the commodity at face value. Neither the face values of, nor the specified cash outlays on, the vouchers need be the same for all eligible households.

Suppose that an eligible household with a money income of Y may purchase a voucher with a face value of V for an outlay C. If p_i and q_i are the price and quantity of the ith good, and if the voucher must be spent on the nth good, then the voucher scheme changes the budget constraints faced by this household from

$$\sum_{i=1}^{n} p_i q_i \leqslant Y \tag{6.12}$$

to

$$\left[\sum_{i=1}^{n} p_i q_i \leqslant Y \right] \quad \text{or} \quad \left[(\sum_{i=1}^{n} p_i q_i \leqslant Y + S) \text{ and } p_n q_n \geqslant V \right] \tag{6.13}$$

If the household purchases the voucher, then the public subsidy S is equal to V minus C. There are three possible outcomes of this change in the houshold's budget constraint and these are depicted in figures 6.2, 6.3 and 6.4.

The household depicted in figure 6.2 will not purchase the voucher since it prefers its original consumption vector b to any of the new consumption vectors made available by the voucher scheme. The household depicted in figure 6.3 will purchase the voucher and will consume the same quantity of each good as it would had it been

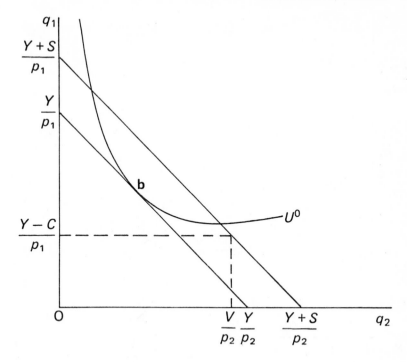

Figure 6.2

given a cash grant equal to the public subsidy. The consumption vector a is preferred to the original consumption vector b and is the most preferred consumption vector available, given the new budget constraint. In this case, as is evident from figure 6.3, the household's total spending on the subsidised good will exceed the face value of the voucher. The household depicted in figure 6.4 will purchase the voucher and will spend exactly the face value of the voucher on the subsidised good. The consumption vector a is preferred to the consumption vector b and is the most preferred consumption vector available, given the new budget constraint. If the household had been given a cash grant equal to the voucher subsidy it would have chosen the consumption vector c, implying an expenditure on the subsidised good less than the face value of the voucher.

Let us now apply these results to the public good problem on the assumption that there is no feasible system of unrestricted cash grants that will induce a set of households to consume its optimal quantity of such a commodity. Olsen has demonstrated that the attainment of the optimal allocation of resources requires: (i) that the face value of the voucher be just sufficient to permit its recipient

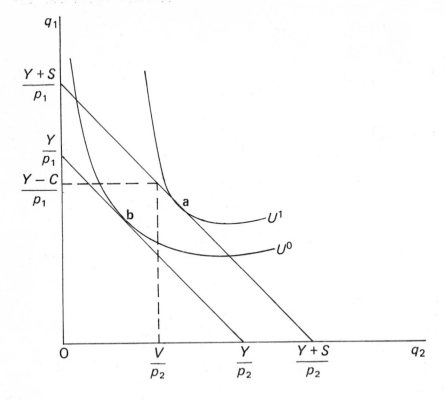

Figure 6.3

to purchase the optimal quantity of the nth good at its market price; and (ii) that the amount charged to the recipient for his voucher must leave the household with just enough money to purchase the optimal quantities of other goods. For, if V and C were set so as to leave the household as in figure 6.2, the voucher is irrelevant. If V and C were set so as to leave the household as in figure 6.3, the voucher is equivalent to a cash grant which, definitionally, cannot satisfy an optimum. Only if V and C are set so as to leave the household as in figure 6.4, with the face value of the voucher equal to the optimal quantity of the nth good, will the household consume that optimal quantity. Similarly, only where $Y - C$ is just sufficient for each household to purchase the optimal quantities of the first $n - 1$ goods will the overall optimum attain. A necessary condition for the voucher scheme to result in an overall optimum, therefore, is that:

$$C_j = Y_j - \sum_{i=1}^{n} p_i q_{ij}^{0} \tag{6.14}$$

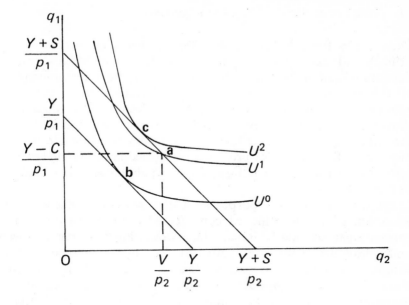

Figure 6.4

where C_j is the amount charged the jth household for its voucher, Y_j is the income of the jth household, p_i is the price of the ith good and $p_{ij}{}^0$ is the optimal quantity of the ith good for the jth household.

To determine the optimum set of vouchers for the whole community in practice is an impossible task, requiring as it does an intimate knowledge of the configuration of household preferences and a highly flexible pattern of voucher provisions. For this reason, many Paretians are sceptical of the voucher principle and prefer to fall back upon their collective choice nirvana. But in a comparative institutions assessment the voucher has much to support it, even for Paretians, preserving, as it may do, competitive markets and rooting out X-inefficiency while controlling to a tolerable extent the public good problem. To liberals the voucher principle is very much a second-best solution, involving almost an 'in kind' transfer with its implicit reduction in freedom of choice. But, if the alternative is collective choice, liberals will willingly endorse voucher solutions, which maintain much greater freedom of individual choice both in consumption and in occupation while restricting the coercive power of Leviathan. Education provision affords an excellent example of the strength of the voucher principle, even where other alternatives to collective choice are rejected.[21,22]

iii   British education: a liberal reassessment

State policy towards formal education is clearly defined in Britain. Primary and secondary education is provided by the State, through a network of nationalised schools, and is a compulsory requirement for all children between the ages of five and sixteen years, save those who are in receipt of approved private education. State education is provided at zero prices on a zoned basis for all children within the prescribed age range, and is financed by general taxation and by local rate levies. This system of provision is justified in economic terms by reference to the alleged non-private and public good characteristics of formal education.

Let us assume, for purposes of the present discussion, that education provision is indeed complicated both by the presence of conventional external benefits, which would involve straightforward under-provision in the market situation, and by the presence of more complex 'atmospheric' externalities with marked public good characteristics — the product of such social objectives as 'equality of opportunity' and 'social cohesion' — which pose less tractable problems for the private market place. To the conventional Paretian state provision at zero prices may appear appropriate. But the liberal will have other ideas.

Certainly, a bargaining solution is out of the question in a market as extensive and complex as that in education provision, even if the full force of the Paretian dogma is to be modified by liberal criteria. But this does not imply the blind acceptance of a collective choice alternative, especially since education is not a decreasing cost industry and lends itself well to the maintenance of competitive markets. In so far as the problem is simply that of straightforward external benefits, for example, one solution is compulsory education legislation, whereby all households are required to purchase a minimum quantity of education services for the children entrusted to their care. Legislation of this kind is frequently associated even with collective choice solutions and indeed is an important facet of the British approach to education provision. Liberals do not rejoice in compulsory legislation of this kind, which is not designed to maintain other freedoms. Nor do they believe necessarily that the government is either sufficiently well informed or well intentioned to select a rate of compulsory education consumption that reflects the preferences of the voting citizens. Nevertheless, minimum education laws at least do not imply the destruction of competitive markets and their replacement by central or local government hegemony as is the case with the collective choice solution.

An alternative solution, applicable to the externality problem, is via public finance, internalising the externality by an appropriate tax subsidy intervention. A choice exists between subsidising the education producers (and presumably taxing those who receive the externality benefits of an extended education system) and subsidising the households with children of educable age. For Paretians the choice is a difficult one at the present level of discourse. But for the liberal, the difficulty of distinguishing between producer subsidies that relieve externalities and those that finance X-inefficiency, coupled with the power thereby afforded to the State to coerce producers to provide particular patterns of education, establishes a clear-cut case for consumer subsidies. If parents, for whatever reason, are deemed to be unwilling to use cash subsidies to extend education consumption for their offspring, the voucher principle can obviate the problem, though liberals cannot be entirely easy about the curtailment of household freedoms incumbent on such an intervention.

The case for state provision does not rest, therefore, on the externality issue, but rather upon the publicness characteristics of two widely supported social objectives, namely equality of opportunity and the quest for common values, or social cohesion. Equality of opportunity is an imprecise social objective — does it imply equality of treatment or equality of attainment, or differential treatment for children of differing intellects (an élitist notion which certainly dominates the present British collective choice solution)? Most educationists reject the notion that an unfettered market can provide equality of education opportunities in any of the senses here defined, and probably they are right, though much would depend upon the precise configuration of tax remissions that would follow the withdrawal of state education expenditures. But the same cannot be said in the case of private education markets buttressed by minimum education laws and non-supplementable education vouchers. In principle, such a system could satisfy any of the relevant definitions of equality of opportunity far more effectively than the present system which suffers in an extreme form from all the discriminatory distortions predicted by Breton—Downs theories of representative government. It could do so without many of the coercive implications of collective choice solutions.

The quest for common values is here defined as directing the education process toward the understanding and toleration of widely accepted values; i.e., we exclude indoctrination objectives from consideration. Does this objective — which is widely though not universally supported — constitute a sufficient case for collective choice? The answer to this question is an unequivocal negative, even though the free-market solution does not stand up well to scrutiny on this issue. For the voucher principle can be utilised to obtain any measure of social mixing considered desirable, simply by attaching suitable conditions to the issued vouchers. In principle, such a system could achieve social cohesion far more effectively than the present British solution which, not infrequently, zones children from highly homogeneous home backgrounds into a single school, thereby attaining a degree of class isolation which even the most exclusive private schools would avoid.

In conclusion, therefore, it is our contention that the collective choice solution for education fares badly in any comparative-institutions analysis by comparison certainly with the various market regulation alternatives, and even with the free-market solution. as viewed from the strictly Paretian viewpoint. Once liberal considerations are given weight with equality of opportunity now strictly defined as equality of treatment, and with the quest for common values sharply discounted, the voucher solution, in an appropriate form, presently dominates the field as the most attractive means of education support. With growing affluence, and with parents increasingly experienced in exercising choices in the expenditure of their vouchers, liberals indeed have faith that the free education market in due course of time could reassert itself as the rationale for voucher-type coercion slowly disappeared.

iv   The economics of political decentralisation

For those areas of economic provision where collective choice is to remain, the issue arises as to the appropriate degree of political decentralisation — on which both the Paretians and the liberals have taken up positions. For many Paretians, indeed, this is the only issue countenanced in connection with the provision of public goods, a view which recently pervaded the thinking of the British Royal Commission on the Constitution, which was established in 1969 and charged with examining possible changes in the institutions both of central and of local government in the light of the desires and aspirations of voters. In its *Report*,[23] in 1973, the Royal Commission refused even to countenance the possibility that voter alienation from the operations of government might be a function of the growth of government intervention. The problem of devolution, as viewed by the Commission,[xi] therefore, was that of deciding which functions, if any, might be transferred from Westminster to the Scots and Welsh nations and to the English regions. The possibility that certain of these functions might be returned, with or without surveillance, to the private sector was not deliberated upon at all.

Paretian discussions on the optimal degree of decentralisation in collective choice has centred to a considerable extent on the controversial model of Charles Tiebout,[25] published in 1956 in a paper which has become a classic in the public finance theory of local government. Tiebout tried to prove the proposition that, as long as local government was appropriately assigned the task of providing certain public goods and as long as individuals retained the freedom of personal migration among jurisdictions, there were efficiency-generating processes at work despite the publicness of the goods provided. On the extreme assumptions of Tiebout — most notably concerning constant costs in production and an absence of inter-jurisdictional spillovers — a careful matching by potential migrators of the particular mix of public good—tax price provisions with their own preferences seemed to ensure that the necessary conditions for Pareto optimality are met in the localised public sector of the economy. The essential similarities between the Tiebout model and the economic theory of clubs are too striking to be ignored, at least in the absence of locational fixity.

The problem of locational fixity in the real world of local government cannot, however, be ignored. For individuals locate themselves in space on a balanced assessment of their overall welfare. Their incomes are not drawn exclusively from dividends, as Tiebout assumes, and their allocation over space influences the total value of private goods product in the economy. Local governments have geographic as well as membership dimensions — a fact that can be largely ignored in the theory of clubs. Let us illustrate the potential inefficiency of a Tiebout solution by reference to a simple model, due to Buchanan and Goetz,[8] which incorporates the locational fixity assumption.

The necessary conditions that must be satisfied for Pareto-optimality are that for each person i and for each pair of locational alternatives, X and Y

$$MVP^i_X + MVG^i_X = MVP^i_Y + MVG^i_Y \qquad (6.15)$$

where the MVPs refer to marginal private goods value or product and the MVGs refer to marginal public goods value or product generated by an individual location in the subscripted community. Designating the number of persons in a local fiscal community by N, the total benefit that the person secures from the public good or service made available by that community by B, and the total tax payment made by the individual by T, the MVG term may be broken down as follows:

$$MVP_X^i + (B_X^i - T_X^i) + \left[\frac{\partial(\Sigma B^j)}{\partial N_X} - \frac{\partial(\Sigma T^j)}{\partial N_X}\right] = MVP_Y^i + (B_Y^i - T_Y^i)$$

$$+ \left[\frac{\partial(\Sigma B^j)}{\partial N_Y} - \frac{\partial(\Sigma T^j)}{\partial N_Y}\right], \, i, j = 1, 2, \ldots, N \qquad (6.15a)$$
$$i \neq j$$

The individual contemplating migration will take account of the fiscal surplus $(B^i - T^i)$ available in the designated jurisdiction. However, he will not take into account the fiscal externalities summarised in the bracketed terms in (6.15a). Instead, the following conditions will be satisfied in a Tiebout-like equilibrium:

$$MVP_X^i + (B_X^i - T_X^i) = MVP_Y^i + (B_Y^i - T_Y^i) \text{ for all } i. \qquad (6.16)$$

Whatever the precise assumptions — as to the degree of publicness of the goods in question or the ability of local communities to vary the rate of public provisions to reflect the number and preferences of their residents — the necessary conditions for Pareto optimality are as defined in equation (6.15a) and will not be satisfied by private adjustment. Furthermore, as Buchanan and Goetz establish, it is impossible to generalise concerning the direction of distortion that the Tiebout process will produce. As they put it, 'the world with local public goods is not an analogue to the competitive market in private goods.' (p. 34). Only in so far as the locality was able to differentiate among persons so as to internalise all fiscal externalities — divorcing individual tax shares from all objective criteria that reflect internal demands for non-excludable goods — could this inefficiency be remedied. A situation in which total taxes of persons depended on relative fiscal alternatives, bearing no relationship to incomes, assets owned or expenditure on private goods, is less than credible from the real-world viewpoint. Moreover, it violates the central notion of free migration in which individuals are free to choose among local government jurisdictions on the basis of non-discriminatory fiscal treatment. Yet it is a necessary complement to the Tiebout adjustment process if a Paretian-optimum is required.

Once real-world assumptions are allowed full play, the Paretian case for political decentralisation disintegrates in its entirety. For the world in which local governments are provided only with partial taxation powers, supplemented by substantial grants-in-aid from central government, and in which the process of fiscal decentralisation is one in which decisions about the scope of provision are made at central government level, and only decisions about the design of activity are delegated to lower layers, is not the world of Tiebout. Nor are the inevitable distortions of representative government both at the central and at the local level allowed any role in the Tiebout adjustment model. Yet these are the dominating features of the real-world environment.

Liberals, aware of such distortions and apprised of the risks of discrimination in collective choice, both at central and at local government levels, must remain agnostic on the decentralisation issue, at least in the absence of detailed information on the coercive powers of the lower layers of government. And this despite the natural preference of liberals for smaller communities in which individuals hold greater sway in collective choice decisions. For, at the general level, there can be no assurance that the outcome of 'representative' government will be less coercive and discriminatory at the local than at the central government level. The committed decentraliser has only to ask himself whether a local Northern Ireland or a central United Kingdom government would provide the greater degree of equality before the law to raise questions as to the validity of his conviction. For the liberal, *ad hoc* assessments based on political realities must take precedence over general principle on the decentralisation issue. But the justification for such agnosticism rests far more upon uncertainties concerning the balance of freedoms than upon ambiguities concerning the Paretian efficiency implications in the centralisation—decentralisation solutions.[18]

NOTES

i J. M. Buchanan and Gordon Tullock, of the Center for Study of Public Choice at the Virginia Polytechnic Institute, have both played highly influential roles in developing the so-called public choice approach. There are now many practitioners.

ii See Buchanan and Tullock[9] (p. 313):

Although Spinoza is often described as a follower of Hobbes, we do not find Hobbes' work at all similar to Spinoza's in relation to our own construction, ... it seems essential that some separation of the constitutional and the operational level of decision be made before politics, as a social science, can be satisfactorily divorced from moral philosophy. If sovereignty is conceived as being necessarily undivided and indivisible, this essential separation cannot be made readily. The contractual apparatus to Hobbes becomes an excuse or a justification for political obedience of the individual and little more.

iii In a recent contribution, David Barton[1] has modified the Buchanan and Tullock model to allow for frequent voter contracting. With his modification, the simple majority decision rule will be adopted with greater frequency than would be predicted in the original model.

iv To be fair, Buchanan's recent contributions do not reflect this compromise. In his latest text, for example, Buchanan does not deviate from the strict unanimity requirement.[7]

v But there are other important considerations which are reviewed in the final section of this chapter.

vi To a considerable extent, Breton's use of political participation in response to public policy provisions is the counterpart of Downs's reliance upon information inadequacies as an explanation of pressure group activities in his earlier model.

vii The non-vote maximising arguments in the politicians' utility function are also given some play in this process, especially where discretionary power is non-trivial.

viii As Demsetz himself clearly indicates.

ix Merely as a basis for analysis.

x Largely as a consequence of free-rider problems and of the costs of securing agreement among members of sharing groups.

xi With the important exception of Alan Peacock, who was a member of the Royal Commission and who was co-signatory of a Memorandum of Dissent.

REFERENCES

1. Barton, D. 'Constitutional Choice and Simple Majority Rule: Comment' *Journal of Political Economy* (March/April 1973)

2. Breton, A. *The Economic Theory of Representative Government* London, Macmillan (1974)

3. Buchanan, J. M. 'Positive Economics, Welfare Economics and Political Economy' *Journal of Law and Economics* (October 1959)

4. Buchanan, J. M. *Public Finance in Democratic Process* Chapel Hill, North Carolina, University of North Carolina Press (1967)

5. Buchanan, J. M. *The Demand and Supply of Public Goods* Chicago, Rand McNally (1968)

6. Buchanan, J. M. 'An Economic Theory of Clubs' *Economica* (February 1965)

7. Buchanan, J. M. *The Limits of Liberty: Between Anarchy and Leviathan* Chicago, University of Chicago Press (forthcoming)

8. Buchanan, J. M. and Goetz, C. J. 'Efficiency limits of fiscal mobility: an assessment of the Tiebout model' *Journal of Public Economics* (April 1972)

9. Buchanan, J. M. and Tullock, G. *The Calculus of Consent* Ann Arbor, University of Michigan Press (1965)

10. Burrows, P. 'On External Costs and the Visible Arm of the Law' *Oxford Economic Papers* (March 1970)
11. Demsetz, H. 'The Private Production of Public Goods' *Journal of Law and Economics* (October 1970)
12. Demsetz, H. 'Reply to Professor Thompson' *Journal of Law and Economics* (October 1973)
13. Downs, A. *An Economic Theory of Democracy* New York, Harper and Row (1957)
14. Hobbes, T. *Leviathan: or the Matter, Forme and Power of a Commonwealth* (1651)
15. Ng, Y.-K. 'The Economic Theory of Clubs: Pareto Optimality Conditions' *Economica* (August 1973)
16. Ng, Y.-K. 'The Economic Theory of Clubs: Optimal Tax/Subsidy' *Economica* (August 1974)
17. Niskanen, W. A. *Bureaucracy and Representative Government* Chicago, Aldine (1971)
18. Oates, W. *Fiscal Federalism* New York, Harcourt, Brace Jovanovich (1972)
19. Olsen, E. 'Some Theorems on Efficient Transfers' *Journal of Political Economy* (January/February 1971)
20. Peacock, A. T. 'Cost-Benefit Analysis and the Politics of Public Investment' in N. Wolfe (ed.) *Cost-Benefit and Cost Effectiveness Analysis* London, National Bureau of Economic Research (1970)
21. Peacock, A. T. and Wiseman, J. *Education for Democrats* London, Institute of Economic Affairs (1964)
22. Rowley, C. K. 'The Political Economy of British Education' *Scottish Journal of Political Economy* (June 1969)
23. Royal Commission on the Constitution *Report* London, HMSO (1973)
24. Thompson, E. 'The Private Production of Public Goods: A Comment' *Journal of Law and Economics* (October 1973)
25. Tiebout, C. 'A Pure Theory of Local Expenditures' *Journal of Political Economy* (October 1956)
26. Tullock, G. 'Constitutional Choice and Simple Majority Rule: Reply' *Journal of Political Economy* (March/April 1973)

7. Justice

> The principle of distributive justice, once introduced, would not be fulfilled until the whole of society was organized in accordance with it. This would produce a kind of society which in all essential respects would be the opposite of a free society — a society in which authority decided what the individual was to do and how he was to do it. [F. A. Hayek *The Constitution of Liberty* London, Routledge and Kegan Paul (1960) p. 100]

For many individuals, distributive justice takes pride of place in the category of social objectives, even dominating the objective of economic efficiency. Yet, this pre-eminence is not reflected in the welfare economics literature of the Western world, which centres attention almost exclusively upon efficiency considerations. The explanation of this 'distortion' of emphasis is to be found in the self-denying ordinance of the conventional Paretian approach, which entirely precludes consideration of the primary structure of rights. Only recently has there been evidence of fundamental rethinking by economists on the issue of distributive justice,[i] in an attempt to make an economic contribution to the policy debate. In this chapter, we shall review the more important of these contributions as a prelude to presenting our own view of the liberal approach to justice.

I JOHN RAWLS AND A THEORY OF JUSTICE

To Rawls,[12,13] society is a more or less self-sufficient association of persons who in their relations to one another recognize certain rules of conduct as binding and who for the most part act in accordance with them. In this sense, society is marked by a conflict as well as by an identity of interests. The identity of interests exists since social co-operation makes possible a better life for all than any could achieve solely by his own efforts. Conflict of interests exists since individuals are not indifferent as to the distribution of the benefits of their collaboration. The resolution of this conflict is the essence of social justice.

To Rawls a society is well-ordered when not only is it designed to advance the good of its members, but it is also effectively regulated by a public conception of justice. The latter conception implies (i) that every individual accepts and knows that all other individuals accept the same principles of justice and (ii) that the basic social institutions generally satisfy and are generally known to satisfy these principles. Rawls is fully aware that existing societies are not well-ordered in the sense outlined, that individuals born into different positions have different expectations in life, that the institutions of society favour certain starting places over others, and that these discrepancies are not universally accepted by members of society. In no sense is his treatise to be considered either as an explanation of or as a defence for the *status quo*. Rather is Rawls concerned with a conception of justice for the basic structure of society which generalises the theory of the social contract as found in the writings of Locke, Rousseau and Kant, and which he labels 'justice as fairness':[12]

... the guiding idea is that the principles of justice for the basic structure of society are the object of the original agreement. They are the principles that free and rational persons concerned to further their own interests would accept in an initial position of equality as defining the fundamental forms of their association. These principles are to regulate all further agreements; they specify the kinds of social cooperation that can be entered into and the forms of government that can be established. [p. 11]

Thus, Rawls would have us imagine that those who engage in social co-operation choose together, in one joint act, the principles that are to assign basic rights and duties and to determine the division of social benefits. The choice that rational men would make in this hypothetical situation determines the principles of justice. In justice as fairness, the original position of equality corresponds to the state of nature in the traditional theory of the social contract — an entirely hypothetical situation characterised so as to lead to a certain conception of justice — in which no individual knows his place in society, his class position or social status, nor does any individual know his fortune in the distribution of natural assets and abilities, his intelligence, strength and the like. Rawls even assumes that the parties involved do not know their own conceptions of the good or their special psychological propensities. The principles of justice thus are chosen behind a 'veil of ignorance' which ensures that no individual is advantaged or disadvantaged in the choice of principles by the outcome of natural chance or the contingency of social circumstances. These principles form the basis for all constitutional and post-constitutional decision-making by the society in question:[12]

... a society satisfying the principles of justice as fairness comes as close as a society can to being a voluntary scheme for it meets the principles which free and equal persons would assent to under circumstances that are fair. In this sense its members are autonomous and the obligations they recognise self-imposed. [p. 13]

In most essentials, this part of 'justice as fairness' is acceptable to those Paretian economists[4] who extend the scope of their analysis to the pre-constitutional situation, since they also have emphasised a contractarian approach. Rawls, however, is not content to rest his discussion at the choice-making level but is anxious to derive policy implications from his decision-making model. This — as we shall outline in a subsequent section — is an important departure point between Rawls and public choice Paretians.[ii]

Rawls suggests that the principles of justice selected in the 'original position', as it is defined above, will be formally constrained by what he calls 'the concept of right', namely the requirement that certain axioms should not be violated. For Rawls, the axioms of generality, universality, publicity, completeness, transitivity and finality (i.e. no higher standard) are seen to apply. The close proximity between these axioms and those of the Arrow Possibility Theorem — though ignored by Rawls — is evident. We have already explored the dubious value basis upon which axioms such as these frequently are grounded.[iii] He further assumes that the rational person will not be motivated by envy or by benevolence while negotiating under the veil of ignorance; i.e., he returns to the solipsist assumption of conventional Paretian welfare economics. Moreover, since each negotiator is deemed to be unaware even of his temporal position, he is assumed to choose for everyone at all points in time and in space (within the society in question). Finally, Rawls defines a valid agreement as one which the parties must be able to honour under all relevant and foreseeable circumstances.

In such circumstances, Rawls suggests — as far as is disclosed on the basis of introspection alone — that two principles of justice will be agreed upon by parties negotiating in the original position, namely that (i) each person is to have an equal right to the most extensive basic liberty compatible with a similar liberty for others and (ii) social and economic inequalities are to be arranged so that they are both (a) reasonably to be expected to be to everyone's advantage, and (b) attached to positions and offices open to all. Let us, with Rawls, explore these very general statements in closer detail, first as to their priority and secondly as to their content.

Rawls is less than consistent in his discussion on the ordering of the principles of justice, in our view because he is not clear about the nature of freedom. At first (p. 63), he urges that the ordering is in serial or lexicographic form, implying that the first principle must be fully satisfied, whatever the implications for the second, with no trade-off possibility where the two turn out to be in conflict. This he subsequently and categorically reaffirms:[12]

By the priority of liberty I mean the precedence of the principle of equal liberty over the second principle of justice. The two principles are in lexical order, and therefore the claims of liberty are to be satisfied first. Until this is achieved no other principle comes into play. [p. 224]

Very quickly, however, when actually confronted with a potential trade-off situation in which the maintenance of liberty might involve deleterious social consequences, Rawls backs down and concedes that certain liberties justifiably may be sacrificed in the pursuit of alternative objectives, at least in the short and medium terms (not defined). Rawls seems to be entirely unaware of the importance for his theory of justice of this substantial concession:[12]

Under certain conditions that cannot be at present removed, the value of some liberties may not be so high as to rule out the possibility of compensation to those less fortunate. To accept the lexical ordering of the two principles we are not required to deny that the value of liberty depends upon circumstances. But it does have to be shown that as the general conception of justice is followed social conditions are eventually brought about under which a lesser than equal liberty would no longer be accepted. Unequal liberty is then no longer justified. The lexical order is, so to speak, the inherent long-run equilibrium of a just system. [pp. 247—8]

With all respect, this restatement of the meaning of lexicographical ordering is nonsense! Rawls's indecision on this matter can be explained by a closer scrutiny of his conception of liberty. From the outset, Rawls explicitly ignores the debate over negative and positive freedom, arguing that this debate is essentially concerned only with the relative values of the several freedoms when they come into conflict. As we have demonstrated in chapter 5, this view is entirely fallacious and confuses freedom with effective power, a confusion that colours Rawls's approach (as outlined above) to the principles of justice:

. . . liberty is represented by the complete system of the liberties of equal citizenship, while the worth of liberty to persons and groups is proportional to their capacity to advance their ends within the framework the system defines. Freedom as equal liberty is the same for all; the question of compensating for a lesser than equal liberty does not arise. But the worth of liberty is not the same for everyone. Some have greater authority and wealth, and therefore greater means to achieve their aims. [p. 204]

Nevertheless, Rawls leans in favour of a definition of liberty in terms of negative freedom (almost, it would seem, despite himself), and certainly it is on this basis that he derives the first principle of justice from individual negotiations in the 'original position'. Essentially, Rawls views mankind as being risk-averse and argues that the conditions of the original position are especially conducive to the resort to maximin-type strategies when choosing from a known set of alternative policies, in that each individual has knowledge neither of his own bargaining position nor even of his objective function. In such circumstances, since no one can know at the time of negotiation whether or not he would be part of a coerced group, Rawls supposes that all individuals would vote for the maximum possible freedom, save only where the freedom of intolerance might jeopardise the basic structure itself.

With the problem of the conflict of freedoms (and the need for ranking) Rawls does not seriously concern himself — a weakness indeed in his theory of justice. In other respects, there seems to be no substantial conflict between his views on 'the equality of liberty' and our views as expounded in chapter 5. Throughout his discussion, Rawls emphasises that the parties to the agreement are concerned with 'the equality of liberty' within a social context.

Now let us direct attention to the second of Rawls's principles of justice, which usefully may be summarised, following Rawls, as the 'difference principle'. For Rawls, the difference principle removes the indeterminateness of the Paretian efficiency concept (yes, Rawls is a neo-Paretian) by singling out a particular position from which the social and economic inequalities of the basic structure are to be judged. In essence, the difference principle is equivalent to an asymmetrical use of the compensation principle with the proviso that compensation must be paid. For the principle enunciates that the higher expectations of those better situated are just if and only if they work as part of a scheme which improves the expectations of the least advantaged members of society. Expectations, in the Rawls sense, are to be measured in terms of income and wealth.

According to the difference principle, an arrangement is unjust when higher expectations are excessive. For in such circumstances, if these expectations were decreased, the situation of the least favoured would be improved. The degree of injustice, as Rawls views it, depends on how excessive the higher expectations are and to what extent they depend upon the violation of the other principles of justice, e.g. fair equality of opportunity. At this point, Rawls *qua* interpreter shifts perceptibly to Rawls *qua* social commentator:[12]

A society should try to avoid the region where the marginal contributions of those better off are negative, since, other things equal, this seems a greater fault than falling short of the best scheme when these contributions are positive. The even larger difference between rich and poor makes the latter even worse off, and this violates the principle of mutual advantage as well as democratic equality. [p. 79]

Why this should be so in a society composed of solipsists, Rawls does not explain!

It is important to note Rawls's emphasis upon the position of the least advantaged members of society, especially where the notion of chain-connection of advantages does not apply, i.e. where an advantage to the least advantaged does not raise the expectations of all intermediate positions. In such circumstances, those who are better off should not have a veto over the benefits available for the least advantaged. It is in this respect that the asymmetry of the compensation criterion enters into the Rawls's conception of justice. It is in this respect also that the Rawls's approach lends itself most readily to coercive interventions in the real-world situation.

Closely associated with the difference principle in Rawls's theory of justice is the principle of fair equality of opportunity — which is not to be confused with the notions of 'careers open to talents' and of a 'meritocratic society'. The principle of fair equality of opportunity is grounded in justice and not in efficiency and is to be applied even at some sacrifice in efficiency terms. It expresses the conviction that, if some places were not open on a fair basis to all, those excluded would be right in feeling unjustly treated even though they benefited from the greater benefits of those who were allowed to hold them. Without fair equality of opportunity, the difference principle itself forms an inadequate basis for the second principle of justice, since the system would not satisfy the conditions for 'procedural justice'. Rawls contends that the application of the difference principle safeguards fair equality of opportunity from 'meritocracy' criticisms by requiring that undeserved inequalities call for redress:[12]

In justice as fairness men agree to share one another's fate. In designing institutions they undertake to avail themselves of the accidents of nature and social circumstances only when doing so is for the common benefit. The two principles are a fair way of meeting the arbitrariness of fortune; and while no doubt imperfect in other ways, the institutions which satisfy these principles are just. [p. 102]

Once again Rawls justifies the second principle of justice as being the obvious choice for individuals negotiating under the veil of ignorance and in the original position, on the assumption that they choose on the basis of the maximin decision rule, each fearing that he will be allocated the least advantageous position in society. Rawls further argues that the two principles of justice constitute a basis for the strongest possible contract, which is sustainable even against the worst eventualities, since the least advantaged are provided with substantive safeguards with respect both to liberty and to justice. Moreover, since everyone's good is affirmed, all individuals will acquire inclinations to uphold the scheme, ensuring the widest possible publicity for the basic structure. He concludes that the original position observes the conditions of generality in principle, universality of application, completeness and transitivity, publicity and finality, and in this sense may be categorised as justice as fairness.[iv]

Rawls's theory of justice has met with widespread interest — not to say acclamation — in Western societies, not least because it appears to provide a theoretical underpinning for the egalitarian prejudices of many intellectuals. Certainly, it has reawakened the interest of the economics profession in matters of distributive justice, and in this sense, if perhaps in no other, it has served a useful purpose. In our view, however, it is seriously deficient as a theory of justice and it is susceptible to criticism on at least three important matters, namely (i) internal consistency, (ii) the maximin principle and (iii) relevance.

i Internal consistency

Let us initially accept the framework of the original position and the veil of ignorance as expounded by Rawls, with individuals, solipsist and risk-averse by nature, contracting over an unknown environment. By what manner of contract can they safeguard the second principle of justice? Rawls himself is clear that transaction costs will rule out any system of continuous reassessment of income and wealth designed to keep track of the expectations of the least advantaged — the economic system is too complex for such an exercise. Inevitably, therefore, the contract must relate to an institutional framework and a set of procedures designed to throw up the requisite distribution of income and wealth. But what kind of system? Once again, Rawls has a ready answer:[12]

The intuitive idea is familiar. Suppose that law and government act effectively to keep markets competitive, resources fully employed, property and wealth (especially if private ownership of the means of production is allowed) widely distributed by the appropriate forms of taxation, or whatever, and to guarantee a reasonable social minimum. Assume also that there is fair equality of opportunity underwritten by education for all; and that the other equal liberties are secured. Then it would appear that the resulting distribution of income and the pattern of expectations will tend to satisfy the difference principle. [p. 87]

No economist, of whatever persuasion, would seriously endorse this solution without a tableau of reservations, as a system desired to protect above all else the interests of the least advantaged. For competition, save only in its most perfect form and in long-run equilibrium, does not protect society from quasi-rents, nor does it guarantee a socially acceptable minimum wage, whatever that might be. Minimum wage legislation has been shown to damage the expectations of the least advantaged and to be inimical to high employment policies. Education for all may protect equality of opportunity in the conventional sense; but, without coercive intervention to limit the education of the able, it cannot provide fair equality of opportunity in the sense of Rawls. Yet, coercion infringes his first principle of justice.

The point is simple, but nonetheless important. The relationship between economic structure and economic performance is complex and subject to continuous adjustment. The state of economic knowledge on these relationships at present is not conducive to placing great confidence in institutional adjustments as a basis for achieving complex economic objectives. Probably, there is no institutional framework short of central planning by a benevolent despot that could guarantee Rawls his distributive solution. Presumably, such a system is debarred by Rawls's first principle of justice. If individuals bargaining in the original position are assumed to be aware of these complexities, how can Rawls guarantee that they would reach universal agreement? If they are assumed to be ignorant of structure—performance relationships, on the other hand, presumably they would choose at random, with unknown consequences for justice as fairness. Clearly, economists must make major advances in their understanding of the economic system before universal consensus is to be anticipated even for a closely specified economic objective — which the Rawls difference principle evidently is not.

ii   The maximin principle

The maximin decision-making principle is absolutely essential to tne Rawls theory of justice, since in its absence the difference principle implication no longer holds and the egalitarian thrust of the model is lost. Is the justification advanced by Rawls for the application of this principle convincing? We suggest that it is not and assert that Rawls has confused games between persons with games against nature in applying it to negotiations in the original position.

Rawls[13] defends maximin on five principal grounds, namely: (i) that the special conditions of the original position are conducive to very considerable normal risk-aversion; (ii) that its implications are less demanding than those of any alternative in terms of information requirements; (iii) that it is especially suitable as a 'public principle'; (iv) that it minimises the strains of commitment; and (v) that it best satisfies the aspirations of the free and equal personality. Each ground is suspect or irrelevant as we shall demonstrate.

The risk-aversion issue is easily dispensed with. Rawls argues that, from the standpoint of the original position, 'the parties will surely be very considerably risk-averse'[13] (p. 143). Why? It is true that individuals would have no notion of their eventual place in society; but, presumably, they would have some idea of the likely structure of society, and some impression that the least advantaged members would represent a minority of the total citizenship. As solipsists, they would be concerned to maximise only their own expected utilities — there is no hint of benevolence in the Rawlsian system. The risk-neutral person, no doubt, in such circumstances would apply some version of the difference principle to the mean/median or modal wealth group, while leaving the least advantaged to fend for themselves. The risk-taker would gamble on attaining the upper reaches of the wealth spectrum and would negotiate for zero restrictions. Only the extreme risk-averter would vote for maximin. On what grounds can Rawls assert that 'people will be different', that carefree gamblers will become cringing risk-averters in the original position? The answer is that he cannot. Only in games between persons, where one party is known to adopt maximin, will the others be obliged to do so to protect themselves from major defeat. Nature, by contrast, cannot be considered alien, and there is no need (other than innate risk-aversion which is rarely encountered) to resort to maximin. For Rawls to make his case, 'Sod's Law' must always operate. With nature, at least, we do not accept that it does.

The view that the difference principle minimises information costs we have already dispensed with in discussing the internal consistency of the theory of justice. The view that the difference principle serves well as a public principle, in that citizens generally should be able to understand it and to have some confidence that it is realised, is also suspect essentially for the same reasons. The view that maximin minimises the strains of commitment to the contract perhaps is more credible in that it assures the less favoured that inequalities work to their advantage — but even this assumes a degree of *ex-post* reasonableness by the parties to the agreement that is rarely encountered in practice. The view that maximin best satisfies the aspirations of the free and equal personality is an empty box, once extreme risk-aversion is denied — and attempts to justify an assumption in terms of an implication that is supposed to be derived from the maximin assumption itself — a most suspect manoeuvre in circular methodology.

In short, maximin is indefensible as a universal decision rule for individuals negotiating in the original position. Yet without it, what is left of the Rawls's theory of justice, even when viewed as a simulation exercise to determine the likely pattern of justice in circumstances where the existing advantages and disadvantages of individuals are entirely ignored?

iii Relevance

The above criticisms provide some indication of the essential weakness of the Rawls's theory of justice, even in terms of its own framework. Once real-world considerations are allowed to enter, the approach loses all credibility. For in the real world individuals do not negotiate under a veil of ignorance — indeed, they are only too well aware of their relative income/wealth ranking in society. Nor, for the most part, are they solipsists — modern society is riddled with benevolence and envy, as Paretian economists now readily acknowledge. Nor are they necessarily enraptured by freedom — many individuals would sell themselves into slavery in return for material possessions if the law so allowed, while others would eagerly purchase property rights in coercion. In our view, if Rawls were to attempt to put his theory to the test, he would be severely surprised.

The real danger, of course, is that the Rawls's hypothesis is not designed for testing — indeed, except at the introspective level it is untestable — but the policy implications are readily adoptable. In short, Rawls provides a spurious justification for egalitarianism. For in real-world terms, the distributional outcome essentially *cannot* be discussed in terms of justice as fairness. Rather, it is to be viewed as the outcome of conflict — whether resolved by resort to anarchy or coercion, by contract or revolution. It is to the processes by which individuals resolve such conflict that public choice Paretians[2,3,4,5,14,15,16,17] now devote significant attention in an effort to make positive predictions as to the likely nature of the solution. To this more promising, if in our view also limited, approach we now must turn.

II   DISTRIBUTION AND THE PUBLIC CHOICE INTERPRETATION

Public choice Paretianism, (PCP)[v] for purposes of this section, is defined by reference to the recent contributions by Professors Buchanan,[4,5] Tullock,[17] *et alia* which emphasise the individualistic, contractarian approach to the distribution problem, and which reject any notion of distributive justice introduced as an ethical norm or precept. For this reason, PCP endorses the basic approach of Rawls, which adopts the contractarian principle, but recoils from his policy implications, derived from the conditions of the original position, viewing this aspect of his work as both over-ambitious and susceptible to misinterpretation as actual policy *proposals*.

In its essentially normative role, PCP is subject of course to all the value assumptions of the Paretian approach, including the ban on making interpersonal utility comparisons. In the absence of utility interdependences of the kind postulated in chapter 3, it might appear, therefore, that PCP could have little to say on the distribution problem. In fact, by retracing the development of societies to their anarchistic foundations and by emphasising the economic gains obtainable from distribution contracts, PCP offers a plausible, if not entirely a compelling, explanation of constitutional development which does not deviate from the Wicksellian unanimity requirements. Furthermore, PCP, in marked contrast to Rawls, does not rely upon the unrealistic assumptions which define the original position, viz. the initial equality of all individuals as they negotiate under the veil of ignorance, but develops its explanation from an initial basis of inequality of individual preferences, capacities and environmental settings, in which information exists albeit not always in perfect form. For this reason, PCP is far more closely associated with the real world than is Rawls's theory of justice. Moreover, by emphasising process and procedure, rather than seeking out a policy blueprint, PCP avoids, for the most part, the excess of ambition which characterises Rawls's latest text. To PCP, 'good' is defined as that which emerges from agreement among free men — this indeed constitutes the ethical basis of the PCP theory of justice.

In the initial state of nature (anarchy)[vi] each individual has a 'right' to everything, or to nothing, depending on the view adopted, since property rights, in the conventional sense, do not exist. In such circumstances a natural distribution will emerge as a consequence of the tastes, capacities, environmental setting, strength, cunning and ingenuity of the various individuals comprising society, and some kind of initial equilibrium may be envisaged in which each individual extends his behaviour in providing, securing and defending commodities to the point where his marginal costs and benefits are equal. The natural distribution itself is not to be viewed as a structure of rights — for it is not based upon consent — but it does provide a basis for subsequent contracting. By its very nature, however, the natural distribution is unlikely to be one of equality, as postulated in the Rawls's theory of justice.

There are defence/predation costs involved in maintaining the natural distribution which could be eliminated by co-operation, since the individuals concerned are locked together in a negative-sum game. And once these costs are recognised as a dead weight loss, a necessary condition for contracting exists — this is the logic of the PCP approach. Thus is a genuine basis for the emergence of property rights derived from a situation of anarchy. An agreement on rights in these circumstances essentially reflects a contractual internalization of an externality relationship that existed in the precontract state of nature. Of course, the specific distribution of rights consequent upon the contracting process will be linked directly to the relative command over commodities enjoyed by each individual in the natural distribution — so much for Rawls! The essential point in the PCP analysis is that contracting will occur even if conventional solipsist, self-seeking behaviour is universal within society.

At this stage, however, the public good problem menaces the contractual solution in that the security of rights and claims is not easily made susceptible to the exclusion principle. Each individual has a private incentive to renege on or to violate contractual agreements on rights provided that he can do so unilaterally and thereby obtain a free ride at the expense of those who abide by their agreements. In the large-numbers case, no contracting system could withstand free-riding disruption of this kind and for this reason some form of constitutional contract may meet with universal consent, as individuals recognise again that they will be locked otherwise into a negative-sum game.

The nature of the constitutional contract has received close attention in the PCP analysis, not least because it is recognised that individuals who contract for the services of enforcing institutions necessarily surrender a part of their independence. For enforcement, in this particular public good situation, must include the imposition of physical constraints on those who would violate the structure of rights, and there is no obvious mechanism through which the enforcing institution (the State) can be constrained in its own behaviour. For this reason, the PCP approach designates to the State the role of umpire or referee in the constitutional solution to the distribution problem, with a responsibility only for ensuring that contractual terms are honoured. In particular, the important distinction is underlined between the role of enforcing claims and that of defining those claims in the first instance, with the former only allocated by individuals to the State. The 'protective State', so defined, must be neutral, as must the umpire or referee in the game situation, and, in this limited sense, fairness or justice will emerge from the self-interest of contracting individuals. Once the constitutional contract is established, the basis exists for post-constitutional contracting, which at any point in time will determine the ultimate distributional outcome as viewed in PCP terms. The entire PCP approach to distribution in a two-person but many-commodity society is usefully summarized in figure 7.1 which is due to Buchanan.[4] The utility attained by individual A is shown on the ordinate and that by individual B on the abscissa. The neutral distribution is defined at D. The constitutional contract which underpins the structure of rights shifts the utility positions to C within the bounds defined by the broken lines from D. Post-constitutional contracting further shifts the utility positions to E within the bounds defined by the broken lines from C, at which point the possibilities of mutually beneficial redistribution are exhausted. In terms of figure 7.1, it is assumed that the shift from C to E is accomplished by some combination of private-goods trade and public-goods trade, both of which take place within the framework defined by constitutional contract including the precise voting system which will contain the influence of the collectivity in the post-constitutional situation.

Once the constitutional contract, with all its implications, has been established there is no reason to suppose that it should be retained for all time. The individuals comprising society themselves change with the passage of time as do their material circumstances. Constitutional change may thus be justified, but only where universal consent is forthcoming — this is the PCP value judgement. If, after examination and analysis, no such potential for change exists, the existing constitutional contract must be adjudged Pareto-optimal despite the presence of discontent within society — at this point the scope for adjustment disappears.

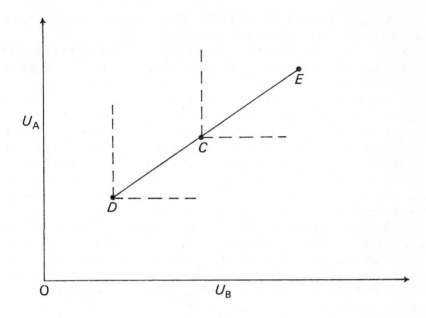

Figure 7.1

A society which in fact developed along the lines outlined above would be immune from criticism, whatever the policy outcomes, in terms of public choice criteria. But the advocates of the PCP approach themselves are aware that no such society exists. Indeed, public choice specialists are in the vanguard in analysing the methods whereby in practice collective decisions are registered, in identifying the inevitable distortions of the political market place and in demonstrating the ubiquitous corruption of bureaucracy. To assess the practical implications of public choice for distributive justice, we now must turn to the darker, positive side of public choice analysis. In this context, distribution is to be viewed as a social dilemma to be resolved in part by contract, it is true, but not necessarily by contracts freely entered into. For, in practice, contractual solutions are influenced/curtailed/imposed by a mix of coercion, theft, revolution, *coups d'état* etc. and/or of threats thereof — hardly a process of agreement among free men! Furthermore, the State cannot in practice conceivably be viewed as a referee, impartially enforcing the constitutional contract. Rather, it must be viewed as a coercive institution, at best reflecting the will of the majority, at worst assuming an independent authority and momentum of its own, redistributing income and wealth according to the passing dictates of the public market place. Between the ideal society of the constitutional contract and the reality of public choice in any contemporary society there is in our view an insurmountable gap.

What then are the discernible redistributive implications of public choice in societies characterised by two-party, majority-vote systems of government? This is at first sight an unanswerable question, requiring apparently intimate knowledge of the entire structure of rights — which defines the distribution of income and wealth — as it would have emerged under a constitutional contract and of the deviations from that structure (together with their distributive consequences), which result from non-contracted state interventions. Information of this order just cannot be derived from a perusal of the recent fiscal measures attributable to central and local government — indeed, it is not conceivably attainable at all. Where empiricism falls down, however, useful insights are often available from *a priori* analysis. Let us illustrate one possible outcome by applying Downsian analysis to a two-party, majority-vote system of government, on the assumption that voter preferences on distribution cluster around the middle-wealth position, are single-peaked, that the middle-wealth group are motivated essentially by solipsist considerations, but gain utility from parading an egalitarian public conscience. What predictions are to be derived from such a model?

Median wealth voters — whose preferences may be supposed to dictate public policy on the distribution issue in the full-information case — may be assumed overwhelmingly to desire a redistribution of rights favourable to themselves with the inference that the public choice outcome will be one of shifting entitlements away from the rich and the poor, both of which form coercible minorities. The desire to subvert entitlements to themselves, however, is accompanied by a desire not to be seen to do so, since this would taint the egalitarian conscience publicly worn by many of the median wealth group. It is predictable therefore that the nature of the redistribution of rights will be such as to present an image of redistribution to the poor while *de facto* increasing median wealth group entitlements. The provision of free or subsidised medicare, education, museums, national parks, theatre, opera, cultural television etc. is clearly identifiable in these terms, as are minimum wage laws and graduated schemes of unemployment and sickness relief. In so far as median wealth group egalitarianism has any reality in such circumstances it is (following Buchanan)[3] not based to any degree upon generalised concern for the poor so much as upon personalised discomfort when confronted with particular modes of poverty, e.g. malnutrition. This would suggest a preponderance of systems of 'in kind' poverty support (food coupons and the like) despite the known efficiency losses that these impose.

In so far as the prevailing structure of rights cannot easily be identified, and the median wealth group thereby located, the political parties may be wary of recommending effective redistribution measures which run the risk of alienating median preference votes. Predictably, their policy pronouncements will be ambiguous and their specific proposals contradictory and self-cancelling, couched in the most complex possible form. Predictably, also, government action will be contradictory, returning in a subsequent intervention entitlements that have been withdrawn by the previous intervention. This would suggest a perplexing range of contradictory and more-or-less self-cancelling redistributions perpetrated upon the middle-wealth group to provide an image of active government without risking a major net loss of votes.

The absence of full information would also provide the rich with an opportunity to engage in effective pressure group activities in defence of their entitlements. Since such activities would be directed to areas where expected net benefits were highest, two consequences follow. First, lobbying will be conducted wherever possible through organisations controlled but not financed by the rich — charitable functions might prove to be much in favour — thereby minimising individual transaction costs and flavouring the campaign with a spurious 'social interest' image. Second, lobbying will be devoted to indirect supports for the entitlements of the rich, and associated with slogans that are designed to enthuse the median voters, rather than to the direct defence of minority interests. Tariff protection, agricultural support programmes, anti-competition programmes, regional support programmes etc. all lend themselves well to this type of activity and are much more likely to win median voter approval than are campaigns directed against progressive income taxation and estate duties. It is predictable, therefore, that the redistribution from rich to median voters will be less than would occur in the full-information situation. The poor, by the nature of their conditions, would have no similar protection.

What then, in such a Downsian-type system, is the limit to the redistribution of entitlements away from the rich and the poor? What are the outer bounds of coercion? No doubt, in part, where a range of policy issues, including distribution, simultaneously are under consideration, log-rolling — which provides a means whereby preference intensities may be reflected in public choice — may moderate the expressed preferences for redistribution on the part of the median wealth groups. For this to be at all effective, however, it would be necessary for the clustering of preferences on the various policy issues to vary with respect to the individual voters in society. By no means is it always clear that this is so, especially where the median wealth group detects the political returns to solidarity in public choice and enters into an implicit coercive conspiracy. It is by no means evident, therefore, that log-rolling would provide the binding constraint upon the redistribution process. The principal alternative is revolution or *coup d'état* or the threat thereof on the part of coerced minorities.

Following Tullock,[17] both revolution and *coup d'état* involve a violent change in government (if successful), and they are distinguished only by reference to the scale of operation, the former large and the latter small. Following the self-interest axiom, we shall also assume that revolution and *coup d'état* both occur not in pursuit of some ethical ideal, but as a consequence of narrow self-seeking on the part of those who are dissatisfied with their distributive situations. On these assumptions, it can be demonstrated that 'popular revolution' is unlikely save in extreme cases of coercive redistribution, essentially because of the public good characteristics of revolution. For the discontented who do not participate in successful revolution avoid the costs of participation (including the finite probability of injury, torture and death) but are unlikely to be excluded from the redistributive benefits. In such circumstances, free-rider problems are likely to erode the threat of popular revolution, and thereby to relax the constraint upon the degree of coercion by the majority of the minority.

For this reason, revolution and *coup d'état* most commonly are intra-government phenomena, usually confined to a small, self-seeking group within the government/military/police establishment. The prospects for successful action will depend upon the ability of the malcontents to offer returns to those who will assist them commensurate with the costs involved. This, more than anything, explains why the successful overthrow of government is always followed by widescale personnel shifts within the reorganised bureaucracy. It also explains the greater incidence of *coups d'état* than of revolutions. Whatever the distributive slogan adopted in the course of revolution to marshall popular support/neutrality, there is no necessary reason to suppose that redistributive consequences will follow. In so far as the new administration is despotic, the distributive consequences are unpredictable. In so far as it relies upon democratic support, it must be driven into the middle ground (albeit perhaps a new middle-ground), implying little in the way of fundamental change from the behaviour of its predecessor. Coerced minorities, save in exceptional circumstances, have little to gain from the overthrow of government, be it violently through revolution or peaceably via the ballot box, given stability of median voter preferences on the distribution issue. Likewise, the threat of violence at best offers only a limited protection against the seizure of rights by majority groupings.

Whither then the contractarian approach of the public choice Paretian to the distribution dilemma as posed in the two-party, majority-vote system of government? How does he reconcile the ideal with practical reality? To answer this, we must turn to the recent important contribution to the debate on liberty, due to Professor Buchanan,[4] and in particular to his final chapter. Essentially, Buchanan urges a return to the eighteenth-century methodological approach to political economy, with its emphasis upon constitutional analysis and a shift away from mid-twentieth-century welfare economics with its narrow and obsessional emphasis upon the theory of market failure. He asks fundamentally for a systematic and non-incremental review of the nature and structure of society as a precondition for the constitutional revolution that may be necessary for survival. With this plea and emphasis, as liberals, we have no criticism — indeed it coincides with our own judgement.

But Buchanan remains committed to the contractarian principle of the Paretian dogma — for constitutional change to be acceptable it must be universally endorsed. There is to be no escape from the Paretian strait-jacket. In essence, Buchanan puts his faith in the essential good sense and judgement of all individuals when exposed to the alternatives that confront them and in their deep-rooted commitment to the democratic ideal, once the constitutional contract has been established. It is clearly his expectation that the process of discussing public choice within a constitutional framework and confronting individuals with the alternative routes that lie before them will generate universal support for a newly-embraced constitutional contract. Thus:[4]

Free relations among free men — this precept of ordered anarchy can emerge as principle when successfully re-negotiated social contract puts 'mine and thine' in a newly defined structural arrangement and when the Leviathan that threatens is placed within new limits.

Would that we felt able to share with Buchanan this optimistic view of the development of society! But in societies such as ours, in which envy plays so great a role in individual motivation, in which true freedom is so little understood and cherished, in which the State and its bureaucracy are so powerful and so corrupt, in which the processes of logic and of reason are so little valued and in which the clever turn of phrase and the empty rhetoric can raise such primitive passion, we are able to place but little faith in the contractarian solution to the distribution problem.

III   A LIBERAL APPROACH

Liberalism we have already defined as a philosophy concerned essentially with the maintenance and extension of individual freedom, in the sense of minimising the degree of coercion of some individuals by others.[6,8] This is the only principle that directs the liberal approach to justice — thus we are at once at odds with Rawls, who feels obliged to invoke a separate principle, other than that of equal access to liberty, as a basis for his theory of justice. We are at odds both with Rawls and with Buchanan, moreover, on a crucial interpretation of individual motivation, namely the extent to which negative freedom is valued in contemporary society. Both Rawls and Buchanan take the essentially optimistic view that individuals need only be faced with the full freedom to architect their society to endorse unanimously the need to provide and protect freedom. We do not accept this view[11] — indeed, if we did liberalism could be viewed as an all-embracing philosophy and this book would be almost unnecessary.

In defining a liberal approach to justice, therefore, we are in a sense following the approach, commended by Buchanan, of presenting a refutable proposition to the voting public. But our proposition is not designed to produce consensus — in our view an impossible objective — but hopefully to convince a majority of the electorate of the validity of our case. For at present the liberal position is one of minority, with its emphasis upon personal responsibility, by its nature, unlikely to appeal to citizens who have experienced several decades of collectivist experience.[vii] Those who find it easier to rely upon centralised decision-makers rather than to make their own free choices now constitute a majority of the electorate, certainly in the European economies, but possibly also even in the USA. To be successful, therefore, liberalism must be sold and liberals must step down from their ivory towers to engage in missionary work[viii] Hence the present text.

We start then with society as it now is and with the existing structure of rights, recognising that this structure is the outcome of all kinds of corruption and coercion, of all kinds of inequalities of birth, ability, luck and misfortune, which in no sense reflect a constitutional contract. What are the implications for justice, if any, that are derivable from liberal principles? To answer this, in part at least, we must consider the implications of the liberal precept of 'equality before the law' advanced in chapter 5 as an important safeguard against coercion by some of others.

i Equality before the law

The precept of equality before the law is not to be confused with any other sort of equality or with any egalitarian philosphy, for indeed its general application must produce an inequality in the structure of rights in societies in which the drive, ability and environmental circumstances of individuals are subject to variation. With important qualifications, which we shall shortly enumerate, liberals endorse inequalities in the structure of rights which do not negate equality before the law. Hayek[6] indeed has urged that if the result of individual liberalism did not demonstrate that some manners of living are more successful than others, much of its justification would vanish. This essentially inegalitarian viewpoint reflects the attitude of John Stuart Mill, who also detested and feared standardisation and who perceived that, in the name of philanthropy, democracy and equality, 'a collective mediocrity' was gradually strangling originality and individual gifts.

Equality before the law requires that those conditions of people's lives determined by the collectivity should be provided equally to all individuals — even though the consequence inevitably is material inequality. This implies, for example, that laws that discriminate for or against individuals by reason of their colour, race or religion infringe the liberal ethic — though freedom of *individual* dissociation is seen as an essential corollary to the freedom of individual association. It further implies, however, that discriminatory interventions designed only to make individuals more alike in their material condition also infringe the liberal ethic — and this indeed is the flashpoint of conflict with egalitarian philosophy, denying as it does the redistributive case for progressive taxation. On this important issue, careful consideration is necessary.

Taxation, in some form, is of course required if a government is to fulfil its minimum responsibilities in the provision of public goods. The danger, in a majority-vote system of government, concerns the opportunity thus provided for a majority to engage in coercive redistributions of wealth and income away from minorities. Equality before the law safeguards minorities from such coercion by providing that such taxation as is enforced will be met in equal proportions by the majority as by minorities. In itself, this does not constitute a case for the proportional income tax, since other taxes may be regressive in incidence, and since public goods may be differentially valued, but it does imply strict limits to the degree of progressiveness allowed. Hayek[6] has suggested, for example, that the highest marginal rate of taxation might be restricted to that proportion of Gross Domestic Product accounted for by the government. Individual liberals will have their own views as to the merit of this particular proposal.[ix] Fundamentally, what is required is a recognisable limit on the extent of coercive taxation that might be enshrined as a constitutional rule, alterable only by a large majority preference and only then following extensive constitutional debate.

Equality before the law has implications also for the pattern of public provision of goods and services, namely that such provisions should be available on equal terms to all citizens. Thus, for example, public education should not discriminate for or against the able or the rich, the black or the white as a means of coercive redistribution; nor, where it is operative, should public medicare provision. Once again, a limit on such coercion might be given constitutional status, thereby safeguarding minorities from the interventions of envious or vindictive majorities.

In all this discussion, however, the plight of the poor is not to be ignored. Most liberals (as most individuals) are concerned to avoid the ultimate human degradations of acute poverty, and recognise that to do so requires a loophole in the proposed constitutional rules. To prevent poverty by providing a means-tested support programme, whether or not reflected in interdependent utility functions, implies deviations from proportionate income taxes (to allow for negative tax rates) on the one side and deviations from equality of access to publicly provided commodities on the other. Fundamentally, however, the poverty problem is seen as requiring special arrangements. It is dangerous to construct an entire constitution on the basis of the needs of a tiny minority of society, thereby exposing all minorities to coercive redistributions.

Where redistribution is justified, by reference to poverty criteria, liberals have a strong preference for redistribution by cash rather than in kind.[10,11] For the most part, however, this preference is *not* grounded on the conventional Paretian efficiency considerations (essentially the reverse of the argument indicating the excess burden of indirect taxes), which demonstrate that an income subsidy places the individual consumer on a higher level of utility than would an equal transfer used to subsidise the price of a commodity.[9,10] Rather, the liberal supports cash transfers because they place the responsibility of choice more firmly in the hands of the individual recipient. Those who are not allowed to exercise choice not unnaturally may never show their capabilities so to do[x] — and liberalism is closely identified with the exercise of freedom of choice. Furthermore, redistribution in kind presupposes an extensive state apparatus designed to facilitate handling the commodities in question, inviting public production as well as public distribution, with all the disadvantages that this involves for those who would contain Leviathan. All this is not to deny Buchanan's point[3] that redistribution in kind is the predictable outcome of democratic politics. But, as we have emphasised before, while liberals will abide by the democratic decision, in no sense must they endorse such decisions or give them their blessing.

ii   Distribution and the liberal hierarchy of economic freedoms

In chapter 5, the essential divisibility of freedom was emphasised, as was the existence of a conflict of freedoms, not least within the economic sphere. In the hierarchy of liberal freedoms, there developed as a means of resolving conflict, the freedoms of markets, of competition and entry, and of freedom of choice (to the extent possible) in consumption and occupation are more important than are the freedoms of contract and coalition, with the inference that liberals will accept coercive intervention to ensure the dominance of the former over the latter freedoms wherever they are in conflict. The distributive implications are significant, in that the structure of rights is highly sensitive to decisions on this conflict.

Thus, liberals will support suitable anti-trust policies,[xi] designed to eliminate coercive power in the commodity markets and in the factor markets, even though such policies are in conflict with policies of contract and coalition and even though they are themselves coercive policies. In fact, such interventions as influence the distributive outcome are incidental and are not instrumental in the policy thrust, which is derived from the hierarchy of freedoms and not in defence of some concept of justice. For liberalism is concerned not at all with the notion of rewarding individuals by reference to merit — at best a subjective concept — nor is it concerned with the egalitarian ethic. It is concerned with the preservation in appropriate forms of individual freedoms — and this cannot be achieved by a policy of *laissez-faire*.

It is to be emphasised that the liberal reliance on anti-trust laws will not provide an egalitarian outcome of the kind envisaged by Rawls. The economic system is in continuous dynamic adjustment, with the notion of long-run equilibrium a convenient analytic device.[xii] Those who are successful in anticipating market adjustment — be it by good judgement or by good fortune — will earn substantial rents which may carry through into the medium term and may be consolidated by subsequent enterprise. Those who are fortunate, by birth or training, in possessing talents that are scarce by reference to market preferences will not be prevented by anti-trust laws from earning quasi-rents, perhaps throughout their occupational lifetimes. The competitive solution does not guarantee that rewards will be in line with merit or with justice — merely that there will be some (imperfect) correspondence between returns and the value of the contribution as measured by reference to market criteria.[xiii]

For the most part, liberals speak with a single voice on the taxation of income, fearing the coercive and discriminatory implications of representative government, and seeking constitutional protection for minorities based upon the postulate of equality before the law. The liberal voice is divided, however, over the vexatious issue of inheritance, i.e. the treatment of wealth at the point of death, with some, like Hayek, supporting the freedom of citizens to leave their accumulated wealth to whomsoever they may choose and with others, like ourselves, supporting *appropriate* redistribution policies as an acceptable price for the preservation of more important freedoms. Let us outline these alternative positions.

Hayek[6] accepts, of course, that inherited wealth is an important source of inequality in all non-socialist economies. He denies, however, that the fact that it confers unmerited benefits on some is a valid argument against the institution. In part, he rests his case on material considerations, ranging from the alleged advantages to the community that only wealthy homes can offer, to the incentives to capital accumulation provided by the absence of death duties. But, in essence, Hayek's case rests upon the maintenance of negative freedom both by allowing testators the fullest freedom of choice and by reducing the incentives for wealthy parents to purchase lucrative and prestigious occupations for their offspring (as occurs in socialist countries) with serious implications for political freedoms.

We take a different view. Given the taxation policies advanced in this section, it will be possible for some individuals to amass considerable wealth within their own lifetime. In the absence of any intervention, accretions of wealth on a sufficient scale can endanger important intellectual and moral as well as political and economic freedoms, as less fortunate individuals succumb to temptation and sell their freedoms for a suitable mess of pottage. Certainly, concentrations of wealth which are sustained over lengthy time periods at the least are a potential source of danger to the liberal ethic. To counter this, we propose that wealth should be redistributed at the point of death as a means of dispersing power — but not by estate duty interventions as currently utilized. For liberals are more afraid of Leviathan than of private power and are unwilling to support methods of redistribution which place additional effective power in the hands of the State. The appropriate solution, therefore (following Mill), is to disallow total inheritances (by will and by gifts *inter vivos*) from all sources by any individual *in excess* of strictly specified amounts (with the limit designed to eliminate the idle rich at each point of death), but to allow each individual to disperse his wealth privately to chosen inheritors as long as this limit is not violated.[xiv] Wealth that is not so dispersed might be transferred to suitable charities which themselves would be subjected to strict antitrust regulations. In this way, great wealth would not confer coercive powers upon certain of the future generations — though inequality in the structure of rights would not disappear — and yet the power of Leviathan would not be advanced.

FOOTNOTES

i Reawakened interest in the distribution issue owes much to the important contributions by Buchanan,[5] Rawls[12] and Tullock,[14,15,16] whose principal ideas are evaluated in this chapter.

ii Viz. Buchanan[4] (p. 128):

Surely we now need a wider recognition of man's inability at playing God. It is a matter for regret that the extension and elaboration of his basically humble, and to this degree, admirable conception of 'justice as fairness' led John Rawls away from rather than toward the contribution to social philosophy that this treatise might have represented.

iii In chapter 2 of this book.

iv For a philosopher, Rawls is surprisingly unrigorous in proving that justice as fairness satisfies these axioms.

v The PCP approach is most comprehensively explored in a very recent text by J. M. Buchanan.[5]

vi The Hobbesian jungle characterised by the 'war of each against all'.

vii For a strong statement of this viewpoint, see Barry[1] (pp. 152–3):

Liberalism rests on a Faustian vision of life. It exalts self-expression, self-mastery, and control over the natural and social environment, the active pursuit of knowledge and the clash of ideas; the acceptance of personal responsibility for the decisions that shape one's life. For those who cannot take the freedom, it provides alcohol, tranquilizers, wrestling on television, astrology, psycho-analysis, and so on endlessly, but it cannot by its nature provide certain kinds of psychological security.

viii Thus Barry[1] (p. 152): 'My own view is therefore that a liberal must take his stand on the proposition that some ways of life, some types of character are more admirable than others, whatever may be the majority opinion in any society.' We would add that Barry himself in our view is not a liberal.

ix Professor Buchanan has suggested in discussion that the precise maximum could be determined empirically by observing the voting behaviour of the wealthy when faced by different public expenditure—taxation packages.

x It is recognised that individuals may abuse this freedom. Where the abuse damages third parties alternative arrangements may be necessary. For example, the wife, rather than the husband, might be designated head of household. If this solution also failed resort to in kind redistribution might be necessary, perhaps as a preliminary to freeing the children from the tyranny of parents.

xi The approach commended recognises the practical difficulties of maintaining effective anti-trust programmes and is grounded on a realistic view of the corruptibility of bureaucracy.

xii Recognition of this feature of markets is important for the liberal approach. Thus Lachmann[7] (p. 102):

There is, of course, no such thing as an 'initial distribution' before the market process starts. The distribution of wealth in terms of asset values at any point of time is the cumulative result of the market process of the past. In the asset markets, the sums of income streams are revalued every day in accordance with the prevailing balance of expectations, giving capital gains to some, inflicting capital losses upon others.

xiii Thus Hayek[6] (p. 97):

A society in which the position of the individuals was made to correspond to human ideas of moral merit would therefore be the exact opposite of free society. It would be a society in which people were rewarded for duty performed instead of for success, in which every move of every individual was guided by what other people thought he ought to do, and in which the individual was thus relieved of the responsibility and the risk of decision. But if nobody's knowledge is sufficient to guide all human action, there is also no human being who is competent to reward all efforts according to merit.

xiv Special provisions might be thought necessary for widows/widowers to protect their positions through their own lifetimes. But care would be required to avoid leaving a loophole in this way through which wealth might remain concentrated over lengthy time periods, e.g. by systematic remarrying with younger spouses. It must be recognised of course that wealth controls are difficult to enforce and would certainly require buttressing with some form of gift controls even though these latter involve coercion of the living.

REFERENCES

1. Barry, B. 'Liberalism and Want Satisfaction: A Critique of John Rawls' *Political Theory* (May 1973)
2. Buchanan, J. M. 'Positive Economics, Welfare Economics and Political Economy' *Journal of Law and Economics* (October 1959) pp. 124—38
3. Buchanan, J. M. 'What Kind of Redistribution Do We Want?' *Economica* (May 1968) pp. 185—90
4. Buchanan, J. M. 'Rawls on Justice as Fairness' *Public Choice* (Fall 1972)
5. Buchanan, J. M. *The Limits of Liberty: Between Anarchy and Leviathan* (forthcoming)
6. Hayek, F. A. *The Constitution of Liberty* London, Routledge and Kegan Paul (1960)
7. Lachmann, L. M. 'Methodological Individualism and the Market Economy' in Streissler, op. cit.
8. Machlup, F. 'Liberalism and the Choice of Freedoms' in E. Streissler (ed.) *Roads to Freedom, Essays in Honour of Friedrich von Hayek*, London, Routledge & Kegan Paul (1969)
9. Olsen, E. O. 'Some Theorems in the Theory of Efficient Transfers' *Journal of Political Economy* (January/February 1971) pp. 166—76
10. Peacock, A. T. and Barry, D. 'A Note on the Theory of Income Redistribution' *Economica* (February 1951) pp. 83—90
11. Peacock, A. T. and Rowley, C. K. 'Pareto Optimality and the Political Economy of Liberalism' *Journal of Political Economy* (May/June 1972)
12. Rawls, J. *A Theory of Justice* Oxford, Oxford University Press (1973)
13. Rawls, J. 'Some Reasons for the Maximin Criterion' *American Economic Review* (May 1974)
14. Tullock, G. *Private Wants, Public Means* Scranton, Pa., Basic Books (1970)
15. Tullock, G. *The Logic of the Law* Scranton, Pa., Basic Books (1971)
16. Tullock, G. (ed.) *Explorations in the Theory of Anarchy* Center for Study of Public Choice (1972)
17. Tullock, G. *The Social Dilemma* Center for Study of Public Choice (1974)
18. Tullock, G. 'Inheritance Justified' *The Journal of Law and Economics* (October 1971)

8. Market Regulation

The end of the law is, not to abolish or restrain, but to preserve and enlarge freedom. For in all the states of created beings capable of laws, where there is no law there is no freedom. For liberty is to be free from restraint and violence from others; which cannot be where there is no law: and is not, as we are told, a liberty for every man to do what he lists. [John Locke *Second Treatise* sec. 57 p. 29]

The liberal approach to market regulation differs fundamentally from that of the Paretians, and not only in terms of the valuation of freedoms. The Paretian approach, in its conventional form, consists of determining, by reference to a set of necessary conditions, whether or not a particular market situation is optimal. If these conditions are not satisfied, the market situation is condemned and remedial measures are proposed, usually without reference to the realities of the political market place — compromise is out of the question in the Paretian catechism, where a bliss point or nothing is the first article of faith. In this sense, Paretians stand justly accused of adopting a nirvana approach to public policy discussion and of paying scant regard to the inevitable imperfections of any humanly devised economic system. First- and second-order conditions take on the role of bread and wine in their professional communion.

By contrast, liberalism — idealistic but not utopian — embraces the compromises inherent in the human condition, recognises that nirvana is unattainable[16,19] and, in any event, is not unique, and emphasises the comparative institutions approach to so-called problems of market failure. From the choice set of realistic institutional alternatives, the element is chosen which appears best able to cope with the economic problem while preserving freedoms and supporting the rule of law. Nor have liberals any false illusions as to human nature, recognising the limits within which institutional changes can be expected to influence human behaviour, and grounding their policy advice upon a realistic interpretation of the human as well as of the institutional condition. Indeed, it is precisely from this perspective that liberals place such emphasis upon the rule of law in approaching the problems of market regulation.

I THE RULE OF LAW AND ITS IMPLICATIONS

The notion that all coercive interventions should conform with the rule of law, and that this requirement should constitute a limitation on the powers of government, was emphasised in chapter 5. Such a requirement implies that laws must always be prospective, that they must be known and certain, and that they must apply with equal force to all individuals without exception or discrimination. It is now urged that regulatory interventions in markets should conform to the maximum possible extent with these conditions of the rule of law — indeed, that for these purposes the rule of law should be given written constitutional form, binding the legislature and the executive by general rules and subjecting regulatory measures to an over-riding judicial review — as is the case essentially in the United States of America.

There are several reasons why liberals[26] favour such an approach to the market regulation problem. First, it restricts the effective power of Leviathan, both by prohibiting discriminatory coercion of minorities (this most important given the predictions of the economic theory of representative government) and by subjecting major extensions of government intervention to judicial review in terms of general principle. Second, it restricts administrative discretion in the implementation of policy, thereby avoiding the more serious outcomes of bureaucratic behaviour. Third, it places over-riding authority for the control of market regulation in the hands of the judiciary, probably the least corruptible of all the possible control organisations and the most committed in term of its intellectual heritage to the maintenance of freedoms.[30] Fourth, by emphasising interventions in the form of clearly defined rules wherever possible rather than by *ad hoc* instruments, the true degree of coercion is widely publicised and all concerned are aware of the implicit diminution of their freedoms.

Of course, we are not dealing with nirvana, and the costs of law by enforcement must exercise some influence, even in a society constructed by reference to the liberal ethic, with inevitable discriminatory implications for the regulatory process. Let us briefly review this problem by reference to Stigler's important paper.[32] The goal of enforcement, as Stigler views it, is to achieve that degree of compliance with the rule of prescribed (or proscribed) behaviour that society believes that it can afford. With this in mind Stigler defines the properties of rational enforcement as follows:

(1) Expected penalties should increase with expected gains so that

there is no marginal net gain from larger offences. Let the criminal commit in a year S crimes of size Q, where Q is the monetary value to the criminal of the successful completion of the crime. The fraction p of crimes completed successfully (or the probability of successful completion of one crime) is a decreasing function of the amount of expenditure E undertaken by society to prevent and punish the crime. Hence $p = p(E,Q)$ or possibly $p = p(E,Q,S)$. The expected punishment is the fraction of crimes apprehended (and punished) times the punishment F. The condition for marginal deterrence is, for all Q:

$$\frac{d(pSQ)}{dQ} < \frac{d(1-p)SF}{dQ} \tag{8.1}$$

(2) The expenditures on prevention and enforcement should yield a diminution in offences, at the margin, equal to the return upon these resources in other areas. An increment of expenditures yields a return in reduced offences:

$$\sum_{Q'} \frac{d(pSQ')}{dE} = \text{marginal return on expenditures elsewhere} \tag{8.2}$$

where Q' is the monetary value of the offence to society.

Although this approach is Paretian in nature — though ignoring the redistributive implications — it has much to commend it from the liberal viewpoint. For at the present time, there can be no doubt in the field of economic regulation that the enforcement agencies use inappropriate and discriminatory techniques in determining the nature and extent of enforcement, usually in the form of seeking numerous, easy cases to dress up the records to the benefit perhaps of the frequent violator and the violator who does much damage. At least, the Stigler formula, or some variant of it, provides nondiscriminatory guidelines for the enforcement agencies and nondiscriminatory penalties for those who are successfully apprehended.

The rule of law, therefore, provides a framework for the liberal approach to market regulation. Liberal ethics provide the basis for the nature and pattern of actual interventions. Let us illustrate by reference to four areas where regulatory intervention is frequently discussed and implemented, namely the organisation of production, pollution externalities, enterprise monopoly and labour monopoly.

II THE ORGANISATION OF PRODUCTION

Despite recent contributions both to the theory of the firm and to the theory of organisational efficiency, Paretian welfare economics still embraces, for the most part, the neoclassical paradigm of the profit-maximising, cost-conscious enterprise, controlled by equity interests with the passive co-operation both of management and of shop-floor labour. Typically, productive services are incorporated into the individual utility function as negative arguments, without reference to the precise organisation of production, despite growing concern about the alleged problem of worker alienation. In chapter 5 we confronted the problem of alienation via the division of labour and suggested that it did not pose serious problems for the liberal economy. It is now necessary to explore a second potential cause of worker alienation — namely the wage system, which establishes an authority relationship between the worker and his employer — and to assess its significance, from the liberal position, for the organisation of production.[20]

The authority relationship consists in the worker's agreement that within some limits (defined both explicitly and implicitly by the terms of the employment contract) he will accept as the premises of his behaviour orders and instructions supplied to him by the organisation. From this standpoint, it follows that Marx was justified, at least in part, in contending that the employee's labour is 'not voluntary, but coerced; it is forced labour'. This is so even when the employment contract itself is accepted voluntarily, for, as we have argued repeatedly in this book, individuals do not necessarily value freedom as highly as liberals might wish.

Let us accept, with Dolan,[20] that alienation is a phenomenon resulting from certain aspects of economic organisation which are a function less of the type of property relations prevailing in society than of the level of industrial and technological development which it has attained. Clearly, in such circumstances those who value freedom highly will opt at the margin for occupations less susceptible to coercive authority. But what of those who are less overtly concerned about freedom, but who nevertheless will suffer 'wage system' alienation? Levy[28a] has argued, following Paretian methodology, that the prevailing level of alienation — the outcome of the worker's freedom of choice under conditions of scarcity — is optimal and that there is no incompatibility between alienation and freedom. Dolan,[20] for reasons with which we have sympathy, disagrees and asserts that liberals indeed should be concerned about coercion within the firm. The worker may, for example, achieve only a local optimum, unaware as a consequence of imperfect information that better solutions exist, and lock himself into an alienation syndrome, losing all initiative as a choosing individual. Serious external effects may flow from this syndrome when the habits of deference to authority are combined with a democratic political system, as we have already argued in this text. Furthermore, the individual who fails to make his life 'an act of meaningful self-expression' may well develop a hostility towards those who succeed. Thus Dolan:[20]

In many sectors of our society, the love of individual freedom has been replaced by the fear of the free individual. Lack of freedom breeds fear of freedom, and that in turn breeds intolerance, violence, and repression, making it impossible for the libertarian to do his own thing in peace. [p. 1093]

Thus liberals must be concerned about the existence of alienation, even if Paretians are not, and should seek out their own solutions to the problem, while recognising that choices may be required as a consequence of the conflict of freedoms. Let us now evaluate the implications of wage-system alienation by reference to the property rights model of economic organisation as outlined recently by Alchian and Demsetz:[1,22]

Typically, the firm is an organisation designed to increase productivity through team production — with team production of a product Z by two factors X_i and X_j defined by the condition

$$\frac{\partial^2 Z}{\partial X_i \partial X_j} \neq 0. \tag{8.3}$$

For obvious reasons, it is costly in team production to measure directly the separate marginal products of co-operating inputs, with the inference that 'shirking behaviour' cannot easily be discerned and regulated via simple market exchange. On the realistic assumption that arguments other than pecuniary wealth enter into individual utility functions, undetected shirking clearly is desirable and will occur in the absence of intervention. In the event that it is economical to estimate marginal productivities indirectly by observing or specifying input behaviour, there are returns to all factor inputs from some sort of central supervision designed to prevent the pursuit of non-pecuniary objectives to the pecuniary detriment of the entire team; in essence this is the coercive response to a public good problem. Fundamentally, this is the basis for the contractual organisation of inputs known as the classical capitalist firm, characterised by: (i) joint input production, (ii) several input owners, (iii) one party who is common to all the contracts of the joint inputs, (iv) who has rights to renegotiate any input's contract independently of contracts with other input owners, (v) who holds the residual claim, and (vi) who has the rights to sell his central contractual residual status.

The classical capitalist firm, thus defined, is created because of the need to monitor the activities of the team members. For each input member has a greater incentive to shirk in team production than in situations where his marginal product is more easily discerned since the effect of relaxing on his realised (reward) rate of substitution between output and leisure will be less than the effect on the true rate of substitution, to the detriment of others in the team. By appointing someone to specialise as a monitor of performance — and by inducing the person appointed to monitor efficiently via his entitlement to the residual claim on group earnings — the problem of shirking is minimised, to the advantage of all members of the team. The monitor's position is further strengthened by the provision of special contracting rights — as outlined in (iii) and (iv) above — and by allowing him the final entitlement to sell his central contractual status should the team situation so warrant. The classical capitalist firm is the outcome undoubtedly of free contracting between individuals, though the contracts provide the monitor with coercive property rights over the productive behaviour of fellow contractors. In so far as the classical capitalist firm has survived — and where capital requirements are not extensive it is still the typical organisational form — it has done so by providing a hierarchical structure in which one factor input is induced to maximise the difference between revenue and cost. No alternative so far has proved as effective in maximising organisational efficiency.

The classical capitalist firm is no longer typical of the advanced economies: the economies of raising large sums of equity capital by selling promises of future returns have accelerated its decline in favour of the corporate enterprise. Inevitably, however, the associated diffusion of ownership has brought with it severe monitoring problems which have necessitated the introduction of complex procedures designed to transfer decision authority to a small group within the enterprise. Incentives for the decision authority to monitor shirking (and not to shirk itself) are provided both by allowing the unrestricted sale of stock and transfer of proxies so that disgruntled stockholders may vent their disapproval, and by encouraging across-market and intra-firm competition from new groups of would-be managers, as well as by providing the present decision authority with some claim upon present and future residual returns. A vast literature in management science is devoted to the implications of alternative monitoring mechanisms for the maintenance of organisational efficiency. Inevitably, shirking can be controlled in the large corporation only at a cost in terms of the use of coercion as well as of incentives, with the precise balance between these measures varying from situation to situation. Significantly, however, the advent of corporate enterprise in no sense has disturbed the hierarchical form of business organisation — and this is indicative of the strength and persuasiveness of the shirking disposition.

In no sense is the foregoing analysis to be viewed as an apologia for the classical capitalist and the corporate enterprise organisation of production — indeed, nothing is further from our intention. There is nothing in our discussion that denies the right to any team to try out alternative organisational forms — labour control and profit-sharing spring readily to mind in view of the alienation issue — only to cast doubt upon their survival capacities in competitive conditions. Let us justify this pessimistic prediction for each in turn by reference to the shirking issue — recognising that the predictions do not run counter to twentieth-century experience.

Although the notion of 'workers' democracy' has a lengthy pedigree in Western social thought, the analytical concept of the labour-controlled firm only recently has been subjected to intensive consideration by economists. The idea that workers themselves should jointly undertake the monitoring responsibilities and should share in the residual returns of their team production has an intuitive appeal to many people who are perturbed by the alienation problem — why is it not more extensively employed? The answer lies in the shirking implications of such a change in the monitoring arrangements, especially in the large-team situation. There are two offsetting effects. Labour control on the one hand reduces the incentive to the central monitor to control shirking within the enterprise — in the event that the hierarchical monitoring procedure is retained at all — by reducing its claim upon the residual returns, thereby invoking shirking losses within the enterprise. However, the general sharing in the residual, implicit in labour control, on the other hand provides anti-shirking incentives, thereby reducing shirking losses. Presumably, the losses exceed the gains, since labour-controlled firms are rarely found in Western economies where such organisations in no sense are banned or penalised. Intuitively, such a result seems likely, given the public good problem implicit in such a widespread sharing of the returns to organisational efficiency.

Similarly is the profit-sharing organisational firm doomed in the large-team situation, with the losses at the central monitoring level almost certainly outweighing individual incentives, and with a predictable net increase in shirking losses to the team. Profit-sharing is more viable where small team sizes are involved and where the cost of specialised monitoring inputs is large relative to the associated improvements in organisational efficiency. Predictably, therefore, profit-sharing partnerships most frequently are encountered in the arts and in the professions, where a relatively freer rein is required on individual behaviour and where team co-operation is less important than individual performance.

Whatever the form of organisation, the shirking phenomenon will be the more pronounced the larger are the discretionary spoils available for subversion and the more protected is the organisation from competitive pressures. This feature of team production is now fully reflected in the anti-trust literature, where X-inefficiency is directly associated with corporate market power. For, when competition is unrestricted, the fear of potential bankruptcy, with ensuing unemployment and all the associated costs of job dislocation, will drive both management and labour into a fuller co-operation with the central monitoring objectives. Similarly, an efficient capital market, by exposing inefficient management to a takeover bid when the existing monitor is ineffective, will induce management co-operation at zero cost to the team. Thus is the personal and often highly coercive intervention of the central monitor substantially eliminated under competitive conditions — and arguably with some reduction in welfare losses from alienation. For, contrary to popular fantasy, it is quite possible to run a tight but happy organisation, especially when the team's livelihood is at risk.[11] Evidently, it is possible to run a slack but unhappy organisation disrupted by conflict and pervaded by central monitoring coercion. In this respect, competition is seen by liberals as offering increased freedoms in the organisation of production.

The dilemma concerning the organisation of production is not always so simply resolved in practice, however, since many organisations do not face the survivorship ordeal. Let us therefore confront the most difficult case of all as a means of demonstrating the liberal position. Suppose that coercion is more severe in capitalist and corporate organisations than in labour-controlled and profit-sharing organisations and that alienation is more pronounced, but that efficiency is greater — arguably, this is indeed the case. Would this justify liberal action to support the latter and to restrict the former organisation forms? At first sight, there seems to be a straightforward conflict between freedom of contract and freedom from coercion, as property rights in coercion are exchanged for material considerations — and previously we have urged that such a conflict ought to be resolved in favour of freedom from coercion. In fact, however, another, and in our view a decisive, factor must be considered. If labour-controlled or profit-sharing solutions were to be made viable, in the assumed situation, the arbitrary intervention of Leviathan is required, with damaging implications both for equality before the law and for the curtailment of public power. By leaving the organisational form to be determined by private contracting, no such implications follow. For the liberal, desirous of chaining Leviathan — especially with respect to arbitrary interventions — there is but one solution. The most efficient organisation form must be allowed to evolve, and to dominate less efficient forms, always provided that it is the product of freely negotiated contracts, even at some cost in terms of individual freedoms. Liberals no doubt will emphasise the advantages of policing via the chequebook rather than the whip, and some will devote their ingenuity to developing non-coercive techniques for moderating X-inefficiency.[11,12,13] But, in essence, liberals are neutral and open-minded as to the organisation of production within the private sector.

III   THE PROBLEM OF POLLUTION EXTERNALITIES

Let us assume an initial situation in which a large number of producers possess property rights in the effluent-carrying capacity of a particular tidal water which they utilise by discharging degradable effluent to the detriment of a large number of consumers of the river environment. To simplify discussion, let us assume that the producers and consumers in question are identified and are aware of the existence of Pareto-relevant marginal externalities. Figure 8.1 depicts the initial position. The curve BC is the horizontal summation of the marginal valuation curves of the separate producers, since pollution is entirely private in its economic good capacity. OA is the vertical summation of the negative marginal valuation curves of the separate consumers, since environmental quality here is a public good. In the initial property-right situation, the equilibrium market situation is at C, where the marginal benefits to the dischargers reach zero, and losses represented by the triangle OAC are imposed upon consumers of the river environment. The Pareto-optimal rate of discharge, in the given property-right situation, however, is at E, where the marginal valuation curves intersect. If bargaining were possible, the environmental consumers would bribe the producers to abate their rates of discharge from C to E, thereby eliminating the mutual gains from

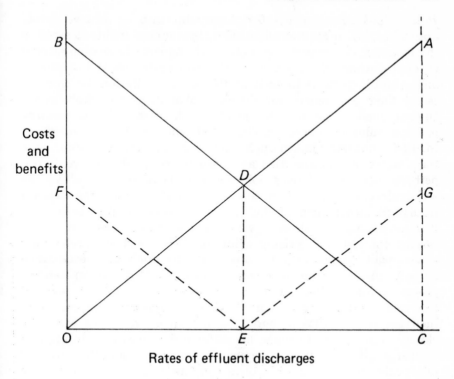

Rates of effluent discharges

Figure 8.1

trade and internalising the externality. This is ruled out, in our example, on grounds of free-riding in the large-numbers situation and of prohibitive bargaining costs. Nor is the problem to be resolved by reversing the property rights; for similar bargaining impediments then would imply that suboptimal discharge rates would attain. In such circumstances, the conventional Paretian response is collective intervention to shift the rate of effluent discharge from C (or O) to E. The traditional policy instrument (ignoring the redistributive consequences for the most part) is the imposition of a Pigovian tax price on discharges such as to shift the discharge benefit curve from BC to FE. Buchanan and Stubblebine[8] have pointed out that such a solution fails to satisfy the full optimality conditions which require a simultaneous marginal subsidy to the environmental consumers such as to shift the marginal cost curve from OA to EG. We have already argued (in chapter 2) that the Buchanan—Stubblebine solution is the more sensitive to the Paretian ethic.

In practice, of course, the deterministic elegance of figure 8.1 has only limited value when dealing with problems of river pollution with serious consequences for those who wish to achieve Pareto optimality. When natural scientists themselves are unable to agree on the technical consequences for the environment of specified rates of effluent discharges, consumers of the river environment, not surprisingly, find it difficult to evaluate the cost of pollution, let alone to reveal their preferences for discharge abatement accurately in the large-numbers situation. In practice, therefore, the consumers' marginal valuation curve is unlikely to be more than a figment of the theorist's imagination. In such circumstances, resort to some arbitrary water quality standard as a basis for collective intervention is perhaps inevitable, if river pollution is to be attacked at all via the economic calculus. And in this second-best situation the case for regulation rather than pricing has been advanced from within the Paretian dogma. To this issue, we must now address attention.

The conventional pricing solution,[2,3,4,5,31] once preliminary water quality standards are established, is for prices to be established initially on a trial-and-error basis and to be adjusted in an iterative process as information on producer reactions accrues. Charges would be levied on all polluters according to the volume and composition of their respective effluent, and their abatement reactions would be closely monitored. Changes in preference intensities for effluent discharge, given the pricing scheme, would show up in the under- or over-achievement of the objective and this would constitute a case for reappraising the tax prices. The provision of a uniform charge per unit of effluent discharged — with profit-maximising polluters abating discharges to the point where marginal abatement costs are equal to the established price — ensures a minimum cost solution with the cost of abatement, at the margin, equal in all firms. Until recently, environmental economists, almost without exception, have emphasised the efficiency advantages of pricing over regulation even in second-best situations.

But no longer so. In a challenging paper, perhaps the first of many such, given the dirigiste tastes of certain welfare economists, Burrows[9] has thrown down the regulation gauntlet, in presenting a reasoned case for a consent solution. He has pointed out, for example, that if the initial price, in the pricing solution, is not close to that eventually established firms will be induced to adopt more or fewer pollution prevention processes than are required to minimise production cost subject to the overall water quality objective. Costly lock-in effects may ensue as firms react to prices that are not maintained in the longer term. If, to avoid this, producers were to bide their time until equilibrium prices emerged, however, the iterative process would not identify the appropriate tax price solution. To counter the suggestion that arbitrary consent decisions would result in wide variations in the marginal abatement costs of separate producers — with consequential inefficiencies — Burrows suggests that the regulators might impose uniform consents on all dischargers unless the discharger was able to demonstrate 'exceptional' abatement costs. In this way, preferences might be revealed and lock-in effects avoided, and the water quality objective might be achieved more efficiently than in the pricing solution.

Inevitably, the debate between pricing and regulation, conducted within the Paretian ground rules, centres attention exclusively upon the respective efficiency implications of the two approaches, posing the empirical issue as to which is the more cost-effective in achieving water quality objectives. No other considerations enter in this Paretian nirvana. Scant regard is paid to the public choice implications of the two approaches and none at all to the freedom consequences. Yet once these issues are incorporated into the policy debate, as they must be following liberalist philosophy, the scenario quite dramatically is changed.[4]

In devising corrective measures to be imposed by the State in cases of pollution externalities, environmental economists for the most part have been remiss in failing to recognise the possible effects of individual maximising behaviour in the political process, arguably with significant implications for the pricing—regulation debate. Recent papers have attempted to redress this omission by incorporating public choice criteria into the pollution control debate, with results that are directly relevant to the present discussion.

The first, by Goetz,[24] utilizes economic models of political behaviour to describe the nature of equilibrium political decisions about environmental pricing systems, and defines important difficulties in securing allocatively efficient solutions via state intervention. In particular, employing the two-party, majority-voting model, and assuming that the preferences of voters over the various environmental states is single-peaked, political equilibrium can be predicted by reference to the median preference theorem previously discussed. On this basis, Goetz determines that consistency between political equilibrium and Pareto-optimality requires that, for the median voter, the marginal personal benefits from the effluent charge revenues must precisely equal the marginal personal damages imposed by the environmental pollutant. This would happen only if 'compensation payments' derived from effluent charge revenues were distributed to members of a majority voting bloc in strict equality with the marginal evaluation that each voter places on changes in environmental quality — an occurrence the probability of which is close to zero.

Furthermore, the cost and the benefit functions for environmental pollution are not characterised by perfect knowledge, and this also has damaging consequences for environmental pollution control by political action. The producer valuations, it is true, are derivable via market tests — such as those discussed above — since pollution benefits are assumed to satisfy privateness conditions. The consumer valuation curves, however, are not so easily derived, for public good reasons, and attempts to estimate the aggregate valuation curve will be distorted by all the usual preference-falsification problems. In the Goetz situation, where compensation is paid out of effluent charge revenues, voters will overstate their marginal pollution costs, with the inference that pollution abatement will be excessive. In an alternative formulation,[31] where effluent charges are lost in general revenues, free-rider problems will imply inadequate pollution abatement. In either case, the impact of pressure group lobbying must also be accounted for. A Pareto-optimal outcome, from all this confusion of inefficiencies, would be the product of chance indeed.

The implications of the Goetz contribution are applicable equally to the pricing and to the regulatory solution in so far as the predictable rate of abatement is concerned. But, as Beavis and Rowley[4] have demonstrated, there are further public choice implications, which impinge differentially upon the two approaches. In the United Kingdom, certainly, the most seriously polluted tidal waters are located in regions of relatively high labour unemployment, and regulatory bodies are susceptible to a general temptation to accede to increased pollution as the price to be paid for creating new or retaining existing job opportunities. Any public authority charged with the task of pollution control in such locations would be confronted by employment pressure group activities supported by readership-conscious regional press campaigns. A pricing solution to the effluent discharge problem, especially one featuring a uniform charge per unit of discharge, offers protection against the browbeating of regulators into discriminatory practices — and the risk of excessively low rates of charges in high unemployment areas could be obviated by central government decisions as to the water quality objective. By contrast, any consent scheme — other than the hopelessly uneconomic rule of uniform discharge rates for all producers — provides immense discretionary power to the regulators, exposing them to the greatest possible pressure and temptation. The likely combination of weakness and corruption, in such circumstances, will

provide ample opportunity for powerful, unscrupulous and em-
ployment-intensive but dirty corporations to subvert the regulatory
process.

The intervention of liberal criteria into the pollution control
debate further strengthens the case for a pricing solution, where
collective intervention is countenanced to all. For the pricing
solution — with its emphasis upon uniformity of effluent charges —
satisfies the liberal precept of equality before the law, while
simultaneously minimising the discretionary power of the regulatory
body, whose function is reduced to that of providing metering
mechanisms in the equilibrium situation. By contrast, the consent
solution provides almost inevitably for inequality of treatment as
consents are more or less arbitrarily allocated and adjusted, and it
offers immense powers to the regulators and to those who manage to
control them — powers that foster corruption and coercion. To the
liberal, therefore, consent regulation is anathema in the pollution
externality situation. No feasible increase in economic efficiency
(itself unlikely anyway) could compensate for the loss of freedom
that consent regulation implies.

Three alternatives to the tax price solution yet remain for liberal
consideration. The first simply is to take no action concerning the
externality other than clearly to determine property rights in favour
of or against the 'polluters'. In the absence of negotiated settlement,
it might then be presumed that preferences were insufficiently
intense, in whatever direction, to counterbalance the initial property
right decision — which itself would reflect median voter preferences
as expressed in an imperfect political market. Given the many
weighty problems of public intervention — transaction costs, inefficiency, corruption and coercion — this solution cannot be ruled out
for the less tractable but small-numbers case of pollution externality,
and indeed it is frequently employed in practice. In the large-
numbers situation, however, severe problems of under- or over-
pollution — with implied losses of efficiency — might remain un-
resolved as a consequence of bargaining impediments. A second
alternative, due to Buchanan,[7] is designed explicitly to reduce
bargaining costs and overcome the free-rider problem in the
large-numbers case. It deserves close liberal consideration.

Essentially, Buchanan recommends a shift in the institutional
setting which is designed to eliminate the publicness aspects of
large-numbers negotiations on externality issues — and this involves a
shift from a many-consumer to a one-consumer model. The
institutional changes require only that a single bargaining agent be
authorised to act on behalf of the 'consumers' with no directions as

to the specific outcomes that may be forthcoming in his negotiations with the separate 'producers' of the externality. The size of the coalition would be determined by the limit of 'publicness' inter-action and the agent would act on behalf only of his constituents, thereby enabling separate negotiations for groups unrelated by publicness interactions. The agent would be empowered to bargain for either *more* or less of the externality-generating activity with property rights defined on a *status quo* rate of pollution at a stipulated point in pre-intervention time. If that rate turned out to be excessive, the agent could purchase from the producers agree-ments for reductions; if it proved suboptimal, the producers could compensate the agent for extensions. The final outcome, whatever the direction, would rest on the process of bilateral bargaining between agency and producers.

The agent cannot act, of course, in the absence of information as to the preferences of the members of his consumer coalition, whether he is assessing tax shares or compensation shares in the financial settlement. Here, the uncertainty surrounding the property-right outcome is instrumental in eliminating the problem of eliciting true preferences, which is implicit in the public good situation, by making the free-rider dilemma work in offsetting ways. If individuals believe they will be taxed they have an incentive to understate their preferences for pollution abatement. If they believe they will be recompensed, they have an incentive to overstate their true evalua-tions. Uncertainties as to just which solution will evolve should force them to compromise on a close approximation to their true preferences, especially where periodic renegotiations are allowed.

We do not pretend that the Buchanan approach is simple, or that its transaction costs are low; nor do we believe that it is universally applicable — indeed, where the consumers themselves are not easily identified, or where they are 'unreasonably' hostile to the coalition, it cannot be applied. But in many areas of pollution, where the parties are easily identified and where the costs of large-numbers bargaining otherwise are prohibitive, it merits liberal attention. By helping individual citizens to help themselves, in an institutional setting that minimises coercion and extols the maximum possible degree of decentralisation, the liberal precepts are satisfied without noticeable loss to the Paretian welfare calculus.

The third alternative, due to Dales,[15] consists of creating a water control board which would establish a market in pollution rights. Initially, the board would survey the quantity and nature of effluent pollution in the river, and would establish some common denomi-nator of pollution units as a reference base. On this basis, a total number of pollution-equivalent shares for one year's discharges would be derived. By issuing only a proportion of these shares, the board could engineer water quality improvement and give the shares a market value, to be determined at an auction attended by all potential polluters. Firms would be required to own at least enough shares to match their effluent discharges, and would be required to bid shares away from other firms if this appeared to be less costly than implementing pollution abatement measures. In essence, the Dales solution achieves the same result as the tax price solution, but more precisely in terms of target achievement and probably at a lower cost in administration. In the small-numbers case, however, it is susceptible to producer collusion, though such collusion could result only in inefficient abatement processes and not in any failure to achieve the board's water quality target, always provided that the penalties for transgressions were appropriately steep.

In principle, the Buchanan—Dales alternatives to tax prices appear to be attractive when viewed in terms of liberal criteria, in that they satisfy efficient abatement conditions without the coercive implications of explicit government tax price decisions. Certainly, pilot experiments should be encouraged to test out the reliability of these instruments in real-world conditions. In cases where, for particular reasons, they cannot be effectively implemented, liberals strongly advocate the preferability of the tax price to the consent solution, whatever the respective Paretian efficiency merits of the two policy instruments.

IV   THE PROBLEM OF ENTERPRISE MONOPOLY

Profit-maximising monopolies violate the necessary conditions for a Paretian optimum with respect both to exchange and to technical (X) efficiency.[10,11,12,13,28] As such, they have been the butt of much criticism in the welfare economics literature, with interventionist recommendations ranging from anti-trust to public regulation and even public ownership. Recently, however, with the formal incorporation of scale economy possibilities into the welfare calculus, the Paretian position on enterprise monopoly has become ambiguous, and complex welfare trade-offs are now seen to be necessary.[11,30] For this latter purpose, the Harberger social welfare function[25] (cf. chapter 3) has been extensively applied. Within this framework, the only criterion is economic efficiency. Only in so far as individuals themselves valued freedom and introduced it explicitly as a relevant argument could freedom considerations influence the policy outcome. Needless to say, freedom considerations are not so introduced in the Paretian literature.

Clearly, this is the point of departure for liberals, who deny that individual sovereignty is to be identified with individual liberty, and who see a major threat to important freedoms in the concentration of economic power, whether in the hands of private parties or of the State. To take account of the freedom issue, while yet upholding the trade-off approach, it would be necessary to moderate the Harberger social welfare function. Let us illustrate by reference to the problem of natural monopoly.[14,17,18,29,30,33,34]

i   The natural monopoly problem

Natural monopoly is defined as a situation in which production is characterised by falling long-run marginal cost throughout the relevant output range. In such situations, a policy of *laissez-faire* must result in monopoly and efficiency losses for society. The conventional Paretian solution to market failure of this kind is public regulation (in the USA) or public enterprise (in the United Kingdom). Liberals reject both alternatives as being incompatible with important freedoms. Figure 8.2 summarises the policy dilemma.

The demand curve and the associated marginal revenue curve in the monopoly solution are as conventionally drawn. The long-run average cost curve AC_c and marginal cost curve MC_c reflect the cost conditions attainable in competitive markets, with X-inefficiency minimised. The long-run average cost curve AC_x and the marginal cost curve MC_x reflect the cost conditions attainable in monopolised markets (both private and public). *Laissez-faire* would provide price OP_1 and output OQ_1 and not, as textbooks typically still suggest, price OP_1' and output OQ_1'. Anti-trust-enforced competition would provide an average cost-price solution, without X-inefficiency and with price located on AC_c, at a position reflecting the degree of fragmentation required by anti-trust. A 'competitive bidding' solution[17] designed to enforce average cost pricing without X-inefficiency while preserving single-firm production, would provide price OP_3 and output OQ_3. Public regulation designed to enforce marginal cost pricing with losses made good by lump sum transfers would provide price OP_2 and output OQ_2, frustrated by X-inefficiency from satisfying the marginal conditions of price OP_2'. and output OQ_2'. The Harberger trade-offs for each of these solutions are depicted in figure 8.3.

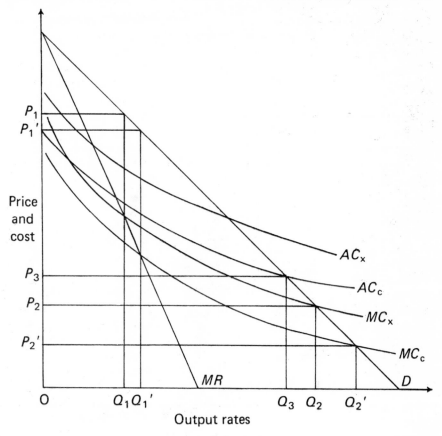

Figure 8.2

Here, the market demand curve D and the marginal revenue curve MR are as in figure 8.2. In the absence of intervention, the natural monopolist would operate on the X-inefficient short-run cost curve, AC_M, at price OP_1 and at output OQ_1. By comparison with the theoretical optimum price OP_2 and output OQ_2, there is a welfare loss (entirely at the expense of consumers) reflected approximately by the triangle $AHAC_1$, and by the X-inefficiency loss of P_2P_3CH. The additional transfer from consumers to the producer — P_3P_1AC — is neutral from the Harberger social welfare standpoint.

Public regulation would provide price OP_3 and output rate OQ_3, with X-inefficient marginal cost (long-run) equated with price. By comparison with the theoretical optimum, there is a welfare loss reflected in the triangle AC_MJAC_1 and in the area $P_3AC_MJP_2$. By

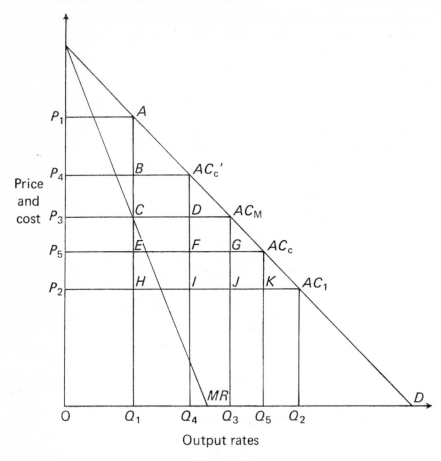

Figure 8.3

comparison with *laissez-faire*, however, regulation provides an un-ambiguous gain (to consumers) of $ACAC_M$.

Anti-trust fragmentation, involving production on the short-run cost curve AC_c', would provide price OP_4 and output OQ_4. By comparison with the theoretical optimum, there is a welfare loss reflected in the triangle $AC_c'IAC_1$ and in the area $P_4P_2IAC_c'$. By comparison with *laissez-faire*, there is ambiguity, with gains of $ABAC_2'$ but losses of P_4P_3CB. By comparison with public regula-tion, there is an unambiguous welfare loss reflected in the triangle $AC_c'DAC_M$ and in the area $P_4P_3DAC_c'$.

Competitive bidding would provide price OP_5 and output OQ_5 with X-efficient long-run average cost equated with price. By comparison with the theoretical optimum, there is a welfare loss reflected in the triangle AC_cKAC_1 and in the area $P_5P_2KAC_c$. However, competitive bidding is unambiguously superior, in this example, to *laissez-faire*, to regulation and to anti-trust in terms of the welfare trade-off criterion.

The Harberger social welfare function thus is seen to offer a useful analytical framework, given its value premises, for a comparative institutions approach to the natural monopoly problem. Of the alternative solutions scrutinized — other than the theoretical nirvana optimum itself — much clearly depends on the relative cost levels from which the price/output outcomes are derived — and this is an empirical problem of some considerable complexity. Nevertheless to those who endorse the approach — and after all this is the Harberger 'final solution' — the signposts are clear if the road itself is somewhat winding and uneven. Pragmatic investigation, on a case-by-case basis, is to be employed — no doubt to the delight and the pecuniary advantage of the cost—benefit analysts.

For those who endorse the pragmatic, piecemeal approach to policy problems, while adhering to liberalist values, the Harberger social welfare function may be utilised following appropriate adjustment.[29] In principle, the required adjustment is simple. The benefits arising from large-scale production, as trapped by the Harberger social welfare function, should be discounted by a factor which increases (in our view at an exponential rate) as the degree of associated market power (appropriately defined) itself increases. There is sufficient flexibility in the choice of discount exponent to satisfy all liberal viewpoints, for the rate is bounded only by the limits of zero and infinity. It *is* important, however, that a standard discount exponent should be chosen (despite inevitable controversy), that this exponent should be widely publicised and that it should be applied universally. Otherwise, the precept of equality before the law will be transgressed, with all that implies for the potential coercion of minorities.

The thorny problem remains, of course, of defining market power and of devising an effective index of changes in such power — a problem common to all but the *laissez-faire* solution. To this there is no easy answer. On the assumption that the market itself is tolerably well defined — with some regard for cross-elasticities of demand — and that potential as well as actual commodity substitutes are taken into account, we suggest that an index of market power should incorporate some assessment of the probabilities of effective price leadership and collusion as well as of single firm dominance.

Following Stigler, the most appropriate barometer of these various sources of market power is the Herfindahl Index:

$$H = \sum_{i=1}^{i=n} S_i^2 \qquad (8.4)$$

where S_i is the market share of the ith firm in an industry comprising n firms.

The Herfindahl Index is a measure of relative concentration which is highly sensitive to changes in market structure, ranging from a value of zero in the case of perfect competition to a value of unity in the case of pure monopoly. If the liberal discount factor were to be based upon the Herfindahl Index, the freedom implications of growing market power would be effectively included in the analytics of the social welfare trade-off. Following liberal philosophy, we would further suggest that the enforcement mechanism should be entrusted to the courts in order to maintain the precept of equality before the law and to protect individuals from unnecessary extensions in the arbitrary powers of Leviathan. Furthermore, in the event that public regulation yet should prove the most attractive solution, following a liberalist assessment, we would urge that the regulatory authority should be required to satisfy the conditions of the rule of law as outlined both in chapter 5 and in sections of the present chapter.

ii   Non-discretionary anti-trust

By centring attention exclusively on the polar extreme of the enterprise monopoly problem, we have presented the case for pragmatic inquiry in its most favourable light. It is now time to extend the liberal discussion to the problem of enterprise monopoly as a whole, arguably with significant implications for the pattern of intervention. For, at best, pragmatic investigation is a complex exercise — costly, time-consuming and ultimately subjective — and of only passing validity, given the speed of economic change. At worst, it creates discretionary power, which even courts upon occasion may be tempted to abuse, with the possibility of inequality of coercion which is offensive to liberal prejudices. As we have urged in chapter 5, clear-cut rules are essential if the judicial approach is to function effectively in the delimitation and the protection of freedoms.

Inevitably, any approach other than that of pragmatism must involve harsh decisions in which beneficial monopolies are destroyed or in which detrimental monopolies are tolerated. We are fully aware of this limitation of the constitutional rule. Yet, in our view, there is a compelling case for such an approach to the enterprise monopoly problem.[30] Recent evidence[28,30] suggests that the incidence of scale economies has been exaggerated by conventional texts on industrial organisation but that X-inefficiency — which until very recently was ignored — is widely evident in monopolistic markets. If accepted, this evidence tips the balance, even of the unmodified Harberger approach, in favour of anti-trust, at least in markets equivalent in size to those of the USA and of the European Economic Community. Once transaction cost considerations and liberal prejudices are further accounted for, the balance of advantage shifts decisively in favour of the anti-trust solution.

Non-discretionary anti-trust rejects the notion of reviewing enterprise monopoly pragmatically in favour of a dogmatic treatment based on rules. Essentially, such an approach would prohibit all agreements in restraint of trade, penalising infringements by criminal action in the courts and by multiple damage civil suits, as in the United States. Court discretion would be allowed only as to whether or not an agreement could be said to exist, and even this discretion would be circumscribed by rules. Mergers, acquisitions and even the internal expansion of independent corporations would be prohibited where the result was a market share, correctly defined, in excess of a prescribed percentage, which would be universally applicable and widely publicised. In the United States the merger guidelines established by the Department of Justice might provide acceptable safeguards, once they became unequivocally applicable. Once free trade is fully established within the European Economic Community, the same guidelines — based on EEC market definitions — might be applied for domestic purposes by the United Kingdom and other member countries. Transgressions, unless clearly accidental, would be penalised and would be rectified by divestment procedures. Court discretion would be restricted to the process of estimating the market shares of corporations suspected of infringing the law.

In countries where non-discretionary anti-trust formerly was non-existent (as in all of Western Europe) or was not forcefully applied (as in the USA) existing monopolies would have to be dispersed, if equality before the law was to be actuated. In these instances, however, penalties are inappropriate, in that they would be retrospective, and divestments even may be unnecessary. Attacks on entry barriers, on tariff protection and on other subsidies, supported by prohibitions on enterprise growth and on all further acquisitions, would normally suffice to restore competitive markets. Once the anti-trust structural conditions are satisfied the normal non-discretionary rules would be applied. Within a decade, all but a handful of monopolists — each characterized by stagnant or by declining total markets — would be rooted out by such procedures.

No doubt the critics of the structural approach to the enterprise monopoly problem will point to the uneven link between structure and performance and will re-emphasise the truism that suitable structural conditions cannot guarantee competition. We do not deny their point. But, with coercive taxation eliminated (see chapter 7), considerable incentives would exist for active competition, if not always with market expansion objectives, then certainly with profit motives to the fore. Competition in the sense here implied would not achieve Pareto-optimality, since it would result in average and not in marginal cost pricing solutions. X-inefficiency would be a prime sufferer in such a market environment — and the freedoms of choice in consumption and in occupation undoubtedly would be maximised.

Realistically, a small residual of markets — far fewer than the conventional regulation literature would allow — would be characterised by technical scale economies sufficiently marked as to present an insurmountable barrier to anti-trust procedures — in certain respects paralleling the public good problem. As we have urged in chapter 6, this does not imply necessarily the public provision of the commodity in question, nor even its public regulation. Indeed, in cases where the exclusion principle is operative, a competitive bidding solution[17] has much to recommend it, especially to those of liberal persuasion. Potential suppliers of the decreasing cost commodity would be required to bid for contracts with prospective buyers through a representative agency, over time periods designed to minimise dislocation costs while avoiding long-period lock-ins. The rival who offered buyers the most favourable terms (as determined by buyer representatives on some majority vote basis) would obtain the entire production contract, hiring the capital and labour required to fulfil their contracts. The bids submitted, of necessity, would relate prices inversely to the required scale of operation (suitably defined) and no doubt would be indexed for inflation over the period of the contracts. Where the number of bidders was large the competitive bidding solution would simulate the competitive market while preserving single-firm production. The role of the courts would be restricted to that of ensuring that contracts were honoured and that breaches were appropriately penalised.

We have suggested elsewhere[29] that the practical problems associated with competitive bidding are considerable and rule out its general applicability to the natural monopoly problem. As a residual solution in the least tractable cases, however, it is an attractive proposition at least by comparison with the collectivist alternatives. It provides considerable protection for freedom of choice in consumption and minimises the risk to political freedoms commonly associated with enterprise monopoly. Unfortunately, competitive bidding does not protect freedom of choice in occupation — though it does not worsen it by comparison with the collectivist solutions. As always, perfection is unattainable in the practical situation and the best is the enemy of the good.

Finally, we would comment on the public choice implications of non-discretionary anti-trust as here outlined. On this we have no illusions. Utopianism would suggest that universal consent should be obtained for the non-discretionary anti-trust approach as a decision rule for enterprise monopoly before enshrining it as a constitutional rule. This, we recognise to be impossible. Practical politics would suggest that the median preference voter must be convinced of the benefits of the decision rule, and liberals must do battle in this realm if they are to succeed. The task is no easy one, since voters typically are ill-informed on anti-trust and ambivalent as to its application, whereas producer pressure groups are quite clear as to the benefits from monopoly and recognise the returns to successful lobbying. At a time of economic crisis, such as is now the case, the climate perhaps is most receptive to proposals of institutional change. Let liberals take the fullest possible advantage of current voter doubts as to the benefits to be derived from giant enterprise!

V   THE PROBLEM OF LABOUR MONOPOLY

Although the unionised proportion of the working population has declined consistently in most Western economies throughout the postwar period, this does not imply — as liberal economists like Friedman[21] have suggested — that the problem of labour monopoly is one of declining importance. Rather, the high-employment commitments of all postwar governments — implying in certain extreme instances that governments stand prepared to finance any rate of inflation that arises from the collective bargaining process — have rendered society extremely vulnerable to union monopoly power. Let us review the economic impact of unionisation upon the wage rate bargain on certain simplifying assumptions, before subjecting the labour monopoly problem to a liberal re-examination.

According to the neoclassical economic paradigm, labour receives a wage rate equal to the value of its marginal product only in perfectly competitive markets — as a direct consequence of the inability of individual firms to influence either commodity or factor prices. We have already emphasised (cf. chapter 1) that perfect competition is a theoretical construct, rarely if ever encountered in the real world. Once commodity demand functions take on a negative slope at the enterprise level, and this may be the result of enterprise monopoly or of brand differentiation in otherwise competitive markets, labour receives a wage rate equal only to its marginal revenue product, with consequential 'monopolistic exploitation' as defined by Joan Robinson. In the further event that a single enterprise should dominate the market for a particular category of labour, that category of labour receives less than its marginal revenue product, with consequential 'monopsonistic exploitation' as defined by Joan Robinson. It is noteworthy that anti-trust interventions may remove monopsonistic exploitation but cannot remove monopolistic exploitation except by imposing perfectly competitive markets. These alternative outcomes are depicted in figure 8.4. VMP_L represents the value of the marginal product of labour curve, MRP_L its marginal revenue product curve, S_L its supply curve, and MEI_L its marginal expense of input curve under conditions of monopsony. OW_c and OL_1 represent respectively the wage rate and the labour employed in perfectly competitive markets, OW_M and OL_2 the wage rate and labour employed when monopolistic competition exists in the commodity market, and OW_{MN} and OL_3 the wage rate and labour employed with monopoly in the commodity market and with monopsony in the labour market. The unionisation of labour can eliminate 'monopsonistic exploitation' essentially by persuading or by coercing labour to act as though the relevant section of the labour supply curve was infinitely elastic at the chosen wage rate. Unionisation cannot obviate 'monopolistic exploitation', which is a feature of conditions in the commodity market. There is no unique unionisation solution, since much depends upon the objective function of those who represent their labour membership. At one extreme, the union may attempt to achieve maximum employment for its members, by establishing the *de facto* supply curve at $W_M a S_L$ and the associated MEI_L curve of $W_M ab MEI_L$, achieving the wage rate OW_M and the labour employment OL_2. At another extreme, the union may decide to maximise the wage rate at the existing labour employment level by establishing the *de facto* supply curve at $W_x d S_L$ and the associated MEI_L curve at $W_x de MEI_L$, with a consequential wage rate OW_x at labour employment OL_3. Evidently,

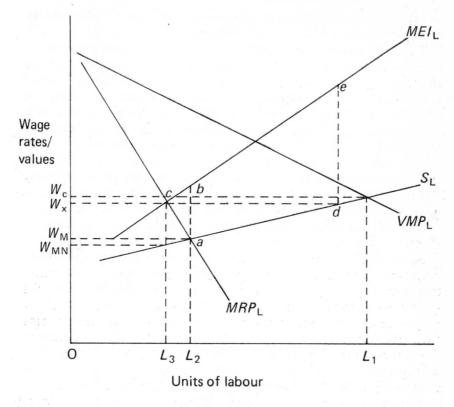

Figure 8.4

there are many other outcomes. Clearly, however, in neoclassical terms, unionisation cannot avoid the essential trade-off between wages and employment which is given by the slope of the *MRP* curve, once 'monopsonistic exploitation' has been eliminated — and much will depend upon union voting rules as to which objective is adopted, given the inevitable conflict of interest among the union membership.

These alternative outcomes all rest of course upon the assumptions of the neoclassical paradigm, which themselves are far from always satisfied by real-world conditions. For instance, profit maximisation does not necessarily operate in non-competitive markets, nor does the assumption of cost efficiency necessarily apply. Nor is the real wage rate—employment equilibrium necessarily stable, even when it is attained, in economies where the interrelationship between microeconomic wage-rate decisions and macroeconomic inflation is close and where inflation exercises a differential impact upon the various markets. How must the theory of union behaviour be adjusted to take account of such realities?

First, the presence of discretionary profit, in the case of private or of public monopolies, implies that union concern will extend beyond the wage-rate issue to the task of subverting profit in the form of X-inefficiency.[11] Individuals themselves can shirk, it is true, but their shirking is much more susceptible to policing measures than is organised union shirking designed to establish an unnecessarily slow work rate, overmanning and excessively lengthy work breaks and to defend individuals who adhere to such restrictions by collective solidarity. Furthermore, where individuals who find shirking irksome run the gauntlet of their union endeavours (or reject the union) it is predictable that coercive measures will be applied by union officials to prevent the disintegration of their policies. Where the union is powerful, such coercion may not be preventable.

Secondly, where the competitive pressures to maximise profit are inoperative, as is often the case with public enterprise, bureaucracies and private monopolies, the unions may be able to avoid the employment—wage rate trade-off, or at least to soften its impact, by bargaining on redundancy constraints as one facet of the wage-rate deal. Size-conscious management, sheltered from the criticism of their government employers or shareholders, may be more than willing to engage in such a contract, especially where subsidies are confidently anticipated in the event of commercial difficulties.

Thirdly, once the expectation is established that high wage settlements will be cushioned by inflation as vote-conscious governments scramble to satisfy the high-employment prejudices of the median voters, such trade-off constraints as formerly existed will be weakened for both the enterprise and the union in collective bargaining, and the structure of society itself may be in jeopardy — but we shall abstract ourselves from the inflation problem in the present section, reserving this topic for the final section of the book.

What then, should be done to handle the problem of union monopoly in a democratic society? On this important issue, the Paretians have almost nothing to offer, constrained as they are by their inability to tackle problems with income distribution implications. In principle, top-level Paretian optima cannot obtain unless labour receives the value of its marginal product (necessary if the income—leisure relationship is not to suffer) and unless production satisfies the conditions of technical efficiency. In both these respects, union behaviour presently is deleterious, since high wage-rate objectives typically dominate high-employment objectives and shirking measures are actively defended by union representatives.

Strangely, Paretians remain, for the most part, silent on such matters, preferring to pass judgement on enterprise rather than labour monopolies. Liberals, however, are not afflicted by this apparent inconsistency.[26]

Liberals pass judgement upon the unions fundamentally in terms of their impact upon the freedoms outlined in chapter 5, and on this basis they find them wanting. The fault does not lie in unionisation and collective bargaining itself, which is justifiable by reference to the handicap of labour when negotiating with capital owing to relative lack of capital reserves. Rather, unions are to be condemned for acts of coercion, which are not central to their existence, but which occur in the pursuit of their objectives. Essentially, coercion arises in an attempt to monopolise the supply of labour to an enterprise.

Figure 8.4 illustrates that unions will be the more successful in their collective bargaining the more they are able to control all labour potentially available to the enterprise — in the limit providing a horizontal supply curve at the selected wage rate. Unfortunately, from the union viewpoint, a complete labour monopoly is rarely attainable on the basis of free association, since there are always those who stand to gain from private negotiations with prospective employers. Inevitably, the unions wish to coerce such recalcitrants into co-operation with their chosen strategies, if not on the basis of special property rights in coercion, then by the violation of individual rights by more or less violent means. In this process, fundamental liberal freedoms are transgressed.

The methods of coercion are various, their consequences more or less severe. At the minimum, a worker may be coerced into union membership, restrictive practices, go-slows and strikes by moral suasion and by social pressuring which only peripherally are open to liberal suspicion. At the other extreme, conformity may be extracted via the threat and implementation of violence to his person, to his relatives and to his property, as union members contemptuously ignore the protection of the rule of law. Equally effectively, but with greater guile, coercion may be gilded with the trimmings of legal protection as unions extract from governments special privileges — the right to the closed shop, to conspire, to picket, to trespass and to victimise spring easily to mind — which constitute a basis for effective monopoly behaviour. Such developments are in conflict with equality before the law, which is a cornerstone of liberal philosophy and essential to the preservation of freedoms.

There can be no doubt that, in the not-too-distant past, unions themselves suffered damaging discrimination and that they have had to struggle hard for equality before the law. In no sense do we advocate a return to such coercion. It must be recognised, however, that unions have now won *more* than equality before the law, that they now have extracted for themselves *special* privileges available to no other section of society. Only by withdrawing such special privileges from unions and by enforcing the laws that protect individual freedoms, even when ignored by the most powerful of unions, can the union threat to the liberal order be contained and controlled. To this end, the liberal solution would require the following measures, where they do not already exist.

First, any rights to the closed or union shop would have to be withdrawn, since freedom to associate implies freedom to dissociate in individual relationships without an implied occupational restriction. Secondly, any requirement that a contract between the union and the enterprise must apply to all employees would have to be struck down, with individuals free, if they so wished, to negotiate a different combination of returns. Thirdly, all coercive actions such as secondary strikes and boycotts, designed to coerce other workers into compliance with union restrictions or to coerce employers into dismissing non-compliant workers, would have to be prohibited. Fourthly, *all* rights to picketing, peaceful or otherwise, would have to be withdrawn, freeing individual workers to act independently on a union strike decision without the menace of coercion. Unionists who then break the law would be fully exposed to the laws of trespass, assault and conspiracy, as are other members of society. Fifthly, though the right to strike would be preserved, all public subsidies to strikers and their families would have to be withdrawn, thereby requiring unions to finance their own collective bargaining manoeuvres.[6] In the case of means-tested proven hardship, loans, recoverable by automatic deduction from wages and bearing interest at market rates, would have to be substituted for grants, such as the supplementary benefits currently available in the United Kingdom. Finally, unions would be required to submit themselves to formal incorporation and to be susceptible to the general rules applying to corporate bodies, thereby returning themselves to full equality before the law. By such measures only would union monopoly be made tolerable to a liberal order and would the discriminatory coercion of worker by worker be dissipated and destroyed. Liberals should be under no illusions. The political obstacles to implementing such a programme of reform in democratic countries are formidable. Perhaps, as a component part of an overall liberal policy proposal, it stands the best chance of obtaining the support of the majority vote.

VI   THE MONETARY FRAMEWORK

The main thrust of our analysis requires a comparison between the liberal and the Paretian positions in real terms, whereas the inflation problem dominates contemporary policy discussion. It is important therefore that we conclude this book by a reference, however brief, to the greatest of all potential menaces to the liberal order, the most effective of all the agents of coercion, namely the spectre of inflation. Thus J. M. Keynes:

There is no subtler, no surer means of overturning the existing basis of society than to debauch the currency. The process engages all the hidden forces of economic law on the side of destruction, and does it in a manner which not one man in a million is able to diagnose.

We take the view that inflation is essentially and everywhere a monetary phenemenon,[27] that there is a stable demand for money in real terms, into which the rate of inflation enters as a cost of holding real balances, which cost influences the quantity of real balances held. Given this function, the rate of increase of the nominal stock of money eventually determines the rate of inflation, with the public eventually adjusting its expectations to that rate of inflation and adjusting its stock of real balances to that rate. Any government, if it so chooses, can moderate the rate of inflation by exercising an appropriate restraint on the rate of increase in the supply of money. But to do so, when the rate of inflation already is significant, is to accept a transitional period of bankruptcies and high unemployment. Democratic governments, fearing that voter hostility to unemployment outweighs that to inflation, will be tempted to finance ever-increasing rates of inflation, while attempting to control the symptoms of the disease by disruptive, discriminatory and highly coercive interventions in the goods and factor markets.

Once money illusion disappears and inflation expectations predominate, those who can exert coercive power will do so in the scramble to protect own-property-rights at the cost of those of the more vulnerable sectors of the economy. The conflict will be most apparent at the union level and, in the collective bargaining process, union will follow union in the battle to beat inflation, while governments will choose to finance further inflation in the belief that this will curb the violence of the conflict situation that they have helped to create.

What can liberals recommend to combat such a vicious set of interactions? Clearly, persuasion will cut little ice with governments desperately seeking to retain power by satisfying the majority vote.

One solution, only, is practically available, namely that of enshrining the control of inflation in the form of a monetary constitution, which eliminates governmental control over the money supply in favour of nondiscretionary expansion at rates that reflect the underlying rate of real growth of the economy in question. Such a constitution, by reducing the scope of Leviathan, in fact would protect citizens from short-term political manoeuvres in a finite election period and, in a fundamental sense, would safeguard the democratic order. For the historical message is clear. Hyper-inflation is the road to dictatorship, be it fascist or socialist in nature. Liberals more than any other individuals in society have a vested interest, therefore, in mounting a campaign in favour of monetary constitutionalism, without which such remnants as now remain of the liberal order surely must be destroyed.

REFERENCES

1. Alchian, A. A. and Demsetz, H. 'Production, Information Costs, and Economic Organisation' *The American Economic Review* (December 1972)
2. Baumol, W. J. and Oates, W. E. 'The Use of Standards and Prices for Protection of the Environment' *The Swedish Journal of Economics* (March 1971)
3. Baumol, W. J. 'On Taxation and the Control of Externalities' *The American Economic Review* (June 1972)
4. Beavis, B. and Rowley, C. K. 'The Control of Industrial Discharges to Tidal Rivers and Estuaries' *Long Range Planning* (November 1974)
5. Beckerman, W. *Minority Report: Royal Commission on Environmental Pollution: Third Report* Cmnd 5054 London, HMSO (1972)
6. Brittan, S. *Government and Market Economy* London, Institute of Economic Affairs (1971)
7. Buchanan, J. M. 'The Institutional Structure of Externality' *Public Choice* (Spring 1973)
8. Buchanan, J. M. and Stubblebine, W. C. 'Pareto-Optimality and Gains-from-Trade' *Economica* (May 1972)
9. Burrows, P. 'Pricing Versus Regulation for Environmental Protection' in A. J. Culyer (ed.) *Economic Policies and Social Goals* London, Martin Robertson (1974)
10. Comanor, W. S. and Leibenstein, H. 'Allocative Efficiency, X-Efficiency and the Measurement of Welfare Losses' *Economica* (1969)
11. Crew, M. A., Jones-Lee, M. and Rowley, C. K. 'X-Theory versus Management Discretion Theory' *The Southern Economic Journal* (1971)
12. Crew, M. A. and Rowley, C. K. 'On Allocative Efficiency, X-Efficiency and the Measurement of Welfare Losses' *Economica* (May 1971)

13. Crew, M. A. and Rowley, C. K. 'A Note on X-Efficiency' *The Economic Journal* (December 1972)
14. Culyer, A. J. 'Pareto, Peacock and Rowley, and Policy Towards Natural Monopoly — Comment' *Journal of Public Economics* (February 1973)
15. Dales, J. H. *Pollution, Property and Prices: An Essay in Policy Making and Economics* Toronto, University of Toronto Press (1968)
16. Demsetz, H. 'The Exchange and Enforcement of Property Rights' *Journal of Law and Economics* (1964)
17. Demsetz, H. 'Why Regulate Utilities?' *Journal of Law and Economics* (1968)
18. Demsetz, H. 'On the Regulation of Industry — A Reply' *Journal of Political Economy* (1971)
19. Demsetz, H. 'Information and Efficiency: Another Viewpoint' *Journal of Law and Economics* (April 1969)
20. Dolan, E. G. 'Alienation, Freedom and Economic Organization' *Journal of Political Economy* (September/October 1971)
21. Friedman, M. *Capitalism and Freedom* Chicago, University of Chicago Press (1962)
22. Furubotn, E. and Pejovich, S. 'Property Rights and Economic Theory: A Survey of Recent Literature' *Journal of Economic Literature* (December 1972)
23. Galbraith, J. K. 'Power and the Useful Economist' *The American Economic Review* (March 1973)
24. Goetz, C. *Political Equilibrium vs. Economic Efficiency in Effluent Pricing* (1974)
25. Harberger, A. C. 'Three Basic Postulates for Applied Welfare Economics' *Journal of Economic Literature* (1971)
26. Hayek, F. *The Constitution of Liberty* London, Routledge and Kegan Paul (1960)
27. Johnson, H. G. *Essays in Monetary Economics* London, Allen & Unwin (1967) Chapter III
28. Leibenstein, H. 'Allocative Efficiency vs. X-Efficiency' *The American Economic Review* (1966)
28a. Levy, D. 'Marxism and Alienation' *New Individualist Review* (Winter 1968)
29. Peacock, A. T. and Rowley, C. K. 'Welfare Economics and the Public Regulation of Natural Monopoly' *Journal of Public Economics* (1972)
30. Rowley, C. K. *Antitrust and Economic Efficiency* London, Macmillan (1973)
31. Rowley, C. K. 'Pollution and Public Policy' in A. J. Culyer (ed.) *Economic Policies and Social Goals* London, Martin Robertson (1974)
32. Stigler, G. J. 'The Optimum Enforcement of Laws' *Journal of Political Economy* (May/June 1970)
33. Telser, L. G. 'On the Regulation of Industry: A Note' *Journal of Political Economy* (November/December 1969)
34. Telser, L. G. 'On the Regulation of Industry: A Rejoinder' *Journal of Political Economy* (March-April 1971)

Index

Alchian, A. A., 164
alienation, 72, 93-4, 109; via the wage system, 163-4, 166
allocation of resources: change in, to improve welfare, 9, 47; control by consumers, 12; efficiency, 26, 60; methods, 18; optimal, 123-4; *see also* redistribution of commodities
anarchy, 144-5
anti-trust policies, 155, 156, 158n., 180-3, 184
arbitrage activities, 117
Arrow, Kenneth, 36, 39, 40, 43n., 56, 82; Impossibility Theorem, 25; Theorem, 36-41, 108, 136

bargaining model, conventional, 29
Beavis, B., 172
Bergson, A., 40; social welfare functions, 56-9
Berlin, Isaiah, viii, 79, 84, 98n.
bidding, competitive, 182-3
Boulding, K., 23n., 51
box diagrams, Edgeworth, 12, 13, 15
Breton, A., 108, 110, 112, 113, 127, 132n.
Bronfenbrenner, M., 76n.
Buchanan, James M., viii, 11, 23n., 32-5 *passim*, 43n., 55, 62n., 104-8 *passim*, 118, 121, 129, 130, 131n., 132n., 144, 146, 151, 152, 155, 157n., 158n., 169, 173
bureaucracy, corruption of, 147, 158n.
Burrows, P., 170, 171

capitalism, market, 73, 74
capitalist firms, classical, 164-5
charities, private, income redistribution through, 53, 54
choice, collective, *see* collective choice
choice, freedom of: importance to liberals 155; obstacles 80; restriction, 95-6; safeguarding, 79, 183; *see also* social decision functions
clubs, economic theory of, 118-21
coalitions, political, 110, 111
coercion: conformity with the rule of law, 161; justification, 79; liberal view, 95-7, 155; minimisation, 78,

111, 149; of minorities, 161; necessity, 88; Paretian approach, 11; as protection of power, 85; as source of political participation, 110, 115; in unions, 187; *see also* freedom: restrictions; threats
collective bargaining, 187, 189
collective choice, 28, 81, 82; alternatives to public provision, 115-25; degree of political decentralisation, 128-31; educational provision, 127-8; liberal approach, 113-31; public choice Paretian approach, 104-8; representative government theory, 109-13; and state intervention, 114; *see also* decision-making; majority voting; social choice
collective intervention, 103, 104
collective rationality, 36, 39
commodities: production, 12, 13-17; types, 26; *see also* public goods
commodity redistribution, 49, 54; *see also* allocation of resources
community indifference curves, 47, 48
comparative institutions approach, 94-5, 121, 125, 128, 160, 179
compensation payments, 171-2
compensation principle, 46-51; asymmetry of criterion, 139
competition, freedom of, 87, 88, 90
competition, perfect, *see* perfect competition
competitive bidding, 182-3
conflict resolution, 79
consensus requirements, 10
constitutions: development, 144, 145-6; less-than-unanimity, 38; unanimity, 36
consumption ownership, 118
consumption vectors, 122, 123
control-loss phenomenon, 112
corporate enterprises, 165-6
cost efficiency, 185
coups d'état, 150-1

Dales, J. H., 174
Davis, O. E., 21, 22
death tax, 156-7

193